The Curse of the Law and the Crisis in Galatia

Todd A. Wilson

The Curse of the Law and the Crisis in Galatia

Reassessing the Purpose of Galatians

WIPF & STOCK · Eugene, Oregon

Wipf and Stock Publishers
199 W 8th Ave, Suite 3
Eugene, OR 97401

The Curse of the Law and the Crisis in Galatia
By Wilson, Todd A.
Copyright©2007 Mohr Siebeck
ISBN 13: 978-1-5326-5865-5
Publication date 5/22/2018
Previously published by Mohr Siebeck, 2007

To Katie

Ἀλλήλων τὰ βάρη βαστάζετε
καὶ οὕτως ἀναπληρώσετε τὸν νόμον τοῦ Χριστοῦ

Preface

Felix Jacoby once observed that Herodotus 'is not a subject for *dissertationes inaugurales*, the young authors of which appreciate one side only of this complicated figure (which is at the same time so simple as a whole), and see that side incompletely or from a wrong angle'.[1] One is tempted to say the same of the Apostle Paul. Yet I have come to believe that the reward to be gained by engaging with so complex and fascinating a figure surely justifies the endeavour, even if it does not entirely excuse a certain incompleteness of presentation.

The writing of this monograph, which began life as a doctoral thesis, would not have been possible without the generous support of a number of people. I owe an enormous debit of gratitude, first of all, to my doctoral supervisor Professor Graham N. Stanton. I could have hardly asked for a more gracious and encouraging person with whom to work. I would also like to thank my examiners, Professor Markus Bockmuehl and Dr. Simon Gathercole, who helped me refine the argument of the thesis in several places.

I have also benefited from my association with the Tyndale House, Cambridge. I owe a word of thanks to the Warden, Dr. Bruce Winter, the librarian Dr. Elizabeth Magba, Dr. David Instone-Brewer, Dr. Peter Head and too many readers to be mentioned here by name.

Special thanks should go to Mr. Paul Adams, Mrs. Claire Lea, and Mr. Wayne Coppins, who helped me to improve the presentation of the monograph considerably. I am also grateful to Prof. Jörg Frey for accepting the manuscript for publication in the *Wissenschaftliche Untersuchungen zum Neuen Testament* and to the editorial staff of Mohr Siebeck for their assistance.

I would like to thank those who have provided financial support during my three years of full-time research, including the Colleges and Universities UK, the Master and Fellows of Fitzwilliam College, Cambridge, the Divinity Faculty, University of Cambridge, and, not least, my mother and father and mother and father-in-law, who are a constant reminder that I am anything but a self-made man. Thank you!

I also owe a warm word of thanks to the elders, staff, and congregation of College Church in Wheaton for their support and encouragement with this project.

---

[1] Jacoby, *Atthis* (1949), 321 n. 5; cited in Harrison, *Herodotus* (2000), vii.

Our three children, Ezra John, Liza Rae, and Annie Clarendon, greatly enriched the entire experience of research and writing. Their delightful diversions played a vital role in keeping me both sane and motivated!

It is only fitting that I save my final word of thanks for my wife, Katie. She has been steadfast, courageous and ever-supportive. What more can I say than that by bearing burdens she has fulfilled the Law of Christ. To her I dedicate this work.

Soli Deo Gloria

October 2006
Wheaton, Illinois

Todd A. Wilson

Table of Contents

Preface VII
Notes XIII

Chapter 1: Introduction 1
  Galatians 5.13–6.10 within the Letter to the Galatians 2
  Various Rationales for Paul's References to the Law in 5.13–6.10 4
    Paul invokes the Law as an abiding standard of behaviour 4
    Paul shows that his Law-free gospel does not entail lawless living 8
    Paul wants to continue his polemic against the Law 9
    Paul demonstrates the superfluity of the Law for ethics 10
  Approach and Method 16
  Thesis and Overview of the Argument 18

Part 1
The Curse of the Law and the Crisis in Galatia 21

Chapter 2: The Curse of the Law in the Letter to the Galatians 23
  Curse and Blessing in the Epistolary Framework of the Letter 23
    Double Anathema (1.8-9) 24
    Conditional Blessing (6.16) 26
  Concentrated Curse Terminology in 3.10-14 28
  The Curse of the Law as a Leitmotif in Galatians 30
    'Under Law' as rhetorical shorthand
      for 'under the curse of the Law' 31
    The Son came 'under Law'
      and redeemed us from 'under Law' (4.4-5) 34
    'We were kept under Law' (3.23) 37
    'Those who want to be under Law' (4.21) 40
    'Under Law' elsewhere in Paul 44
  Conclusion 44

Contents

Chapter 3: The Curse of the Law and the Message of the Agitators 47
   A Word on Method 48
   Compelling Circumcision:
      Paul's Portrayal of the Tactics of the Agitators 53
   The Threat of a Curse as Part of the Agitators' Use of Scripture 56
      Curse and Covenant: The Agitators' use of Abrahamic traditions 58
      Curse and Law: The Agitators' use of Deuteronomic traditions 62
   The Threat of a Curse as Part of the Agitators' Polemic Against Paul 64
   Conclusion 67

Chapter 4: The Curse of the Law and the Galatian Converts 69
   The Galatian Audience 70
   Anatolian Popular Religiosity and the Fear of Divine Vengeance 72
   Suffering and the Situation in Galatia 79
   The Curse of the Law and the Interpretation of Suffering in Galatia 89
   Conclusion 93

Part 2
The Curse of the Law and the Purpose of Galatians 95

Chapter 5: The Fulfilment of the Law and the Galatian Converts 97
   The Whole Law and the Law of Christ 97
      The whole Law 98
      The Law of Christ 100
   The Fulfilment of the Law and the Threat of a Curse 104
      The expression ὁ πᾶς νόμος 105
      The significance of the verb πληρόω 107
   The Crucified and Cursed Christ and the Law of Christ 112
      Burden-bearing as cruciform, suffering love 112
      The Law of the crucified and cursed Christ 114
   Conclusion 115

Chapter 6: The Curse of the Law and the Leading of the Spirit 117
   'If you are led by the Spirit, you are not under Law' (5.18) 117
   'The Law is not against such things' (5.23b) 120
   Wilderness Topography in 5.16-24 125
      The 'works of the flesh' and disinheritance (5.19-21) 127
      The 'fruit of the Spirit'
      and the transformation of the wilderness (5.22-23) 130
   Conclusion 137

Chapter 7: Conclusion 139
   Implications 141

Bibliography 145
Index of Sources 161
   Old Testament 161
   New Testament 163
   Apocrypha and Pseudepigrapha 167
   Dead Sea Scrolls 168
   Philo of Alexandria 168
   Flavius Josephus 169
   Rabbinic Literature 169
   Early Christian Literature 169
   Classical and Other Ancient Writings 170
Index of Modern Authors 171
Index of Subjects and Key Terms 175

Notes

Citations in this monograph are in the form of *Author Surname, Short Title* and *Date*. Full details can be found in the bibliography. Abbreviations follow the listing given in P. H. Alexander et al. (eds.), *The SBL Handbook of Style: For Ancient Near Eastern, Biblical and Early Christian Studies*. The NA^{27} convention is followed of excluding accents where manuscript variants are cited. Biblical references are in the form of *chapter.verse*. Where no book is mentioned, the reference is from *Galatians*.

Chapter 1

Introduction

> Why then does Paul bring up the matter of the Law again at this point?
> As far as his own theology is concerned, he could do well without it.[1]

The above epigram, taken from H. D. Betz's monumental *Galatians* commentary, poses the question this study seeks to answer: why does Paul return to the issue of the Law in 5.14?[2] Given his sustained and at times fierce polemic against the Law earlier in the letter, why does he take up the issue again at this point? This move can hardly be explained as an idiosyncrasy of Galatians or a slip on Paul's part, since 5.14 is followed by *three more* references to the Law (5.18, 23; 6.2) in the so-called ethical section of the letter.[3] In fact, the issue of the Law appears to be an 'undercurrent' in 5.13–6.10.[4] This study must therefore address the question of why there is any further mention of the Law in 5.13–6.10 as a whole. What is the rationale for Paul's four references to the Law in the ethical section of Galatians?

This is a crucial question for our understanding of Galatians because it has a direct bearing on several classic problems of interpretation, including (1) how 5.13–6.10 relates thematically to the rest of Galatians, (2) how 5.13–6.10 contributes to the rhetorical function of the letter, and (3) how 5.13–6.10 helps to redress the crisis in Galatia. In addition, an answer to the question of the rationale for Paul's four references to the Law in the ethical section of Galatians will inevitably inform how one understands the perennial issue of the place of the Law in Paul's theology and ethics.

---

[1] Betz, *Galatians* (1979), 275, commenting on 5.14.

[2] Throughout this study I shall use the capitalised 'Law' only to refer to the Law of Moses. Here I anticipate the conclusions of Chapters 5–6, where I argue that all four references to νόμος in 5.13–6.10 refer to the Law of Moses. Occasionally, I shall also use the term Torah as a synonym.

[3] For convenience I shall on occasion follow the convention of referring to 5.13–6.10 as the 'ethical section' of Galatians, yet acknowledging the difficulties with this particular designation. See, for example, the discussion in Martyn, *Galatians* (1997), 482–84, 482 n. 41. On 5.13–6.10 as a discrete unit within Galatians, see Barclay, *Obeying* (1988), 24. On 5.13 as the beginning of the ethical section (or parenesis), see the oft-cited study by Merk, 'Beginn der Paränese' (1969), 83–104.

[4] Winger, 'Law of Christ' (2000), 538; cf. Eckert, *Verkündigung* (1971), 134; Mussner, *Galaterbrief* (1974), 370; Lührmann, *Galatians* (1992), 100; Hansen, 'Ethic of Freedom' (1997), 220.

Galatians 5.13–6.10 within the Letter to the Galatians

Before considering the various rationales for Paul's four references to the Law in 5.13–6.10, it is worth briefly discussing the current state of the question regarding the relevance of 5.13–6.10 to Galatians. This will prove useful for at least two reasons. First, the central question of this study, the rationale for Paul's four references to the Law in 5.13–6.10, is actually a subset of the larger question of the rationale for 5.13–6.10 in Galatians as a whole. Secondly, identifying the current state of the question with regard to the role of 5.13–6.10 in Galatians should, in turn, clarify how the results of this study contribute to that classic interpretative conundrum.

In the last twenty years, particularly within English-speaking scholarship, a widespread consensus has emerged on the question of the relevance of 5.13–6.10 to Galatians and to the situation in Galatia. In short, most scholars now agree that 5.13–6.10 is both *integral* to the letter and, at least to some extent, *relevant* to the situation.[5] Few follow the lead of those who have claimed, in various ways, that 5.13–6.10 is more or less unrelated to the rest of Galatians or that it has little or no specific bearing on the situation in Galatia.[6] Instead, it is commonplace for interpreters to affirm without further ado that this section of the letter is not only vital to the argument of Galatians but also pertinent to the situation in Galatia; indeed, for some these closing chapters constitute the *Höhepunkt* of the letter.[7]

While most scholars now affirm that Galatians contains a unified argument, they account for the coherence of the letter in different ways. In her recent monograph, *Die Galater zurückgewinnen: Paulinische Strategien in Galater 5 und 6* (2005), S. Schewe identifies three models scholars use to explain the thematic and functional unity between 5.13–6.10 and the rest of the letter: (1) the dogmatic model, which treats 5.13–6.10 as a necessary exposition of the ethical shape of the Christian faith;[8] (2) the rhetorical model,

---

[5] While several factors have contributed to this changed landscape in Galatians studies, Barclay's highly influential monograph, *Obeying the Truth: A Study of Paul's Ethics in Galatians* (1988), is often referred to as having played an important role. See further below.

[6] For a succinct survey of these approaches, see Barclay, *Obeying* (1988), 9–16.

[7] Suhl, 'Galater und Geist' (1989), 284; Matera, 'Culmination' (1988), 79–91; Engberg-Pedersen, *Paul and Stoics* (2000), 131; Barclay, *Obeying* (1988), 216–20. Fee, *Presence* (1994), 420, claims that 5.13–6.10 is 'the crux for understanding Galatians as a whole'.

[8] Schewe, *Galater 5 und 6* (2005), 16–26, points to the commentaries by Becker, *Galater* (1998) and Mussner, *Galaterbrief* (1974) as exemplary of this approach. Cf. Longenecker, *Triumph* (1998), 80 n. 13: 'Paul's discussion of Christian moral identity arose as a consequence of his own theological presentation'. The exposition of 5.13-26 proffered by Engberg-Pedersen, *Paul and Stoics* (2000), 131–77, should be included here as well, even though he utilises a model derived from Stoic ethics rather than Christian theology. In 5.13-26 Paul explicates his vision of the 'genuinely Christ-believing form of life' (131).

which when Galatians is classified as deliberative rhetoric, understands 5.13–6.10 as Paul's climactic appeal to the Galatians to desist from certain behaviour and to adopt a different course of action;[9] and (3) the historical model, which interprets 5.13–6.10 against the backdrop of a particular reconstruction of the exigencies of the situation that calls forth this section of the letter.[10]

However, Schewe takes issue with each model for failing to provide a satisfying account of the *thematic and functional unity* of Galatians. In different ways, all three approaches, she argues, end up treating 5.13–6.10 as a *Fremdkörper* within the body of the letter. While insisting on the essential unity of Galatians, each of these models assumes some kind of a *Themaverschiebung* between the earlier parts of the letter and 5.13–6.10. Even the historical model employed by Barclay, arguably the most successful account of the unity of Galatians on offer, supposes that Paul deals with basically *two different issues* in the two different sections of the letter (roughly speaking, chapters 1–4 and 5–6). Thus, for Barclay the alleged unity of the letter depends to a large extent upon his particular reconstruction of the situation (see further below). As a result, however, as Schewe rightly points out, 'Hauptteil und Schlußpassus haben unüberbrückbar *zwei* Themen, wenn sie nicht mehr über die historische Adressatensituation zusammengehalten werden'.[11]

---

[9] Schewe, *Galater 5 und 6* (2005), 26–48. Kennedy, *Interpretation* (1984), 144–52, has been particularly influential in propagating the view that Galatians is deliberative rather than forensic, as Betz argued. According to Kennedy, *Interpretation* (1984), 146: 'What Paul is leading to in chapters 1–4 is the exhortation of chapters 5–6. This is the point of the letter'. Cf. Hall, 'Rhetorical Outline' (1987), 277–87; Vouga, 'Rhetorischen Gattung' (1988), 291–92 (with comparisons to Demosthenes); Vouga, *Galater* (1998), 5–7; Smit, 'Deliberative Speech' (1989), 1–26 (though he claims that 5.13–6.10 was a later addition). On the propriety of analysing Galatians according to the ancient rhetorical handbooks, see especially Kern, *Rhetoric and Galatians* (1998); though see also Mitchell, 'Reading Rhetoric' (2001), 333–55, who, drawing upon John Chrysostom's *Galatians* commentary, provides critical interaction with Kern's thesis and concludes, somewhat provocatively: 'On the matter of the rhetorical genre and imagined situation of Galatians, Chrysostom clearly sides with Betz' (355). See also most recently Tolmie, *Persuading* (2005).

[10] Schewe, *Galater 5 und 6* (2005), 49–59, identifies Betz as the forerunner of the historical approach (cf. 42–48), but takes Barclay, whose debt to Betz she rightly detects, as the prime exponent of this approach, especially insofar as Barclay, *Obeying* (1988), 26, explicitly eschews dependence upon rhetorical analysis: 'It is clear that our question can only be solved through careful exegesis and historical reconstruction'.

[11] Schewe, *Galater 5 und 6* (2005), 57 (emphasis original). Hays, 'Law of Christ' (1987), 269, already identified this as a problem with Betz's understanding of the relationship between 5.1–6.10 and the rest of Galatians: 'Betz seeks to establish a connection between the parenetic material and the rest of Paul's argument by a hypothesis about the occasion and purpose of the letter'.

Therefore, the question now for students of Galatians is not *whether* 5.13–6.10 relates to the earlier parts of the letter, but *how* it does so. While the focus of this study is more narrowly circumscribed around the issue of the rationale for Paul's four references to the Law in 5.13–6.10, we shall want to bear in mind this discussion and in the end ask how an answer to the question of the rationale for Paul's references to the Law may shed light on this ongoing and perennial issue in the interpretation of the letter.

Various Rationales for Paul's References to the Law in 5.13–6.10

There are essentially four ways in which scholars have explained the rationale for Paul's four references to the Law in 5.13–6.10. The first of the four views considered below operates on the assumption that Paul's references to the Law in 5.13–6.10 are in one way or another the expression of his own convictions about the perpetuity of the Law for the believer, while the latter three views tend to give more prominence to Paul's attempt to address the various exigencies of the situation in Galatia.

Paul invokes the Law as an abiding standard of behaviour

On this first view, Paul's appeal to the Law to sanction a charge to love (5.13–14; 6.2) is hardly surprising. Instead, this is precisely what one would expect from someone like Paul who insisted on the Law as an abiding moral norm. 'It is characteristic of Paul's mode of thinking that he should return to the law at this point [5.14], and bind the command of love upon the hearts of the Galatians by an appeal to the law'.[12] While the Mosaic Law no longer enslaves believers with its curse or binds them with its 'ceremonial' stipulations and legal sanctions, it still reveals the moral will of God. Believers are, therefore, to fulfil the Law insofar as it no longer serves as a national charter for Israel but has been transposed to a new setting within the life of the church, where, if it is rightly understood and interpreted, it can serve as a standard for the behaviour of believers.[13]

Paul can thus call for the fulfilment of the Law within the context of Christian exhortation since the Law itself is an expression of God's will for

---

[12] Ridderbos, *Galatians* (1953), 200. See the classic essays by Cranfield, 'St Paul' (1964), 43–68, and Wilckens, 'Entwicklung' (1982), 154–90 (cf. 174); and, more recently, Martin, *Christ and Law* (1989), 147–54; Schreiner, *Law and its Fulfillment* (1993), 145–78; Bayes, *Weakness* (2000), especially 165–74.

[13] Hong, *Law* (1993), 182; Thielman, *Paul & the Law* (1994), 139–42; Das, *Jews* (2003), 166–86; George, *Galatians* (1994), 380: 'Paul's ethical argument throughout this entire passage [5.13-26] is based on the premise that the moral law of God, far from being abrogated by the coming of Christ, remains the divinely sanctioned standard for Christian conduct and growth in grace'.

his people and centres upon the love of one's neighbour (5.14; Lev 19.18).[14] As a result, Paul's statement in 5.18 that believers are not 'under Law' should be taken to refer to a particular function of the Law – not the Law *per se*.[15] Similarly, Paul's comment in 5.23 (often translated: 'Against such things there is no Law') implies that the 'fruit of the Spirit' actually meets the moral requirement of the Law.[16] The Law of Christ in 6.2 is likewise to be taken as a reference either to that aspect of God's Law which persists into the new era of salvation or to the Mosaic Law itself as it is now reinterpreted by Christ and fulfilled through bearing one another's burdens.[17]

This basic line of interpretation has been prominent among Patristic and Reformed exegetes, who in one way or another are happy to affirm what in Reformation nomenclature came to be referred to as the 'third use' of the Law.[18] Augustine was little troubled by Paul's continued references to the Law in 5.13–6.10, since the Law contained both 'sacramental works' and 'works having to do with good morals', the latter of which, when properly understood, continued to be obligatory for believers.[19] Calvin makes similar sorts of distinctions in order to uphold the moral obligation of the Law for the life of the Christian.[20]

A variation of this basic approach can be found among some scholars known as supporters of the New Perspective on Paul. J. D. G. Dunn, for example, insists that Paul's criticisms of the Law are carefully targeted, not wholesale, and should not be taken to imply a complete disavowal of the Law for the Christian.[21] What has changed is the Law's function within the new era of salvation-history. 'With the transition to a new epoch, the law's role as

---

[14] Cf. Hong, *Law* (1993), 190–91.

[15] Cf. Hong, *Law* (1993), 184; George, *Galatians* (1994), 388.

[16] Ridderbos, *Galatians* (1953), 208: 'The reference presumably is to the curse, the spoliation, which the law brings upon the disobedient (cf. 3:10, 13). Hence the law is not *against* those who walk by the Spirit because in principle they are fulfilling the law (verse 14). In this again it is evident that the requirement and the strength of the law continue'.

[17] Hong, *Law* (1993), 173–76.

[18] Cf. Ebeling, '*Triplex Usus Legis*' (1963).

[19] Plumer, *Augustine's Commentary on Galatians* (2003), sections 43–44 (on 5.13-14). Cf. Aquinas, *Galatians* (1966), 172, who, when discussing 5.18, argues that the believer is obligated, though not *motivated*, by the moral precepts of the Law. Schnabel, *Law and Wisdom* (1985), 274–79, 310–23, adopts essentially this same approach: the Law is no longer the *conditio salutis*, but it does provide moral guidance.

[20] Calvin, *Galatians* (1993), 164 (on 5.18). While the believer's conscience is not bound by the Law for salvation, this does not, Calvin insists, render the Law superfluous for Christian living; see especially Calvin, *Institutes* (1960), 3.19.2. Cf. Hesselink, 'Calvin and Christian Freedom' (1995), 77–89. This was evidently the consensus among Puritan divines; see Kevan, *Grace of Law* (1964), 167–223.

[21] Dunn, *Paul* (1998), 632. Cf. Sanders, *Jewish People* (1983), 93–122.

guardian of Israel's distinctiveness was at an end. The obligation to walk in a way appropriate to the relationship given by God remained'.[22]

Another variation of this same approach is to argue that Paul, in keeping with many of the other earliest Jewish followers of Jesus, believed that the Law was obligatory for Jews and Gentiles in different ways: that is, for Jews *as Jews* and for Gentiles *as Gentiles*.[23] The Jewish theologian M. Wyschogrod explains this approach:

> Over the centuries, Christian debate about the law has revolved around the before-Jesus and after-Jesus axis. The idea was that the law was in full effect before the coming of Jesus, but that with his coming, large parts of it were suspended. The problem then was which parts were declared inoperative and which not. This question was never answered with the requisite clarity, though not a few Christian authors have tried. There is yet another way of looking at the problem which may be more productive for Jewish-Christian relations. Jews have long believed that the full Mosaic law was binding only on Jews. Non-Jews were duty-bound to obey the Noachide commandments, and if they did so, God was fully pleased.[24]

According to Wyschogrod, the Noachide commandments constitute for Paul, and for much of the early church (cf. Acts 15), the Law for Gentiles.[25] While Jews are under obligation to observe, in Paul's terms, the 'whole Law' (5.3), i.e., to live as Jews, Gentiles are to conform to the basic moral standards of the Law, which includes avoiding things such as incest, murder and robbery. Thus, when Paul refers to Gentiles fulfilling the Law, he has in mind the Law *as it applies to Gentiles* (cf. 1 Cor 7.19).[26] And when he warns the Galatians that the 'works of the flesh' exclude one from the 'kingdom of God' (5.19-21), he identifies behaviour that overlaps considerably with those 'cardinal'

---

[22] Dunn, *Theology*, 116.

[23] See Wyschogrod, 'Jewish Postscript' (1988), 185–87; Wyschogrod, 'Mosaic Law' (1993), 451–59; Wyschogrod, *Abraham's Promise* (2004), 160–64, 188–201; Tomson, *Jewish Law* (1990); Tomson, 'Law Teaching' (1996), 251–70 (cf. 268); Tomson, *From Heaven* (2001), especially 179–90; Bockmuehl, *Jewish Law* (2000), 145–73; Bauckham, *James* (1999), 148–51; Segal, *Paul the Convert* (1990), 187–223; Segal, 'Universalism' (1994), 1–29; Finsterbusch, *Lebensweisung* (1996), 97–184; Müller, *Tora* (1998), 174–99. Cf. Reinmuth, *Geist und Gesetz* (1985), 54–66.

[24] Wyschogrod, *Abraham's Promise* (2004), 162.

[25] It is, of course, somewhat anachronistic to speak of Noachide commandments during the NT period, since the earliest explicit formulation of the doctrine comes not until the second century C.E. While there are important precursors to this later rabbinic formulation (cf. especially *Jub.* 7.20-21), probably the most that can be said for Paul is that something like a pre-rabbinic equivalent of the Noachide commandments may have informed his 'halakhic' approach to Gentiles. Cf. Bockmuehl, *Jewish Law* (2000), 145–73; van de Sandt and Flusser, *Didache* (2002), 238–70 (especially 265–69).

[26] Tomson, *Jewish Law* (1990), 175–78.

sins proscribed by the Law, which Jews, generally speaking, believed even Gentiles were to observe.[27]

On the question of Paul's rationale for continuing to refer to the Law in 5.13–6.10, then, each of these approaches comes out looking somewhat similar. While scholars within the Reformed tradition tend to utilise the distinction between various aspects of the Law, some of which are now obsolete,[28] those who identify with the New Perspective on Paul tend to mark different priorities within the Law, some of which now take precedence over others.[29] The third approach mentioned above takes a slightly different tack by distinguishing between different aspects of the Law along the Jew-Gentile axis. In the end, however, each of these readings depends upon a similar line of argument: Paul's positive affirmations of the Law in 5.14 and 6.2 (and perhaps 5.23) refer to the Law as, in some sense, an abiding standard of behaviour, while Paul's negative comments in 5.18 (and elsewhere) should be taken to refer to a particular feature or function of the Law.

Much can be said for this basic approach, not least its ability to take at face value Paul's 'positive' appeals to the Law within the context of his discussion of Christian ethics. This view also rightly questions whether Paul's language of the fulfilment of the Law (5.14; 6.2) can be regarded simply as an *ad hoc* device used to score points over his opponents, rather than something that emerges organically from and thereby reflects his own theological convictions. The principal setback with this whole approach, however, has been, and continues to be, the difficulty it has providing convincing readings of Paul's seemingly dismissive comments about the Law in Galatians (2.19; 3.23-25; 5.1). Perhaps equally problematic for this view is the fact that Paul nowhere appeals simply and directly to the Law itself to sanction his ethical injunctions, something one might have expected him to do from time to time if the Law was for him really an abiding standard of behaviour. Even his comments about the fulfilment of the Law in 5.14 and 6.2 are not prescriptive, but descriptive.[30]

---

[27] On 5.19-21, see Müller, *Tora* (1998), 175–78; Bockmuehl, *Jewish Law* (2000), 168. Neyrey, 'Bewitched' (1988), 88, comments in passing that the 'works of the flesh' are infractions of 'basically the Ten Commandments'. Cf. Stuhlmacher, *Biblische Theologie* (1992), 260.

[28] Thielman, 'Coherence' (1992), 252: 'Paul could distinguish between aspects of the law which were obsolete and aspects of continuing validity'.

[29] Dunn, *Paul* (1998), 656: 'Where the requirements of the law were being interpreted in a way which ran counter to the basic principle of the love command, Paul thought that the requirements could and should be dispensed with'.

[30] Betz, *Galatians* (1979), 235; Westerholm, 'Fulfilling the Law' (1986-87), 235–37; Barclay, *Obeying* (1988), 142.

Paul shows that his Law-free gospel does not entail lawless living

The second approach finds the climax of Paul's polemic against the Law in Galatians in his clarion call to Christian freedom in 5.1 and 5.13. Freedom, however, can easily be misconstrued as license, permission to dispense with moral norms of whatever kind. Paul was keenly aware of this danger. Therefore, after reminding the Galatians of their call to freedom (5.13a), Paul immediately turns to warn them of freedom's misuse (5.13b). He then appeals to the standard of the Law itself to press the point that Christian freedom carries its own moral requirements, which are not at odds with what the Law itself upholds (5.14, 18, 23; 6.2).[31]

This is, at any rate, the explanation of those who are convinced that Paul refers to the Law in the ethical section of Galatians in order to avoid misunderstandings or respond to objections.[32] As S. Westerholm suggests, Paul's references to the Law in 5.13–6.10 reveal that he still has his 'nomistic opponents still very much in mind' and that he has specifically framed his discussion 'in terms designed to meet a potential objection to his call for freedom'.[33] Drane argues similarly: 'Having dismissed the relevance of the Law and the rite of initiation into the Law-oriented community, Paul now feels himself constrained to demonstrate that this does not, in his view, lead to lawlessness'.[34]

J. L. Martyn adopts a similar approach in his *Galatians* commentary, suggesting that one of Paul's main aims in 5.13–6.10 is to answer the Agitators' charge that he has failed to provide the Galatians with detailed guidance in everyday life: 'Being an unfaithful student of the Law-observant apostles in the mother church of Jerusalem, Paul failed to give you the Law, thus allowing you to remain a group of sailors on the treacherous high seas in nothing more than a small and poorly equipped boat'.[35] Thus, while Paul's gospel and pastoral guidance are essentially Law-free, this does not entail

---

[31] Bachmann, *Sünder oder Übertreter* (1992), 119: 'In 5,13-26 sucht der Apostel nämlich in einem ersten Durchgang zu zeigen, daß sittlich vollkommenes Leben der Christen möglich ist und daß es, wenn sie auch nicht ὑπὸ νόμον sind (5,18b), doch nicht in Konflikte mit dem νόμος führt' (cf. 69, 84). Cf. Becker, *Galater* (1998), 83: 'Die christliche Freiheit, wie sie Paulus versteht, ist nicht gegen das Gesetz (5,14.18.23)'; Fung, *Galatians* (1988), 243; Söding, *Liebesgebot* (1995), 187–226 (especially 215–16, 218–19).

[32] Suhl, 'Galaterbrief' (1987), 3119–27, argues that Paul demonstrates for the Galatians in 5.13-25 what he has already shown to be the case for himself in 2.19-20: namely, that his Law-free gospel does not lead to sin. Cf. Wilckens, 'Entwicklung' (1982), 176.

[33] Westerholm, 'Fulfilling the Law' (1986–87), 231. Cf. Westerholm, *Israel's Law* (1988), 201–02, where he stresses the polemical function of these references: 'Paul is concerned to show that the ethical behavior of Christians is better, not worse, than those living "under the law"' (202).

[34] Drane, *Libertine or Legalist* (1975), 52–53.

[35] Martyn, *Galatians* (1997), 481, 305. Cf. Martyn, 'Law-Observant' (1985), 307–24.

lawless living or, in Martyn's own words, becoming enslaved to the 'Impulsive Desire of the Flesh'.[36] In fact, Paul's concrete pastoral guidance outstrips even the very best the Law has to offer.[37]

This way of understanding the rationale for Paul's continued references to the Law in 5.13–6.10 has traditionally been closely connected to a similar way of understanding the role and relevance of the ethical section of Galatians as a whole. The question, then, has often been broader than why the Law in 5.13–6.10, but why this section of the letter at all? This particular question, however, is asked far less frequently than it once was. Galatians scholarship, in fact, appears to enjoy something of a consensus on this point: chapters 5–6 are immediately relevant to the situation in Galatia. Thus, construing the rationale behind Paul's references to the Law in the ethical section (simply) as a means of forestalling misunderstandings or answering possible objections is now generally regarded as inadequate. While there may well be a defensive note to at least some of what Paul says about the Law in 5.13–6.10, there is reason to suspect that there may be more going on in this section.

Paul wants to continue his polemic against the Law

Scholars who advocate this third approach to the question of the rationale for Paul's four references to the Law in 5.13–6.10 will often stress that these references appear between two forceful polemical appeals to resist circumcision and to reject those advocating it (5.1-12; 6.11-18).[38] Therefore, they argue, if we are to read 5.13–6.10 within its context, we should give due weight to this fact, which would suggest that with his references to the Law in 5.13–6.10, Paul is not on the defensive, but on the offensive. He is not defending himself against misunderstandings, but offering a trenchant criticism of those in Galatia who either advocate or embrace the Law.[39] On this reading, Paul's comments in 5.18 and 5.23 are to be understood as 'disparaging references' to the Law,[40] while his remarks about the fulfilment of the Law in 5.14 and 6.2 can be viewed as further distancing the Galatians from the Law.[41] For these scholars, Paul's provocative association of the Law

---

[36] Martyn, *Galatians* (1997), 479–501, 524–40.

[37] Cf. Westerholm, *Israel's Law* (1988), 201–02.

[38] Cf. Matera, 'Culmination' (1988), 79–91.

[39] Russell, *Flesh/Spirit* (1997), 143–70, views 5.13-26 as a polemical contrast between two opposing ways of life based either upon the flesh or the Spirit, thereby bringing Paul's argument against the 'Judaizers' to a climax. Cf. Hamerton-Kelly, *Sacred Violence* (1992), 140–60; Hamerton-Kelly, 'Sacred Violence' (1990), 55–75.

[40] Howard, *Crisis* (1990), 12–13. Cf. Borgen, *New Perspectives* (1987), 241; Hansen, 'Ethic of Freedom' (1997), 220. Kwon, *Eschatology* (2004), 195–98, argues that Paul's polemic against the Law here and throughout Galatians focuses primarily, though not exclusively, upon its moral impotence.

[41] See, e.g., Esler, *Galatians* (1998), 204, 231.

with the flesh in 5.16-18 is particularly significant. By exposing the close affiliation between these two, Paul can press the point that the Law has only deleterious consequences for ethics. Indeed, to turn to the Law is to *return to the flesh*.[42]

The strength of this approach is that it avoids unnecessarily disconnecting 5.13–6.10 from the rest of the letter, not least its immediate context, which includes strong words about both circumcision and the Agitators (5.1-12; 6.11-18). That the issue of the Law is still very much on Paul's mind is strongly suggested not only by his continued references to the Law (5.14, 18, 23; 6.2), but also by his linking the Law with the flesh and contrasting the Law and the Spirit (cf. 3.1-5; 4.21-31). Especially noteworthy is Paul's use of 'under Law' in 5.18, a phrase that has appeared several times earlier in the letter (3.23; 4.4, 5, 21); its use here is doubtless intentional and may invoke these earlier discussions.[43]

It is less clear, however, whether this line of interpretation can adequately account for *each* of Paul's references to the Law in 5.13–6.10. While one could certainly argue that Paul's references to the Law in 5.18 and 5.23 are polemically motivated, this is less clear with his reference to the fulfilment of the Law in 5.14 and 6.2. Of course, one could argue that the Law of Christ in 6.2 is a polemical formulation, but the difficulty with this is that 6.1-5 appears to be particularly bereft of polemics and instead looks like a rather straightforward series of exhortations and admonitions. Therefore, regardless of the extent to which there are polemics in 5.13–6.10, Paul probably had additional reasons for admonishing the Galatians to love one another and thus fulfil the Law (of Christ).

Paul demonstrates the superfluity of the Law for ethics

We come now to the fourth approach, which is also arguably the consensus view among scholars.[44] For those who see Paul more or less dispensing with

---

[42] Lightfoot, *Galatians* (1896), 209; Howard, *Crisis* (1990), 13–14; Mussner, *Galaterbrief* (1974), 378; Lührmann, *Galatians* (1992), 101: 'Paul faults the law also in the realm of ethics for promising more than it can accomplish: bestowing blessing, righteousness, and life'. Elliott, *Cutting too Close* (2003), 287–322, argues that in Gal 5–6 Paul associates the Law and circumcision with the Anatolian Mother of the Gods and self-castration.

[43] Dunn, *Galatians* (1993), 301.

[44] See, though with some variations, Gaventa, 'Singularity' (1991), 147–59; Wessels, 'Responsible Freedom' (1992), 461–74; Lategan, 'Christian Ethics' (1990); Thielman, *Law and New Testament* (1999); Murphy-O'Connor, *Critical Life* (1996), 200; Murphy-O'Connor, *Paul: His Story* (2004), 132; Martyn, *Galatians* (1997), 19 (though see above); Suhl, 'Galater und Geist' (1989), 283; Dunn, 'Covenantal Nomism' (1991), 125–46; Dunn, *Galatians* (1993), 285; Dunn, *Theology of Galatians* (1993), 101–04; Williams, *Galatians* (1997), 28, 144–53; Fee, 'Life of Obedience' (1994), 201–17; Fee, *Presence* (1994), 420–54; Witherington, *Galatians* (1998), 381, 397, 411–12. Cf. Thielman, *Paul & the Law* (1994), 140; Longenecker, *Triumph* (1998), 84.

the Law, or at least rejecting it as an ethical guide for his churches, his four references to the Law in 5.13–6.10 are to be explained primarily, if not exclusively, with reference to the concrete exigencies of the Galatian crisis. As Betz suggests, commenting on Paul's return to the Law in 5.14:

> Why then does Paul bring up the matter of the Law again at this point? As far as his own theology is concerned, he could do well without it. Apparently, however, he cannot avoid the matter, because the Galatians are so preoccupied with circumcision and Torah. If he wants to win his churches back, he cannot ignore the issue that looms largest in their minds and that is central to the theology of his opponents.[45]

Were the issues Paul confronted in Galatia somewhat different, Betz opines that Paul may well have moved straight from 5.12 to 6.11-18 and thereby not included 5.13–6.10, or at least omitted any further reference to the Law. The reason for this is simple: 'For the Apostle there is no longer any Law'.[46] However, it was simply not advisable for Paul to pass over in silence the issue of the Law in the ethical section of the letter. 'If he wants to win his churches back, he cannot ignore the issue that looms largest in *their* minds and that is central to the theology of his *opponents*'.[47] According to Betz, the Galatians were attracted to circumcision and the Torah as a way to deal with cases of 'flagrant misconduct' (cf. 6.1).[48] Paul had therefore to press the point about the sufficiency of the Spirit to deal with the flesh (5.16-17), yet at the same time point out along the way the inadequacy of the Law (5.18).[49]

Betz's explanation of the rationale for Paul's references to Law in 5.13–6.10 was refined and reissued several years later by Barclay in his monograph, *Obeying the Truth: A Study of Paul's Ethics in Galatians* (1988). Barclay's study marks a watershed in the approach to 5.13–6.10 as an integrated part of the letter, even if he is not solely responsible for this present scholarly consensus. His contribution has been highly influential and therefore merits more extended discussion.

Barclay was in essential agreement with Betz on a number of points. He did, however, raise questions about whether the real issue was, as Betz supposed, 'flagrant misconduct'. Instead, Barclay argues that the Galatians were attracted to circumcision and the Torah because they had begun to doubt the adequacy of Paul's ethical instructions and the sufficiency of the Spirit to

---

[45] Betz, *Galatians* (1979), 275.
[46] Betz, *Galatians* (1979), 257.
[47] Betz, *Galatians* (1979), 275 (emphasis added).
[48] Betz, *Galatians* (1979), 8–9, 273–74, 295–96. For a concise presentation of Betz's view of the function of 5.13–6.10 as a whole, see Barclay, *Obeying* (1988), 20–22.
[49] Betz, *Galatians* (1979), 289, summarises the thrust of Paul's argument as follows: 'the introduction of the Torah into the Galatian churches would not lead to ethical responsibility, so long as the people were not motivated and enabled ethically. If they were motivated and enabled, however, the Torah is superfluous'.

enable moral living.⁵⁰ This reconstruction of the situation clarifies the rationale for Paul's continued references to the Law in 5.13–6.10. According to Barclay:

> In giving his exhortation Paul appears intent on demonstrating that walking in the Spirit is a sufficient alternative to living under the law (5:14, 18, 23; 6:2). If the opponents wanted the Galatians to observe the law they probably argued that only the law could properly regulate their daily life.⁵¹

Paul thus needs to convince the Galatians that the Spirit is able to provide them with all the moral direction they need. In fact, he needs to persuade them that the leading of the Spirit actually renders the Law *superfluous* as an ethical resource (cf. 5.18), since the working of the Spirit produces a moral life that fully measures up to the standards of the Law (5.14, 23; 6.2). By arguing in this fashion, Paul is able to provide the Galatians with what they really need (i.e., confidence in the sufficiency of the Spirit), without having to reinstate the Law as a moral guide.

There are obvious strengths with this line of interpretation, attested by its widespread appeal within the guild. Its greatest strength may be its ability to correlate Paul's seemingly dismissive remarks about the Law in Gal 2–4 with his more 'positive' references to the Law in Gal 5–6, while neither surrendering Paul to the charge of blatant inconsistency nor resorting to an appeal to the 'third use' of the Law to explain Paul's return to the Law in the ethical section of Galatians. Furthermore, part of the attractiveness of Barclay's reconstruction of the situation is that it enables one to take seriously *both* the theological *and* the ethical emphases of Galatians, without needing to suppose that he was fighting on two different fronts, as some have suggested.⁵²

This approach also rightly highlights the *assuring* tone of Paul's remarks about the Law in 5.13–6.10. If the Galatians will serve one another in love, they will fulfil the Law (5.13-14; 6.2); if they walk by the Spirit, they are not 'under Law' (5.18); the 'fruit of the Spirit' – 'against such things there is no Law' (5.23). Each of Paul's four references to the Law in this section of the letter are descriptive and affirming. Paul appears, then, to be intent on

---

⁵⁰ Barclay, *Obeying* (1988), 106: 'Paul's ethical policy may have appeared dangerously ill-defined' and 'he appears to be unwilling (or unable) to provide his Gentile converts with the detailed moral advice they often required' (170). Lategan, 'Christian Ethics' (1990), 327, takes this a step further by arguing that the 'ethical deficit' in Galatians is intentional on Paul's part: 'Paul presents an ethical minimum to his readers to stimulate a creative and responsible application of basic theological principles in new situations'.

⁵¹ Barclay, 'Mirror-Reading' (1987), 87.

⁵² Cf. Lütgert, *Gesetz und Geist* (1919); Ropes, *Singular Problem* (1929). Jewett, 'Agitators' (1971), 198, states the issue succinctly: 'The core of the dilemma is that the apparent presence of libertinistic tendencies in the Galatian congregation is difficult to reconcile with the main argument of the letter directed against an orthodox nomism'.

assuring the Galatians of the relationship between the Spirit and love, on the one hand, and the Law, on the other. He seems to be sounding an apologetic note, a point which must be taken into account in any assessment of the rhetorical function of 5.13–6.10.

Despite its obvious strengths, however, Barclay's proposal is not without problems. First, as part of his reconstruction of the situation in Galatia, Barclay suggests that the Galatians were attracted to circumcision and the Torah because of the Agitators' weighty 'theological arguments' and because of the various 'social factors' at work in Galatia (e.g., the Galatians' own social dislocation). However, it is clear that Barclay only makes use of *one* of these when he comes to explain the relevance of chapters 5–6 for the situation in Galatia: namely, social factors.[53] The various theological arguments used by the Agitators to encourage circumcision and observance of the Torah appear to play little or no *direct* role in Barclay's reading of Gal 5–6. Instead, his account of the purpose of these chapters within the context of the crisis relies almost entirely upon various 'social' explanations for the Galatians' attraction to circumcision and the Torah. As Barclay states in his conclusion: '*the problem that lies behind these chapters is not libertinism but moral confusion together with a loss of confidence in Paul's prescriptions for ethics*'.[54] Note that Barclay has identified the issue to which Paul responds in 5.13–6.10 as moral confusion, apparently as distinct from whatever 'theological' confusion the Galatians may have been suffering from as a result of what he refers to as a 'powerful battery of arguments' the Agitators were using to commend the Law in Galatia.[55]

Hence, even though Barclay disavows a 'two front' approach, his own reading appears to amount to something not entirely dissimilar. While Paul confronts a single audience, he nevertheless has to deal with *two different (albeit inseparable) issues*: theology and ethics, or 'identity' and 'patterns of behaviour', which he takes up, roughly speaking, in the *two different (albeit inseparable) parts* of the letter (chapters 1–4 and 5–6, respectively).[56] Put

---

[53] Barclay, *Obeying* (1988), 52–56, 65–67.

[54] Barclay, *Obeying* (1988), 218 (emphasis original). Cf. Barclay, *Obeying* (1988), 106, 142–45, 146.

[55] Barclay, *Obeying* (1988), 68. Murray, *Judaizing* (2004), 37, appears to have misread Barclay by suggesting that he has neglected the 'theological insecurities' of the Galatians as a compelling factor in their decision to undergo circumcision. Barclay discusses this in terms of the issue of 'identity', which he sees Paul dealing with (primarily) in the earlier chapters of the letter. But Barclay has neglected 'theological insecurities' as also being relevant to the interpretation of 5.13–6.10.

[56] Similar criticisms are made by Esler, *Galatians*, 216: 'Barclay has argued that Paul actually faced a dual crisis in Galatia'; Engberg-Pedersen, *Stoics*, 327 n. 6; Kwon, *Eschatology* (2004), 185–91; Schewe, *Galater 5 und 6* (2005), 50–53. Cf. Wakefield, *Where to Live* (2003), 47–49, 183–84. Esler, 'Intergroup Conflict' (1996), 215–40, tries to overcome

differently, Barclay succeeds in integrating Gal 5–6 with the rest of the letter, and demonstrating the relevance of this section for the situation in Galatia, only by postulating a *second* major set of factors contributing to the Galatian crisis: questions over ethics or how the Galatians should live.[57] Barclay's claim, then, to have provided an 'integrated interpretation of the letter', while not entirely unjustified, needs to be carefully qualified.[58] His allegedly integrated reading of Galatians is perhaps more accurately described as a unified understanding of the *situation* in Galatia rather than the *argument* of the letter. Barclay has thus presented us with 'The Dual Problem of the Singular Galatians'.[59]

My second reservation with Barclay's proposal concerns what appears to have been his overreaction to the view that Paul was primarily concerned in 5.13–6.10 with combating libertine abuses, Gnostic or otherwise.[60] Barclay, in fact, doubts that there is any evidence for 'antinomian tendencies' or 'flagrant misconduct' in Galatia.[61] Instead, the primary issue for him is *moral confusion*, which he believes naturally explains Paul's numerous assurances in these closing verses (cf. 5.14, 16-18, 22-24, 6.2). However, Barclay appears not to give due attention to the numerous and direct *warnings* in this same section of the letter (cf. 5.15, 21; 6.1, 3-5, 7-8).[62]

Given Barclay's commitment to reading chapters 5–6 primarily as a means of addressing the Galatians' present moral confusion, it is not entirely surprising that he would (inadvertently) underplay the numerous warnings in these closing chapters. If Paul's chief purpose is to bolster the confidence of those struggling with an acute sense of moral insecurity, then a string of pointed threats and warnings would seem somewhat out of keeping with this overall aim. If the Galatians were so anxious to find directives for their daily lives, why would Paul need to issue such stark warnings? This is, of course, the driving question behind the 'two front' hypothesis, and one to which Barclay does not appear to have provided an altogether satisfactory answer. Barclay's proposal, in other words, does not appear to have taken seriously enough this aspect of Gal 5–6 and to explain the interrelationship between Paul's bold assurances, on the one hand, and his sober warnings, on the other.

---

this difficulty by viewing Gal 5–6 as fundamentally about 'identity-description', while Kwon, *Eschatology* (2004), 185–91, takes the opposite tack, arguing that Paul's polemic against the Law is essentially a 'moral' one.

[57] See Dunn, *Theology*, 101–04, who follows Barclay on this point.

[58] Barclay, *Obeying* (1988), 216, 218 (respectively).

[59] The allusion to F. R. Crownfield's well-known essay, 'The Singular Problem of the Dual Galatians' (1945), is intentional. Note that Barclay, *Obeying* (1988), 73, speaks explicitly in terms of the 'dual aspect of the Galatian crisis'.

[60] Cf. Schmithals, *Gnostics* (1972), 13–64; Jewett, 'Agitators' (1971), 198–212.

[61] Barclay, *Obeying* (1988), 218.

[62] Similarly noted by Thomson, *Chiasmus* (1995), 143.

In fairness, Barclay does note that an integrated reading of the ethical section of Galatians must achieve a certain balance and be able to integrate the various elements of this section into a single coherent reading. Far from ignoring the warnings of the ethical section, Barclay, in fact, mentions that one of Paul's aims is to warn the Galatians of 'moral danger' defined in terms of the flesh.[63] He stresses, however, that these warnings, while genuine, should not be understood 'in the usual manner' as directed against libertine abuses. Yet Barclay does little to correlate this observation with his primary thesis that the ethical section serves as an assurance about the sufficiency of the Spirit. He shows little sign of being troubled by having to read the ethical section as intended both *to warn and to assure* the Galatians simultaneously.[64] Instead, in his concluding summary Barclay appears content to juxtapose these two elements and issue a call for balance.[65]

My third critique is closely related to the second. Barclay's heavy emphasis on ethics or 'patterns of behaviour' as a vital part of the dispute in Galatia appears to have eclipsed the *future eschatological orientation* of Gal 5–6.[66] Again, it may not be entirely surprising to find Barclay lay less stress on the eschatological cast of 5.13–6.10, when, according to his own reconstruction of the crisis, the primary aim of this section of the letter is to provide the Galatians with assurances for the present. Moreover, one suspects that his downplaying of the future orientation of much of chapters 5–6 may owe more to the taxonomy he uses to understand the issues at stake in the Galatian crisis: namely, 'identity' and 'patterns of behaviour'.[67] As Barclay himself acknowledges, this is comparable to E. P. Sanders's own schema of 'getting in' and 'staying in'.[68] This particular framework, however, has recently been subjected to serious criticisms, not least because of its failure to

---

[63] Barclay, *Obeying* (1988), 219.

[64] Schewe, *Galater 5 und 6* (2005), 52–53, takes issue with the fact that Barclay supposes that this one passage has at least three different functions: appeal, warning and assurance. Schewe, however, may be in danger of an overreaction in the opposite direction: a reductionism that insists that Galatians *must have* a single argumentative purpose.

[65] Barclay, *Obeying*, 219.

[66] See Barclay, *Obeying* (1988), 93, and his gloss on 5.6: 'in Christ neither circumcision nor uncircumcision are significant status-indicators'. Kwon, *Eschatology* (2004), 199, not unfairly criticises him for treating the future thrust of this passage as 'irrelevant'.

[67] Kwon, *Eschatology* (2004), 4–7, levels this criticism against 'sociological readings' of Galatians in general, including Barclay's: 'In recent years, the sociological dimension of Paul's argument attracts growing scholarly interest. Being sociological, attention is necessarily focused on the *present*, allowing little room for the future eschatological dimension of Paul's polemic to stand on its own'.

[68] Though note Barclay's criticism of Sanders; Barclay, *Obeying* (1988), 237.

account adequately for the future dimension of Paul's soteriology.[69] While Paul certainly speaks of 'getting in' and 'staying in', or issues of 'identity' and 'patterns of behaviour', he also speaks of a *future* 'getting in', not least throughout Gal 5–6 (cf. 5.5-6; 5.21; 6.7-9).[70] Barclay thus appears not to have taken seriously enough the eschatological orientation of these closing chapters.[71]

Despite Barclay's laudable and in many respects successful attempt to read Galatians in a more integrated fashion, there are several shortcomings with his approach. Perhaps, most importantly, as Schewe has rightly pointed out, Barclay's claim to have provided a unified reading of the argument of the letter may be somewhat overstated. Furthermore, as she also notes, Barclay appears to have leaned too heavily for his exegesis of 5.13–6.10 upon a particular reconstruction of the situation in Galatia. We shall need to consider whether these deficiencies can be redressed in a way that enables one to account more adequately for the unity of the argument of the letter.

In this study I intend to argue that by giving careful attention to how the curse of the Law functioned within Galatians and the situation in Galatia, we shall be able to throw fresh light on the question of the rationale for Paul's four references to the Law in 5.13–6.10 and on Paul's response to the Galatian crisis in general. In addition, a refined understanding of Paul's response to the Galatian crisis will open up a new angle of approach to the question of how 5.13–6.10 relates to the earlier chapters of the letter. Before explaining how I shall develop this argument, I should first describe the approach and method of this study.

Approach and Method

In terms of its basic approach, this study is in essence a piece of historical research, on at least two levels. At one level, it is an attempt to discern an ancient author's intention in writing to influence a particular situation;[72] at

---

[69] See, recently, Gathercole, *Boasting* (2002), whose thesis is in many ways devoted to exposing the inadequacies of this taxonomy, not only for understanding some features of early Jewish literature, but also for understanding certain aspects of Paul.

[70] Kuck, 'Creative' (1994), 296, rightly speaks of 'a string of references to God's future judgement in Galatians 5–6'.

[71] Cf. Kwon, *Eschatology* (2004), 6: 'Ethics is well integrated into the scheme, but future eschatology still does not find any role to play, even in what is arguably one of the most successful attempts to interpret the letter as a unified argument'.

[72] It is, of course, well beyond the scope of this study to engage in a discussion about the viability of being able to discern an author's intentions. The discussion by White, *Human Discourse* (1992), 53–59, strikes me as full of common sense: 'With *careful* digging, one can usually form *reasoned* conclusions about persuaders' purposes' (53, emphasis original).

another level, it is an attempt to (re)construct the exigencies of that situation as a complement to our understanding of the author's perception of the situation. At both levels, I am working with probabilities; indeed, this entire enterprise is an exercise in probability judgements. I thus find R. Evans's likening of historical research to the doing of a jigsaw puzzle particularly useful for what it affirms and for what it denies.

> Doing historical research is rather like doing a jigsaw puzzle where the pieces are scattered all over the house in several boxes, some of which have been destroyed, and where once it is put together, a significant number of the pieces are still missing. The nature of the resulting picture will depend partly on how many boxes still survive and have been tracked down, and this depends partly on having some idea of where to look; but the picture's contours can still be filled in, even when not all the pieces have been located. We *imagine* the contours in this situation, and have to speculate on quite a bit of the detail; at the same time, however, the discovery of the existing pieces does set quite severe limits on the operation of our imagination.[73]

The following study is an attempt to put together some of the pieces of the jigsaw puzzle of Galatians in a way that elucidates afresh its contours and presents the reader with at least a partial glimpse of its picture. This will inevitably involve making some probability judgements and doing a certain amount of guesswork, though not of a completely unfettered kind. As Evans rightly points out, there are a few already existing pieces of the puzzle that place certain constraints upon my results. If the pieces of Galatians only fit together to produce a picture of a steam engine, for instance, it is no good trying to put them together to make a suburban garden: it simply will not work.[74]

The aim of this study determines the methods employed. My goal is to explain the rationale for Paul's four references to the Law in 5.13–6.10. As a result, I shall necessarily be somewhat eclectic in my use of various interpretative strategies. Often students of Galatians adopt a single line of approach to a text, bracketing from view, whether for convenience or from conviction, alternative angles of approach. This appears to be the case with a number of recent studies, which focus exclusively either on the Galatian audience as opposed to the Agitators,[75] or the text as opposed to the context,[76] or the Jewish as opposed to Greco-Roman 'background' of some feature of the letter.[77] One of the contributions of this work is to provide a more

---

[73] Evans, *Defense of History* (1997), 89 (emphasis original).

[74] Adapted from a comment made by Evans, *Defense of History* (1997), 89.

[75] Elliott, *Cutting too Close* (2003).

[76] Kwon, *Eschatology* (2004); Schewe, *Galater 5 und 6* (2005); Tolmie, *Persuading* (2005).

[77] Morland, *Curse* (1995), provides an extensive survey of Jewish curse material relevant to Galatians, but with no attention to non-Jewish material. Davis, *Christ as Devotio* (2002), 139–41, notes this limitation in Morland's study and seeks to redress it by utilising Greco-

balanced reading of the letter by utilising several different and complementary angles of approach to the question under discussion.

In three of the five main chapters of the study I shall employ conventional historical-critical methods of exegesis. Chapters 3 and 4 attempt to throw light on the historical context and require a more extended discussion of method. I shall postpone that discussion, however, for the introduction to each of those chapters.

Thesis and Overview of the Argument

This study examines the rationale for Paul's four references to the Law in 5.13–6.10 in light of a fresh appraisal of the Galatian crisis. As such, it contributes to the continuing debate over the relevance of this section of the letter for the rest of Galatians and for the situation in Galatia. In addition, this study seeks to refine our understanding of how Galatians functioned in its original setting: Galatians is Paul's attempt to confront his apostatising converts with the stark choice between blessing and curse.

The thesis of this study is that Paul intended his four references to the Law in 5.13–6.10 as an affirmation of the sufficiency of the Spirit to enable the Galatians to fulfil the Law and thereby avoid its curse. This study is developed in two parts, the first consisting of three chapters, the second of two chapters.

Chapter 1 has located this study within the broader context of Galatians scholarship and provided a description of the approach taken and an overview of the argument. Part 1 ('The Curse of the Law and the Crisis in Galatia') begins with an exploration of the rhetoric of cursing in Galatians, where it is demonstrated that the curse of the Law is a more prominent and indeed a more pervasive feature of the letter than is generally assumed (Chapter 2). This is then followed by two chapters that explore, from two complementary angles, the relevance of the curse of the Law for the Galatian crisis. Chapter 3 considers whether the threat of a curse played a part in the Agitators' appeal for circumcision, while Chapter 4 considers whether the threat of a curse played a part in the Galatians' attraction to circumcision.

Part 2 ('The Curse of the Law and the Purpose of Galatians') offers a close exegesis of Paul's four references to the Law in 5.13–6.10. Chapter 5 begins with Paul's two references to the fulfilment of the Law in 5.14 and 6.2; Chapter 6 then examines what I shall argue are two references to the curse of the Law in 5.18 and 5.23. These two chapters demonstrate that 5.13–6.10 brings the letter to a climax by affirming that the Galatians will fulfil the Law

---

Roman curse material to elucidate his reading of Galatians; yet he ends up arguing the somewhat far-fetched thesis that 3.13 should be understood in terms of the Roman *devotio*.

and thereby avoid its curse if, and only if, they follow the leading of the Spirit. In a concluding chapter I shall bring together the results of this study and suggest a few possible implications.

Part 1

The Curse of the Law
and the Crisis in Galatia

Chapter 2

The Curse of the Law in the Letter to the Galatians

> I call heaven and earth to witness against you today,
> that I have set before you life and death,
> blessing and curse (Deut 30.19).

In Part 1 we shall explore the relevance of the curse of the Law for the crisis in Galatia. Before turning to the historical situation, however, we should first consider how the issue of the curse of the Law informs Paul's response to the crisis by exploring the rhetoric of cursing in Galatians. In this chapter we shall discover that the rhetoric of cursing is a more prominent and indeed a more pervasive feature of the letter than is generally assumed.[1] This has at least two important implications for the present argument. First, it prepares the way for the exegesis of 5.13-6.10 (Chapters 5–6). Secondly, it provides justification for asking about whether the curse of the Law contributed to the crisis in Galatia (Chapters 3–4).

Although there may be different ways to demonstrate the significance of the curse of the Law for Galatians, I shall draw attention to the following three features: (1) Galatians is framed in terms of curse (1.8-9) and blessing (6.16); (2) one of the letter's leading paragraphs contains an unusually high concentration of curse terminology (3.10-14); and (3) Paul continues to refer to the curse of the Law throughout the remainder of the letter by means of the shorthand expression 'under Law' (3.23; 4.4, 5, 21; 5.18). This last observation is especially important for the argument of this chapter because it demonstrates that the rhetoric of cursing is relatively widespread in Galatians. It is also important for the argument of the work as a whole as it shows that the motif of the curse of the Law extends even into the so-called ethical section of the letter, a possibility which has seldom received much attention.

Curse and Blessing in the Epistolary Framework of the Letter

The first indication of the importance of the curse of the Law to Paul's aims with Galatians is the reference to curse and blessing in the epistolary framework of the letter (1.1-9; 6.11-18).

---

[1] Substantial portions of this chapter are adapted from Wilson, 'Under Law' (2006).

Double Anathema (1.8-9)

Whether one approaches 1.6-9 from an epistolary or a rhetorical angle, it is clear that with this paragraph Paul identifies his main contentions with the Galatians and introduces them to the leading topics he wants to develop as the letter ensues.[2] These are three in number: (1) the apostasy of the Galatians (μετατίθεσθε ἀπὸ τοῦ καλέσαντος ὑμᾶς, 1.6), (2) the influence of the Agitators (οἱ ταράσσοντες ὑμᾶς καὶ θέλοντες μεταστρέψαι τὸ εὐαγγέλιον τοῦ Χριστοῦ, 1.7), and (3) Paul's verdict on the situation (ἀνάθεμα ἔστω, 1.8-9). Paul returns to the first two themes throughout the remainder of the letter, at times together, at times separately (cf. 3.1-5; 4.8-11, 12-20; 5.1-12; 6.11-18).[3] These passages give a good indication of Paul's chief purpose in writing: to halt the imminent apostasy of his converts, incited by those who, as he says, want to pervert the gospel of Christ (1.7).[4]

One should not underestimate the significance of the fact that Paul opens the letter with a double anathema upon anyone who preaches 'another gospel' (1.8-9). To begin with, this abrupt opening salvo marks a sharp contrast in tone to Paul's typical prayers of blessing or thanksgiving (cf. Rom 1.8-15; 1 Cor 1.4-9; 2 Cor 1.3-11; Eph 1.3-14; Phil 1.3-10). Although some of the Galatians may not have been familiar enough with conventional letter-writing habits to register this change in style, they would all have been struck by Paul's stinging rebuke and charge of apostasy (θαυμάζω κτλ., 1.6-7), followed by the pronouncement of an anathema upon anyone preaching contrary to what the Galatians themselves had already received (ἀνάθεμα ἔστω, 1.8-9).[5]

Paul underscores the severity of the double anathema in a number of ways. First, he twice repeats (albeit with slight grammatical variation) the pronouncement of an anathema, which could have easily been viewed as his

---

[2] On 1.6-9 as setting out the thesis of the letter, see Kennedy, *Interpretation* (1984), 148; Hall, 'Rhetorical Outline' (1987), 283–84; Vos, 'Galatians 1–2' (1994), 7.

[3] Morland, *Curse* (1995), 144–48.

[4] Kwon, *Eschatology* (2004), 26–50. Cf. Martin, 'Apostasy' (1995), 437–61 (though his suggestion that the Galatians were returning to paganism is open to question).

[5] So Morland, *Curse* (1995), 151–54, 63–67. Cf. Betz, *Galatians* (1979), 53–54; Martyn, *Galatians* (1997), 114. Originally, ἀνάθημα/ἀνάθεμα (the latter being a Hellenistic variation of the former) meant 'something devoted, something offered', but at some point the term ἀνάθεμα developed to include the semantic field of cursing. The evidence suggests that this occurred within a Jewish milieu since examples of ἀνάθεμα with a negative meaning are rare and late outside Jewish-Christian literature. There are only two early examples of ἀνάθεμα used negatively, one on a lead tablet from Megara (first or second-century C.E.), the other on a curse tablet from Amathous (third-century C.E., though there it is ἀνάθημα), both of which evince Jewish influence. This development in the semantic range of the term may be due to the influence of the translation of the Hebrew Bible into Greek, where חרם is consistently translated by ἀνάθημα/ἀνάθεμα. See Pardee, 'Curse that Saves' (1995), 156–76.

way of strengthening the efficacy of the utterance.⁶ Secondly, and not insignificantly, Paul places himself, his coworkers and even an ἄγγελος ἐξ οὐρανοῦ under an anathema, if any of them were to preach another gospel (1.8).⁷ Thirdly, Paul's solemn reminder that he has already warned the Galatians of this danger (ὡς προειρήκαμεν, 1.9; cf. 5.21) underscores both the gravity and the folly of their present situation (cf. 3.1).⁸ Fourthly, the clear implication of what Paul says is that it is *God himself* who will enforce the anathema.⁹ Fifthly, Paul goes on in 1.10-12 to garner support for the double anathema of 1.8-9, thus revealing his own perception of the importance of the anathema to the situation at hand.¹⁰ Sixthly, in the ancient Mediterranean world, not least in central Anatolia (see Chapter 4), invoking a curse was no light matter; once a curse was uttered, it was bound to take effect, either on the one against whom the curse was directed or on the one who (falsely) uttered it. As a result, the Galatians may have viewed Paul as placing himself at considerable risk by pronouncing an anathema: if he is misguided in his assessment of the situation, he himself is cursed. Thus, we may conclude that the Galatians would have been stunned by hearing these opening words read aloud, perhaps in the presence of those heralding another gospel.¹¹

Furthermore, the use of the term ἀνάθεμα to signify a 'curse' or 'something accursed' is extremely rare outside of Jewish circles. Both the form and content of these verses, as well as the immediate context (1.6-7), suggest that Paul may have been thinking in terms of the legislation of Deut 13, the *locus classicus* on false prophecy. K. Sandnes draws attention to the following parallels:

1. Both Deut 13.1-2 and 1.8 deal with preaching based on revelation.
2. The activity described in Deut 13 involves seducing others into turning to θεοὶ ἕτεροι (Deut 13.3, 7, 14); in 1.6 it is εἰς ἕτερον εὐαγγέλιον.
3. The punishment in both texts is a curse (ἀνάθεμα).¹²

---

⁶ Morland, *Curse* (1995), 148, appeals to the idea of *reduplicatio* to emphasise the solemnity of this warning (cf. *Rhet. Her.* 4.28.38). Perhaps more importantly, repetition was a recognised way of strengthening a curse. Cf. Strubbe, 'Cursed' (1991), 41–45.

⁷ For other examples of self-cursing, see Rom 9.3; Acts 23.14; *1 En.* 6.4-5; Josephus, *Vita* 101; cf. Mark 14.71; Matt 26.74.

⁸ The phrase ὡς προειρήκαμεν καὶ ἄρτι πάλιν λέγω, (1.9) probably refers to a similar warning Paul gave to the Galatians on an earlier occasion. So Lightfoot, *Galatians* (1896), 78; Burton, *Galatians* (1921), 29; Mussner, *Galaterbrief* (1974), 61; Longenecker, *Galatians* (1990), 17; Martyn, *Galatians* (1997), 114–15; Cf. Winger, 'Act One' (2002), 548–67, who attempts to reconstruct Paul's original preaching in Galatia.

⁹ Heckel, *Segen* (2002), 224; Morland, *Curse* (1995), 150.

¹⁰ Dunn, *Galatians* (1993), 48.

¹¹ On the delivery and reception of Paul's letters, see Stirewalt, *Letter Writer* (2003), 11–18; Botha, 'Verbal Art' (1993), 409–28.

¹² Sandnes, *One of the Prophets?* (1991), 71.

In Galatians, Paul portrays his listeners as having been somewhat unwittingly led astray. They have been 'bewitched' (3.1); they have been duped into returning to the 'weak and beggarly elements' (4.9); they have been 'cut in on' and thus hindered from 'obeying the truth' (5.7-8). It would be natural for Paul to perceive the apostasy within his Galatian congregations as akin to the situation envisaged in Deut 13, where one is led astray to worship 'other gods' and thus leads others astray. Little wonder that Paul should have viewed the situation in comparable terms. The double anathema is Paul's effort to put the Agitators under a curse and therefore serves as a means of protecting the Galatians from their corrupting influence. This point becomes more explicit later in the letter: 'Cast out the slave and her son' (4.30; 5.7-12; cf. 1 Cor 5.1-5), something to which we shall return below.[13]

Conditional Blessing (6.16)

One of the more fascinating though least developed features of Betz's analysis of Galatians is his identification of it as a 'magical letter'.[14] According to Betz, this was a well-known letter form in antiquity, though, as he acknowledges, there has been no proper study of it.[15] Betz's reason for placing Galatians in this category is that the letter begins with a conditional curse (1.8-9) and ends with a conditional blessing (6.16). The entire body of the letter is thus framed in terms of blessing and curse.[16]

Whether Betz is correct with his classification of Galatians, it is sufficient for the purposes of this chapter to note that the blessing-curse framework of Galatians offers an important clue as to how Paul intended the letter to function within the situation of crisis in Galatia. Paul addresses the Galatians with a blessing and a curse in response to perceived apostasy (1.6), on the one hand, and the influence of (what he perceives to be) false teachers, on the other (1.7). Invoking the motif of blessing and curse within this particular *Sitz im Leben* bears some similarity to the way this same motif functions as part of the covenant renewal ceremony depicted in other early Jewish texts like 1QS 1.16–2.19 (cf. 4Q286-87; 4Q280; 1QM 13.4-6) and *Jubilees* 1.[17] It is also not unlike what Paul does at the end of 1 Corinthians, where he draws upon covenantal categories to separate out the faithful from the apostates: 'If

---

[13] Cf. Martyn, *Galatians* (1997), 114.

[14] Betz, *Galatians* (1979), 25, 50.

[15] Betz, *Galatians* (1979), 25 n. 125.

[16] Vos, 'Galatians 1–2' (1994), 8, sees the blessing in 6.16 and the curse in 1.8-9 forming 'an antithetic *inclusio*'.

[17] Cf. Nitzan, *Qumran Prayer* (1994), 124–39; Werline, 'Covenant Renewal' (2000), 280–88.

anyone does not love the Lord, let him be anathema (ἤτω ἀνάθεμα). Maranatha. The grace of our Lord Jesus be with you' (16.22-23).[18]

This may suggest that Paul intended the letter to the Galatians, its delivery and reception, perhaps within a liturgical setting of worship (1.5), to function as a kind of 'covenant renewal' ceremony, wherein the entire Galatian community is presented with a stark choice: blessing or curse? 'I call heaven and earth to witness against you today, that I have set before you life and death, blessing (εὐλογίαν) and curse (κατάραν)' (Deut 30.19). Which it will be depends upon how the Galatians respond to Paul's *re-proclamation* of his gospel, which occurs through the delivery of his personal communiqué in lieu of his actual presence (6.11; 4.20; cf. 1 Cor 5.1-5).[19]

But Paul intends his letter to effect not merely a theological change of mind, devoid of social consequences. On the contrary, the conditional nature of both the blessing (6.16) and the curse (1.8-9) signify Paul's intention to *identify* those within the mixed community who are in the right – those who walk according to Paul's apostolic 'rule' (6.16) – and those who are not, but who instead come under his anathema (1.8-9).[20] Upon hearing his letter, the community should divide between the apostates and the faithful, and the subsequent procedure should be clear: the latter group should exclude the former from the life of the community as a dangerous and defiling contagion (4.30; 5.7-12).

In addition, one suspects that part of what lay in the back of Paul's mind as he framed Galatians in terms of blessing and curse was his desire to *legitimate the integrity* of the fledgling Gentile Christ-believing communities in Galatia vis-à-vis the dominant Jewish communities, whether believing or unbelieving, whether in Asia Minor or Palestine (2.1-10; 4.25). Paul's Galatian converts are not to think of themselves as marginal, much less as apostates, at least not by virtue of their lack of circumcision (5.2-4),[21] but as 'sons' of Abraham and heirs of the promise by faith (3.6-9, 26-29; 4.6-7, 21-31). Hence, within the Galatian crisis the language of blessing and curse, somewhat paradoxically, is also intended to bolster the confidence of those who are in the right,

---

[18] Eriksson, *Rhetorical Proof* (1998), 290–97; Thiselton, *First Corinthians* (2000), 1349–52.

[19] Galatians as a re-proclamation of Paul's gospel is a prominent theme in Martyn, *Galatians* (1997); Martyn, 'Events in Galatia' (1991), 160–79. Stirewalt, *Letter Writer* (2003), has argued that Paul's letters are an adaptation of the official letter form in antiquity and thus serve to present him as an emissary of Christ.

[20] Thus, both 6.16 and 1.8-9 contain an element of threat; Martyn, *Galatians* (1997), 566; Betz, *Galatians* (1979), 321; Vouga, *Galater* (1998), 157.

[21] Paul, of course, has other reasons for thinking that the Galatians may be apostates (cf. 1.6-7; 5.19-21). In one sense Galatians is about what constitutes apostasy for Paul. While a lack of circumcision does not (5.5-6), deviating from the 'truth of the gospel' (1.6-9; 2.4; 5.7) or indulging in the 'works of the flesh' certainly do (5.19-21).

especially over and against those who may want to call their status into question. 'For neither circumcision nor foreskin (ἀκροβυστία)[22] is anything, but a new creation. And as many as walk according to this rule, peace and mercy be *upon them*, and upon the Israel of God' (6.15-16).

Concentrated Curse Terminology in 3.10-14

Another way to demonstrate the significance of the curse of the Law in Galatians is to note the unusually high concentration of curse terminology in 3:10-14, one of the letter's leading paragraphs. However, as has recently been observerd, 'The meaning of almost every phrase in 3:10-14 is disputed'.[23] Therefore, I shall focus on only a few particularly relevant observations, lest I find myself sinking into an exegetical quagmire.

Compared to Paul's other letters, Galatians contains a high concentration of curse terminology. In the rest of the Pauline corpus, curse terminology appears on only a few occasions. By contrast, 3.10-14 contains no less than five uses of curse terminology.[24] This paragraph also contains a striking interpretation, found nowhere else in Paul's letters, of Christ's death in terms of him 'having become for us a curse' (3.13a). Paul, moreover, supports this singular affirmation with an enigmatic appeal to Deut 21.23: 'Cursed is everyone who hangs upon a tree' (3.13b).[25]

This paragraph also contains the first use of an 'under' expression in Galatians: 'As many as are of the works of the Law are under a curse (ὑπὸ κατάραν)' (3.10). That Paul chose to use the prepositional phrase ὑπὸ κατάραν in 3.10a instead of the verbal adjective ἐπικατάρατος, which appears in the next phrase in 3.10b, is itself intriguing.[26] There are nine other 'under' expressions in Galatians, including the important and repeated expression 'under Law' (3.23; 4.4, 5, 21; 5.18). And, as Martyn observes, the expression 'under a curse' here in 3.10 serves as an 'important precursor' for

---

[22] Marcus, 'Circumcision' (1989), 67–81 (especially 75), argues that this term would have had a concrete (rather than stative) nuance in this context: i.e., uncircumcised penis (glans).

[23] Young, 'Cursed' (1998), 79.

[24] In 3.10-14 Paul uses κατάρα three times (3.10a, 13a [2x]), ἐπικατάρατος twice (3.10b, 3.13b, both citations from Deuteronomy). Elsewhere in Paul, curse terminology appears only in 1 Cor 12.3 (ἀνάθεμα); 16.22 (ἀνάθεμα); Rom 3.14 (ἀρά, citing LXX Psa 10.7); 9.3 (ἀνάθεμα); 12.14 (καταράομαι). Cf. Matt 25.41; 26.74; Mark 11.21; 14.71; Luke 6.28; John 7.49; Acts 23.21; Heb 6.8; James 3.10; 2 Peter 2.14. Cf. Morland, *Curse* (1995), 139–241; Heckel, *Segen* (2002), 210–36.

[25] Explanations of 3.13 continue to multiply. Cf. McClean, *Cursed Christ* (1996), 113–45; Brondos, 'Redemption' (2001), 3–32; Davis, *Christ as Devotio* (2002), 182–118, 164–98; Finlan, *Paul's Cultic Atonement Metaphors* (2004), 101–14.

[26] Stanley, 'Curse' (1990), 499.

Paul's other 'under' expressions in the remainder of the letter. In fact, as will become clear in our discussion below, this first use of an 'under' expression is in some way paradigmatic for these other uses.[27]

Paul's opening comment in 3.10a ('As many as are of the works of the Law are under a curse') probably looks *back* to the curse of 1.8-9 and *forward* to the conditional blessing of 6.16. Thus, Paul has framed this paragraph in terms of curse and blessing in much the same way he has the letter as a whole. Not only does this reveal the fact that 3.10-14 contains the message of Galatians *in nuce*, it also underscores the *polemical* thrust of this comment within the context of the letter. While Paul probably cannot help but think of the history of Israel under the curse of the Law (cf. 3.13; 3.23-25; 4.1-5; see further below), this verse is also intended to function as a warning or perhaps even a threat to the Agitators and to the Galatians. In addition, by placing curse and blessing in sequence in 3.13-14 Paul reveals that he is interested in how the Gentiles obtain the blessing and thus ties in this paragraph with the larger aim of the letter.

Furthermore, the entire paragraph of 3.10-14 finds echoes elsewhere in the letter. The verbal and conceptual similarities between 3.10-14, 3.23-25 and 4.1-7 are often noted. While these three paragraphs have different roles in Paul's argument, they are each closely related to his principal point about the rightful heirs of the Abrahamic blessing or inheritance. His statement, for example, that 'those who are of faith are blessed with the faith of Abraham' (3.9) is further supported by 3.10-14 (cf. γάρ, 3.10). And his inference in 3.29, 'if you are Christ's, then you are Abraham's offspring, heirs according to the promise', is further explained in 4.1-7 (cf. λέγω δέ, 4.1), where 4.7 reiterates this same point. Moreover, although these paragraphs use slightly different imagery and terminology, the underlying flow of thought is very close. All three paragraphs assume a common redemptive sequence, with the following shared elements: (1) the plight of the group is noted (3.10, 13; 3.23-24; 4.2, 3, 5); (2) Christ or the Son is said to identify with this plight (3.13; 4.4; cf. 3.24); (3) this results in the 'redemption' (ἐξαγοράζω) of the group (3.14; 4.5; cf. 3.25-29), which in turn (4) climaxes with the receiving or sending of the Spirit or 'putting on Christ' (3.14; 3.27; 4.6).[28] Each paragraph, in other words, contains a rudimentary outline of Paul's gospel proclamation.[29] Paul's discussion of the curse in 3.10-14 thus casts a long shadow over the remainder of the letter.

---

[27] Martyn, *Galatians* (1997), 371. Surprisingly, some interpreters can offer readings of 'under Law' without even mentioning the expression 'under a curse'; see, for example, Belleville, 'Under Law' (1986), 53–78.

[28] Cf. Donaldson, 'Curse of Law' (1986), 98.

[29] Cf. Hays, *Faith* (2002), 73–117.

The Curse of the Law as a Leitmotif in Galatians

A third strand of evidence demonstrating the significance of the curse of the Law for Galatians is Paul's use of the expression 'under Law' throughout the letter to refer to the curse of the Law. One of the seldom discussed anomalies of Galatians is the high concentration of curse terminology in 3.10-14 together with an absence of any other reference to the curse of the Law elsewhere in the letter. Has Paul simply dropped the notion of the curse of the Law? This appears to be the tacit assumption for many. Having apparently dealt with the curse of the Law in 3.10-14, many scholars assume that Paul now moves on to other issues in the remainder of the letter.

There are a number of reasons why it is unlikely that Paul would fail to refer to the curse of the Law elsewhere in Galatians. First, as we have already seen, Paul has framed Galatians in terms of curse and blessing (1.8-9; 6.16), which would lead one to suspect that it would be a more pervasive feature of the letter than might at first sight appear. Secondly, as we have seen, 3.10-14 occupies a central place in the development of Paul's argument. One might expect to find, therefore, some resonance of its leading motifs (including the curse of the Law) elsewhere in the letter. Thirdly, as has also just been noted, there is considerable conceptual overlap between 3.10-14 and several other passages in Galatians (e.g., 3.22-29; 4.1-7; 5.1-6), which suggests that the theme of cursing, so prominent in 3.10-14, might also reappear in these other passages. Fourthly, if the Agitators used the curse of the Law and texts like Deut 27.26 (cf. 3.10) to promote the observance of circumcision, as many want to argue,[30] one would then expect to find Paul addressing this issue elsewhere in a letter intended (at least, in part) to answer such threats.[31] Fifthly, since 3.10-14 contains a number of key terms and phrases used elsewhere in Galatians (e.g., 'works of the Law', 'faith', 'life', 'redemption', 'Spirit'), one would expect at least the motif of the curse, if not curse terminology, to appear elsewhere.

There is some *prima facie* support, then, for thinking that Paul would have wanted to continue to refer to the curse of the Law elsewhere in Galatians. Some have suggested that the expression 'under Law' contains a reference to the curse of the Law (3.23; 4.4, 5, 21; 5.18).[32] But no one has provided a satisfactory explanation of *all five* uses of the expression in Galatians understood as a reference to the curse of the Law. I shall try to redress this in what follows by arguing that the phrase 'under Law' not only contains a

---

[30] E.g., Martyn, *Galatians* (1997), 309.

[31] I shall take up this question at greater length in Chapter 3 ('The Curse of the Law and the Message of the Agitators').

[32] Hong, 'Under Law' (2002), 354–72; Hafemann, 'Exile of Israel' (1997), 329–71; Scott, *Adoption as Sons* (1992), 174; Ridderbos, *Galatians* (1953), 144, 204.

reference to the curse of the Law, but in fact serves as shorthand for the expression 'under the curse of the Law' (3.10, 13).[33] If this is the case, it implies that the motif of the curse of the Law pervades much of the letter, including the ethical section (5.18).

'Under Law' as rhetorical shorthand for 'under the curse of the Law'

Galatians is a particularly elusive letter because it contains a large number of enigmatic catchphrases. Betz refers to these as 'theological abbreviations' and identifies over thirty in Galatians, mostly prepositional phrases, including 'according to man' (1.11; cf. 1.1), 'from works of the Law' (2.16; 3.2, 5, 10), 'from faith' (2.16; 3.7, 8, 9), 'in the flesh' (2.20; 4.14; 6.13), and 'in Christ' (1.22; 2.4, 17; 3.14, 26, 28).[34] Paul uses these expressions as a kind of rhetorical shorthand with which to develop the argument of the letter.[35]

Betz includes within this group of theological abbreviations the important and somewhat controversial phrase 'under Law' (ὑπὸ νόμου), which appears five times in Galatians (3.23; 4.4, 5, 21; 5.18), and several times in Paul's other letters (1 Cor 9.20-21; Rom 6.14-15). Regrettably, Betz provides little guidance on how one should go about 'decoding' this phrase. He does, however, offer a number of stimulating suggestions about the use of the phrase in Galatians. But he does not explain *why* he has identified this particular phrase as an abbreviation, nor do we find him explicitly reflecting upon *what* the phrase might be an abbreviation for.

There is good reason to think that 'under Law' (ὑπὸ νόμου) serves in Galatians as an abbreviation or rhetorical shorthand of some kind, indeed it may have been Paul's own coinage. While there is evidence of one or two uses of the phrase prior to Paul, these are rather fortuitous and could hardly have influenced him.[36] The exact expression is not used in the LXX; nor can it be found in early Jewish literature written in Greek.[37] Likewise, there does not appear to be a Hebrew or Aramaic equivalent in early Jewish literature.[38]

---

[33] Hafemann, 'Exile of Israel' (1997), 342–9, suggests something similar, though only with reference to the use of the phrase in 3.23, 4.5. Cf. Hong, 'Under Law' (2002), 354–72.

[34] Betz, *Galatians* (1979), 27. Betz's thesis has been taken up by Lategan, 'Defending' (1988), 420, 429–30; and explored further in Lategan, 'Formulas' (1991), 75–87, where he identifies over fifty abbreviations in Galatians.

[35] I shall use the terms (theological) 'abbreviation' and (rhetorical) 'shorthand' interchangeably.

[36] Pseudo-Plato, *Def.* 415.c.3; Longinus, *Subl.* 33.5.4; noted by Marcus, 'Under Law' (2001), 72 n. 2, and confirmed by an on-line *Thesaurus Linguae Graecae* search (http://www.tlg.uci.edu/; accessed 28/7/04).

[37] For examples of the plural (ὑπὸ νόμους), see Josephus, *C. Ap.* 2.210; 2.174.

[38] Marcus, 'Under Law' (2001), 72–73; similarly noted by Finsterbusch, *Lebensweisung* (1996), 84 n. 136; Gaston, *Torah* (1987), 29, 198 n. 58. Marcus, 'Under Law' (2001), 73 n. 4,

Moreover, the phrase is not used by any other NT author and only begins to appear outside Paul in early Christian writings of the latter half of the second-century C.E., where dependence upon Paul's letters is quite likely, if not explicit.[39]

Depending upon one's chronology of Paul's letters, then, the appearance of ὑπὸ νόμον in Galatians may well be Paul's first use of the phrase, perhaps specially minted for the purpose of responding to the developing crisis in Galatia. Alternatively, the Galatians may have been familiar with the phrase through Paul's earlier ministry, which might explain why so cryptic a phrase can come with relatively little (if any) elaboration.[40] In any event, the compressed and indeed cryptic nature of the expression, especially in light of the virtual absence of the phrase in early Jewish or pagan literature prior to Paul, is reason to think that the phrase may well have been a piece of rhetorical shorthand of Paul's own making.

But this begs an important question: shorthand for what? What does 'under Law' abbreviate? Answering this question requires employing reliable criteria with which to discern the use of shorthand. The following three principles, to my knowledge nowhere else developed in discussions of rhetorical shorthand, may be proposed as at least a partial starting point. First, a shorthand expression obviously must be *shorter* or more condensed than its longhand equivalent. Secondly, a shorthand expression must have some *discernible verbal connection* to its longhand equivalent. For if there is no verbal link between the two expressions, there would be no way to detect whether one particular expression was serving as shorthand for another, as over against any other expression which happens to refer to the same thing. Thirdly, a shorthand expression must have the *same referent* as its longhand equivalent. One can safely assume that a particular expression is shorthand for another expression only when both expressions refer to the same thing. This is not, of course, to deny slight differences in connotation between the two expressions as a result of the various associations that may arise from differences of form; only that an expression cannot be shorthand for another expression without possessing the same referent. Thus, in order for a phrase to qualify as shorthand, it must satisfy all three criteria.[41]

---

also confesses to being unable to identify a Hebrew equivalent in the relevant early Jewish literature (e.g., תחת התורה, תחת התורה, תחת יד התורה).

[39] Justin, *Dial.* 45.3.9; 95.1.6; Clement of Alexandria, *Paed.* 30.3.2; 33.4.10; *Strom.* 1.3; 2.3, 4; 4.2; Pseudo-Justin Martyr, *Quae.* 409.c.1; 413.c.9; 413.d.1; 458.c.5; Origen, *Princ.* 4.1.6; 4.2.6; Gregory of Nyssa, *Psalmorum* 5.47.17; *Canticum* 6.403.16.

[40] It is possible that the phrase was first introduced by the Agitators. So Marcus, 'Under Law' (2001), 73–75.

[41] An author may, of course, use a shorthand expression that does not satisfy the first criterion, but there would be no independent way to confirm the fact.

With this in mind, we can now attempt to 'decode' the shorthand expression 'under Law'. That is, we can seek an answer to the following question: what expression provides the most likely longhand equivalent for the shorthand expression 'under Law'? Since we are concerned primarily with the use of the expression 'under Law' in Galatians, it is perhaps best to take Galatians as our point of departure. Our question can therefore be further refined: is there a phrase in Galatians that might serve as a viable longhand equivalent to the shorthand phrase 'under Law'?

In anticipation of the exegesis to follow, I would like to suggest at this point that the most likely candidate is the expression 'under the curse of the Law' (ὑπὸ τὴν κατάραν τοῦ νόμου, 3.10, 13).[42] With respect to the three criteria outlined above, the following points can be made. First, ὑπὸ νόμον is obviously a shorter, more condensed expression than ὑπὸ τὴν κατάραν τοῦ νόμου, and it is not hard to imagine Paul, for convenience, if not for effect, using the former expression in lieu of the latter, more cumbersome one. Paul could simply drop the middle term κατάραν and create the shorthand expression ὑπὸ νόμον, as here illustrated:[43]

3.10-14:   ὑπὸ ~~τὴν κατάραν τοῦ~~ νόμου (3.10, 13)

3.23–5.18:   ὑπὸ νόμον (3.23; 4.4-5, 21; 5.18)

It is also worth pointing out that there may be significance in the fact that Paul uses the phrase ὑπὸ νόμον *only after* he has first introduced the notion of the 'curse of the Law' in 3.10-14. If 'under Law' had appeared *prior to* Paul's explicit mention of the curse of the Law in 3.10-14, it would considerably weaken my case. As it stands, however, one has reason to suspect that Paul may have resorted to the shorthand expression 'under Law' as a way of being more economical and perhaps even more rhetorically forceful.[44] Moreover, given the exposition of 3.10-14, Paul could have used 'under Law' with reasonable confidence of the fact that the Galatians would have *heard* this expression with the threat of the curse of the Law still ringing

---

[42] While Paul does not use the exact expression ὑπὸ τὴν κατάραν τοῦ νόμου, this surely stands behind the expression ὑπὸ κατάραν (3.10) and is implied by ἡ κατάρα τοῦ νόμου (3.13).

[43] Paul is probably doing something similar with the expressions ἐξ ἀκοῆς πίστεως (3.2, 5) and ἐκ πίστεως (2.16; 3.7, 8, 9, 11, 12, 22, 24; 5.5), and ἐξ ἔργων νόμου (2.16; 3.2, 5, 10) and ἐκ νόμου (3.18, 21).

[44] For reflections on the virtue of brevity within ancient rhetorical theory, see Mitchell, 'Shorthand' (1994), 65–9; Johnson, 'Taciturnity' (1990), 329–336, who includes citations from the Wisdom literature of the OT (LXX), Hellenistic Jewish, rabbinic and early Christian writings.

in their ears, 3.10-14 thus providing a fixed point of reference for all subsequent uses of 'under Law' (3.23; 4.4, 5, 21; 5.18).[45]

As to the second criteria for detecting shorthand, one can of course affirm a close *verbal connection* between ὑπὸ τὴν κατάραν τοῦ νόμου and ὑπὸ νόμον. In some respects, the link is obvious enough that one has little trouble imagining both Paul and the Galatians regarding the use of 'under Law' as shorthand for 'under the curse of the Law' as a rather natural and sensible move to make. Here it is also worth noting that Paul's first 'under' expression in Galatians, as we observed earlier, happens to be the phrase 'under a curse' (ὑπὸ κατάραν) in 3.10. And, again, as Martyn has recently observed, this may well be an 'important precursor' for Paul's other 'under' expressions in Galatians, perhaps in some way paradigmatic for these other uses.[46]

The Son came 'under Law' and redeemed us from 'under Law' (4.4-5)

Perhaps the strongest piece of exegetical support for taking 'under Law' as shorthand for 'under the curse of the Law' comes from a close comparison of the two uses of 'under Law' in 4.4-5 with similar expressions in 3.10-14. The propriety of making such a comparison is based upon the verbal and conceptual similarities between these two paragraphs, which we have already noted.

Paul's statement that 'God sent his Son to redeem those under Law' (4.5a) corresponds to his earlier assertion that 'Christ redeemed us from the curse of the Law' (3.13a). The group identified as 'those under Law' (τοὺς ὑπὸ νόμον) in 4.5a closely parallels the 'us' (ἡμᾶς) who need to be redeemed 'from the curse of the Law' (ἐκ τῆς κατάρας τοῦ νόμου) in 3.13a. Moreover, this apparent conceptual overlap is considerably strengthened by the shared use of the rather unusual verb ἐξαγοράζω, which represents the only uses of this verb in the undisputed letters of Paul (cf. Eph 5.16; Col 4.5).

In 3.13a Christ is the subject of the verb ἐξαγοράζω and the one who effects redemption for 'us'. In 4.5a either God or the Son could be the subject

---

[45] Why did Paul not use the clearer, more explicit phrase 'under a curse' (3.10) when, as I am arguing, it was virtually synonymous with 'under Law'? Paul may have thought that the expression 'under Law' was better suited to Galatians because it had the rhetorical advantage of linking *curse* and *Law*, which might help dissuade the Galatians of their attraction to the Law. Furthermore, one of the disadvantages with using 'under a curse' (3.10) as shorthand in Galatians is that the expression does not explicitly identify either the *identity* or the *source* of the curse under question. Here we do well to remember that the world inhabited by the Galatians was alive with all sorts of curses and cursing (see Chapter 4 below). Clarification about *which* curse was in question and *where* it was coming from would have been of some interest to the Galatians, if not to Paul. The advantage with using the expression 'under Law' to refer to the curse of the Law is that it identifies the threat of the curse as the curse which comes from the Law of the Jews.

[46] Martyn, *Galatians* (1997), 371.

of ἐξαγοράζω, though the latter is more likely.⁴⁷ God sent the Son in order that *the Son* might redeem those 'under Law' (4.4-5). The recipients of Christ's redeeming work are referred to in 3.13a as those who need to be redeemed 'from the curse of the Law' (ἐκ τῆς κατάρας τοῦ νόμου). Presumably, then, on the basis of 3.10a, they are 'under a curse' (ὑπὸ κατάραν). They are, in other words, 'under the curse of the Law' (ὑπὸ τὴν κατάραν τοῦ νόμου, 3.10a, 13a).⁴⁸ Christ redeemed 'us', Paul is thus saying, from the baneful condition of being under the curse of the Law (3.13a).

In 4.5a, on the other hand, Paul describes the recipients of the Son's redeeming work as 'those under Law' (τοὺς ὑπὸ νόμον). This expression most likely refers to the *same group* identified in 3.13a as the 'us' who were redeemed 'from the curse of the Law'.⁴⁹ This enables one to draw the following parallels between 3.13a and 4.5a:

3.13a   Χριστὸς ἐξηγόρασεν ἡμᾶς ἐκ τῆς κατάρας τοῦ νόμου
        =   =   =   =
4.5a ἵνα [τὸν υἱὸν] ἐξαγοράσῃ τοὺς   ὑπὸ νόμον

Given the close proximity between 3.10-14 and 4.1-7 and the strength of this present comparison, it seems rather unlikely that Paul intended to refer to different situations with these two assertions. It is more probable that redemption 'from the curse of the Law' (3.13a) refers to the same plight as redemption from being 'under Law' (4.5a). In all likelihood, therefore, Paul is using the expression 'under Law' in 4.5 as another way to refer to the 'curse of the Law' mentioned in 3.13. More than that, given the obvious verbal similarities between the two expressions, it is probable that the expression 'under Law' serves as shorthand for 'under the curse of the Law'. Just as Christ redeemed 'us' from the curse of the Law (3.13), so too the Son has redeemed those who were 'under (the curse of the) Law' (4.5). Hence, in 4.5 Paul reiterates in abbreviated form what he has already asserted in 3.13: 'Christ redeemed those who were under the curse of the Law'.

Paul's second use of 'under Law' in 4.1-7 is embedded in a participial phrase that defines more precisely the identity of the Son who redeemed those who were 'under Law': 'God sent forth his Son, who was born of a woman, who came under Law (γενόμενον ὑπὸ νόμον)' (4.4).⁵⁰ Paul's statement that

---

⁴⁷ The most immediate grammatical possibility is τὸν υἱόν, and elsewhere in Galatians Christ is portrayed as the agent of redemption (cf. 3.13; 1.4)

⁴⁸ Bonneau, 'Curse' (1997), 72.

⁴⁹ The composition of this group (i.e., inclusive of Gentiles or not) does not affect the essential thrust of the present argument.

⁵⁰ Despite the formal similarities between γενόμενον ἐκ γυναικός and γενόμενον ὑπὸ νόμον, the verb γίνομαι need not necessarily carry the same sense in both expressions (i.e., 'born under Law'). Cf. Burton, *Galatians* (1921), 171. However, treating 4.4d as a reference

the Son 'came under Law' is quite close to his earlier comment that Christ redeemed 'us' by 'becoming for us a curse' (γενόμενος ὑπὲρ ἡμῶν κατάρα, 3.13). While the two participial phrases have slightly different grammatical functions, they nevertheless have the same overall effect: both further explicate Christ's (the Son's) redeeming work.[51] The following comparison of the participial phrases of 3.13b and 4.4d brings this parallelism out more fully:

3.13b   γενόμενος ὑπὲρ ἡμῶν   κατάρα
        =   =
4.4d   γενόμενον   ὑπὸ νόμον

In saying that Christ 'became for us a curse' (γενόμενος ὑπὲρ ἡμῶν κατάρα, 3.13b), Paul wants his hearers to understand that Christ endured 'the curse of the Law' (ἡ κατάρα τοῦ νόμου, 3.13a). Yet one can hardly imagine this was because of his failure to fulfil the Law (3.10b). This of course raises a whole host of questions, not least what Paul means by 'curse' in this context. He provides us with an important clue by disassociating the curse from the triad of 'blessing' (3.8-9), 'life' (3.11-12) and 'Spirit' (3.14); another clue comes from the fact that the curse of the Law is associated with Christ's *death* – which is itself somehow linked with his crucifixion (3.13b; Deut 21.23). This is a notoriously difficult train of thought and will not be pursued further here.[52] Besides, Paul's point is clear enough, even if his 'logic' remains somewhat obscure: Christ redeemed 'us' from the curse of the Law by submitting himself to the Law's curse (3.10a, 3.13).

Like the previous comparison, the strength of this parallelism suggests that when Paul says that the Son came 'under Law' (4.4d) and that Christ 'became a curse' (3.13b), he is probably referring to the same thing.[53] This suggests

---

to the Son being 'born under Law' would not substantially affect the thrust of the present argument. On that reading, the Son would be 'born under (the curse of the) Law' by being born a Jew and thus under the curse of the Law upon Israel (cf. 3.10, 23–25). Cf. Wright, *Climax* (1991), 151, 'The Messiah has come where Israel is, under the Torah's curse (see 4.4), in order to be not only Israel's representative but Israel's *redeeming* representative' (emphasis original).

[51] Hays, *Faith* (2002), 96.

[52] Cf. Hooker, 'Interchange' (1971), 349–61; and, more recently, Brondos, 'Redemption' (2001), 3–32.

[53] The progression from being 'born of a woman' (4.4c) and 'coming under Law' (4.4d) would be a movement from the Son's birth to his death and therefore contain a reference to the Son coming under the curse of the Law upon the cross, an echo of 3.13. Eckstein, *Verheissung* (1996), 236–8. On this reading, the Christologies reflected in these two passages would not be as divergent as is sometimes supposed. Betz, *Galatians* (1979), 150 n. 119, for example, insists that 3.13 and 4.4-5 'must be kept separate' since they 'cannot be harmonized' (207 n. 51).

that the phrase 'under Law' refers to coming under the curse of the Law. Just as Christ redeemed 'us' from the curse of the Law by becoming for us a curse (3.13), so too the Son came 'under (the curse of the) Law' (4.4) in order that he might redeem those 'under (the curse of the) Law' (4.5).[54]

In sum, taking Paul's use of 'under Law' in 4.4-5 as shorthand for 'under the curse of the Law' provides the most economical and straightforward explanation of these striking parallels. Seeing a reference back to 3.10-14 in Paul's use of 'under Law' in 4.4-5 also makes good sense of the immediate context, as has been argued (in different ways) in several recent studies.[55]

'We were kept under Law' (3.23)

Paul's first use of 'under Law' in Galatians (3.23) is significant because it appears alongside two similar expressions: 'under sin' (3.22) and 'under a pedagogue' (3.25). There are, of course, a whole host of issues that could be taken up, but for my present purposes only three will be addressed. How does being 'under Law' relate to being 'under sin'? What implications follow from Paul's comparison of being 'under Law' to being 'under a pedagogue'? Does treating 'under Law' as shorthand for 'under the curse of the Law' make sense within the context of 3.19-25?

Several commentators take 'under sin' to refer to the Law's *condemnation* of sin, thus equating 'under sin' with 'under a curse' (3.10).[56] While I certainly find this a tempting proposal, a close reading of these verses argues against this line of interpretation. First, Paul says that it was Scripture (ἡ γραφή) and not the Law (ὁ νόμος; cf. 3.21; 3.23-25) that enclosed all things 'under sin'.[57] Secondly, he says that Scripture enclosed not just all persons (τοὺς πάντας; cf. Rom 11.32), but all things (τὰ πάντα) 'under sin'.[58]

---

[54] Schweizer, 'υἱός κτλ.' (1972), 383: 'Both formulations [γενόμενον ὑπὸ νόμον, ἵνα τοὺς ὑπὸ νόμον ἐξαγοράσῃ] obviously develop what is said in 3:13'.

[55] Scott, *Adoption as Sons* (1992), 149–86; Hafemann, 'Exile of Israel' (1997), 331–49; Eckstein, *Verheissung* (1996), 233–9. On the relationship between 'under Law' and the other two 'under' expressions in 4.1-7, see especially Hafemann, 'Exile of Israel' (1997), 331–49.

[56] Lightfoot, *Galatians* (1896), 147–8; Burton, *Galatians* (1921), 195–6; followed by Longenecker, *Galatians* (1990), 144. See also Thielman, *Paul & the Law* (1994), 132.

[57] In Galatians, Paul consistently personifies Scripture (γραφή) so that it 'preaches' (3.8), 'encloses' (3.22) and 'speaks' (4.30). This suggests he uses the term as a way to refer to what *God* has done, as witnessed to in Israel's Scriptures. The formal parallels between 3.22 and 3.8, as well as the parallels between 3.22 and Rom 11.32 (cf. Rom 9.17), corroborate this point. Cf. Eckstein, *Verheissung* (1996), 211; Matera, *Galatians* (1992), 135; Belleville, 'Under Law' (1986), 56.

[58] Cf. Cosgrove, *Cross and Spirit* (1988), 71: 'the entire cosmos'. The 'all things' certainly includes 'the whole human situation—man and all his works'; Bruce, *Galatians* (1982), 180. But it should not be limited to this. On the 'cosmic' scope of this statement, see Schlier, *Galater* (1962), 154; Barrett, *Freedom and Obligation* (1985), 34; Dunn, *Galatians* (1993), 194; Kuula, *Law* (1999), 50.

This suggests that Paul may have wanted to include the *Law itself* within the scope of that which Scripture enclosed 'under sin'.

That Paul conceives of the Law itself as 'under sin' is supported by the fact that 3.22 serves as a logical contrast to the condition of 3.21 (cf. ἀλλά, 3.22). Paul denies the possibility that a law was given that could 'make alive' (3.21) by asserting that in reality Scripture has enclosed all things – even the Law itself – 'under sin' (3.22; cf. 1.4).[59] As a prisoner to sin, then, the Law was incapable of producing life and therefore unable to provide 'righteousness' (3.21; cf. 2.15-21; 3.11-12).

It is best, then, to take 'under sin' as a reference, not to the Law's condemnation of sin, but to the *power* or *authority* of sin over all things, including those who possess the Law, those of the Sinai covenant.[60] The expression 'under sin' thus refers to a more general (i.e., universal) condition than that referred to by 'under Law'. The latter is a particular expression of the former; 'under Law' is a subset of 'under sin'. While everyone is 'under sin', only those of the Sinai covenant are 'under Law' – that is, under the penalty prescribed in the Law for failure to observe its precepts, which is itself the direct consequence of being 'under sin' (cf. 3.10; 2.15-16).

This reading makes good sense of the following verse: 'Now before faith came, we were kept under Law, enclosed (συγκλειόμενοι) until faith should be revealed' (3.23). Here Paul repeats the verb συγκλείω from 3.22, though he elides the phrase 'under sin', probably to avoid an unnecessary redundancy. But the point is clear: 'We were kept under Law *by being enclosed under sin*' (3.23). Though controversial, this statement likely summarises Paul's reflections on Israel's own experience with the Law under the Sinai covenant (cf. 3.17-21).[61] Hence, when Paul says that we were kept 'under Law' by being enclosed 'under sin' (3.23), he is probably referring to Israel's inability to escape from the *curse* of the Law because of her inability to come out from 'under sin' (cf. 3.10-12; 4.21-27). In other words, sin foiled Israel's best attempts to find liberation from the curse of the Law *by means of* the Law (cf. Rom 8.3: τὸ ἀδύνατον τοῦ νόμου).

This would then readily explain the metaphor of a 'pedagogue', which Paul uses to describe Israel's relationship to the Law. What does it mean, historically speaking, for Israel to possess the Law and yet be imprisoned 'under sin' and thus enclosed 'under (the curse of the) Law' (3.22-23)? Paul explains by way of a metaphor: 'As a result [of being kept under the curse of

---

[59] Cosgrove, *Cross and Spirit* (1988), 71: 'The Law is by definition included'.

[60] Cf. Paul's two uses of this expression in Romans (3.9; 7.14), where he personifies sin and conjoins it to slavery imagery (cf. Rom 6–7). This suggests that Paul conceived of sin as much as a power that acts *upon* individuals as the discrete acts *of* individuals.

[61] Betz, *Galatians* (1979), 175–76; Hafemann, 'Exile of Israel' (1997), 329–71; Finsterbusch, *Lebensweisung* (1996), 86–87.

the Law, 3.23], the Law became our pedagogue (παιδαγωγός) until Christ' (3.24). Here Paul employs the metaphor of the 'pedagogue' to describe the peculiar *function* of the Law prior to the coming of Christ. While there has been considerable debate over the precise import of this analogy,[62] perhaps Paul's main point is that Israel's confinement under the curse of the Law means that the Law is not a mediator of the promise, but a mere pedagogue, a household slave whose presence reminds the trustee that he is still a minor and thus unable to have access to his inheritance (cf. 4.1-3). Insofar as the Law curses Israel while Israel is 'under sin', the Law serves as a token of Israel's continued estrangement from the inheritance.

In saying this, one should be careful to note that Paul does not describe the *Law itself* as a 'pedagogue', but only the particular historical *function* of the Law before the 'coming of faith' (3.23), when it was itself enclosed 'under sin' (3.22). As Paul says: ὥστε ὁ νόμος παιδαγωγὸς ἡμῶν γέγονεν εἰς Χριστόν (3.24).[63] Thus, Paul's comparison of the Law's function to that of a 'pedagogue' tells us little about whether he thought the Law itself was of a limited duration or not. His only point here is that this particular function of the Law (i.e., to enclose Israel under a curse) is of a limited duration (i.e., εἰς Χριστόν). Despite the widespread assumption to the contrary, the issue of the perpetuity of the Law *after* the coming of faith is not at issue here.

Paul's brief digression in 3.21-25 serves, then, not unlike Rom 7.7-25, to ward off a possible charge against the Law. Given what Paul has said thus far in chapter 3, one might conceivably conclude that the Law somehow opposes the promises (3.21). For Paul has denied that the Law in any way mediates the *blessing* of Abraham (3.6-14), but instead has only brought about the *curse* (3.10-14). This grim reading of the Law's function is further exacerbated by Paul's intervening claim that the Law was secondary to the promises (3.15-18) and added only 'because of transgressions' (3.19), and that by a 'mediator' (3.20). Regardless of the implications one draws from these seemingly disparaging remarks, the question of 3.21 is surely to the point: is the Law against the promises?

Paul's answer to this query, though, is surprisingly straightforward. The Law is not ultimately culpable for the curse – sin is. Sin blocks the reception of the promises by interposing, not the Law, but the *curse* of the Law. This again explains why Paul compares being 'under Law' (i.e., under the curse of

---

[62] Lull, 'Pedagogue' (1986), 481–98; Young, 'Pauline Metaphor' (1987), 150–176; Gordon, 'Παιδαγωγός' (1989), 150–54; Belleville, 'Under Law' (1986), 53–78; though note the incisive comment by Westerholm, *Israel's Law* (1988), 195: 'It is probably pointless to ask which part of the "pedagogue's" task Paul has in mind in applying the figure to the Law'.

[63] Note the syntactical parallel in 4.16: ὥστε ἐχθρὸς ὑμῶν γέγονα ἀληθεύων ὑμῖν. Paul *became* the Galatians' enemy only as a *result* of certain recent developments.

the Law) to being 'under a pedagogue' (3.24-25). In the Greco-Roman milieu, not only was a pedagogue's role over the life of a child temporary, the very presence of a pedagogue was indicative of the child's *inability to access his inheritance*. Not insignificantly, this second nuance is precisely the one Paul develops in both 3.23-29 (cf. 3.29) and 4.1-7 (cf. 4.7).

One of the underlying themes of 3.10-4.7 is that while Israel was 'under Law' (3.23), Israel was unable to gain access to the promise of the inheritance. As such, Israel was, at least with respect to the inheritance, hardly any different than the nations, despite being rightfully entitled to that inheritance (4.1-2). Speaking metaphorically, Israel was 'under a pedagogue' during her protracted childhood (3.24-25; 4.1-2). Alternatively, one could say that for Israel the Law, because of its curse, became for a time a 'pedagogue', which precluded Israel gaining access to the inheritance. In short, until Christ came to redeem Israel from the curse of the Law (3.13; 4.4-5), Israel was kept 'under Law' – under the Law's curse.

'Those who want to be under Law' (4.21)

Paul's fourth use of 'under Law' helps introduce the (in)famous Sarah-Hagar allegory: 'Tell me, you who want to be under Law (ὑπὸ νόμον), do you not listen to the Law?' (4.21). At first sight, this text appears to pose a problem for interpreting 'under Law' as shorthand for 'under the curse of the Law'. How could Paul accuse the Galatians of *wanting* to come under the curse of the Law? Surely nothing was farther from their own intentions!

This is not a problem for those who take 'under Law' as a reference to observing the Law. The Galatians want to be 'under Law' insofar as they want to embrace (some of) the stipulations of the Law.[64] But we need to take seriously the ironic tone of the rhetorical question in 4.21.[65] Nearly all of Paul's rhetorical questions in Galatians are highly polemical and need to be read carefully. Interpreters need to be especially circumspect about Paul's seeming ability to divine the intentions of either the Galatians or the Agitators, bearing in mind that one of Paul's aims with the letter is a *polemical portrayal* of the various players involved in the crisis.[66]

That Paul is speaking polemically and, in fact, ironically in 4.21 is suggested by his use of the verb θέλω to depict what the Galatians 'want' to

---

[64] For many this verse becomes an important datum for reconstructing the Galatian crisis. Cf. Barclay, *Obeying* (1988), 62–63.

[65] Betz, *Galatians* (1979) 241; Ridderbos, *Galatians* (1953), 178; Stanton, 'Law of Moses' (1996), 115; Nanos, *Irony* (2002), 80–81; Hays, 'Galatians' (2000), 300.

[66] Barclay, *Obeying* (1988), 62–63, for example, notes that 'the heavily polemical context of 6.13 should make us extremely hesitant to take this verse at face value'. He does not, however, appear to exercise the same degree of circumspection when reading Paul's comment in 4.21, which he takes as a straightforward statement about the Galatians' actual intentions. This is similarly noted by Mitternacht, *Sprachlose* (1999), 41.

do. Paul uses this verb on a number of occasions to portray the motives of both the Agitators and the Galatians. His strategy with θέλω appears to be twofold. On the one hand, Paul wants to distance the Galatians from the Agitators by exposing the Agitators' fraudulent motives (cf. 1.7; 4.17; 6.12-13). On the other, he wants to warn the Galatians about their present apostasy by projecting their own motives in terms of the negative consequences of their actions (4.9, 21).[67]

While the Agitators no doubt promulgated their teaching under a fair guise, and may well have done so with good intentions, as far as Paul was concerned they simply 'wanted' to pervert the gospel of Christ (1.7), exclude the Galatians (4.17), make a good showing in the flesh (6.12), avoid persecution (6.12) and boast in the Galatians' circumcision (6.13). Paul's tactic with the Galatians, however, is more subtle. By portraying what the Galatians *want* to do in terms of what they are trying to *avoid* in both 4.9 and 4.21, Paul issues a pair of very forceful (albeit highly ironic) warnings.[68] After having been miraculously delivered from servitude to 'beings that by nature are not gods' (4.8), Paul is incredulous over the fact that the Galatians are now observing 'days and months and seasons and years' (4.10). He chides them: 'How are you turning back again to the weak and beggarly elements to whom *you want* (θέλετε) *to be enslaved all over again*?' (4.9). The Galatians, needless to say, had absolutely no intention of returning to slavery of any kind, much less bondage to the 'elements' (4.9). But discerning intentions is not Paul's point here. Rather, he confronts the Galatians with their own foolishness by outrageously asserting that they themselves are eager to be enslaved.

Paul then uses this same technique in 4.21. Following the pathos appeal of 4.11-20, he picks up the bantering line begun in 4.9 by interrogating the Galatians: 'Tell me, you who want (οἱ θέλοντες) to be under Law, do you not listen to the Law?' (4.21).[69] Here Paul warns the Galatians about their present apostasy by threatening them with the prospect of coming 'under Law' (4.21), just as he previously warned them of being 'enslaved all over again' (4.9). To *threaten* the Galatians with the possibility of coming 'under Law' makes best sense, however, if Paul has in mind the *curse* of the Law as the consequence of their present apostasy. Therefore, Paul probably intends 4.21 to serve as an ironic rebuke-warning to be heard along the following lines: 'Tell me, you

---

[67] Cf. Cosgrove, *Cross and Spirit* (1988), 79.

[68] Barclay, *Obeying* (1988) 91, says something similar about Paul's overall strategy in 4.21-31: 'It mirrors Paul's tactic evidenced throughout this epistle, where he attempts to show that the Galatians' attraction to circumcision and the Law will achieve *the very opposite of their intentions*' (emphasis added).

[69] The two rhetorical questions in 4.9 and 4.21 are syntactically and structurally parallel and indicate that Paul has now shifted (returned? cf. 1.6-9; 3.1-5) to a more direct mode of rebuke after the theological exposition of 3.6–4.7. See similarly Wilder, *Echoes* (2001), 105-7.

who are courting the curse of the Law, do you not hear what the Law says to those who are under its curse?'[70]

In 4.22-30, Paul explains what the Law says to those who are under its curse.[71] To begin with, the Law says that those who belong to the Sinai covenant will continue in slavery 'under sin' (3.22) and thus remain under the curse of the Law. As Paul explains: 'Now this is an allegory: these women are two covenants. One is from Mount Sinai, bearing children *for slavery* (εἰς δουλείαν); she is Hagar. Now Hagar is Mount Sinai in Arabia; she corresponds to the present Jerusalem, for she is in *slavery* (δουλεύει) with her children' (4.24-25). Despite the giving of the Law, the Sinai covenant is not able to redeem anyone from either the flesh or sin (cf. 1.4; 3.13-14; 4.4-5). In fact, just the opposite: Sinai has only begotten children 'according to the flesh' (κατὰ σάρκα, 4.23, 29). And because her children are all of the flesh, the Sinai covenant can only enclose its adherents under the curse of the Law (cf. 3.22-25; 3.10-12; 4.1-5). Thus, 'curse begets curse'.[72]

Paul indirectly presses this particular point with his citation of Isa 54.1 in 4.27, which he applies to the eschatological 'above Jerusalem' as a contrast to the 'now Jerusalem' (4.26-27). One of the implications of the use of this citation appears to be that for Paul the 'now Jerusalem' *persists* in a state of barrenness like barren Sarai of old. Hence, the motif of barrenness becomes a salient feature of Paul's explanation of what the Law says to those who are under its curse.[73] To continue under the Sinai covenant (here by metonymy 'Jerusalem') is to remain in a state of barrenness. But this serves as an implicit warning about the curse of the Sinai covenant, since within the biblical tradition barrenness is often associated with cursing (as fertility is with blessing).[74] More importantly, this association is made explicit in the Greek text of Isaiah, where Jerusalem's metaphorical barrenness is described thus: 'Your holy cities have become a wilderness; Zion has become as a wilderness, Jerusalem a curse (εἰς κατάραν)' (LXX 64.9; cf. 65.23).[75] Paul no doubt knew this connection and likely intended to exploit it here to underscore his

---

[70] Scott, 'Galatians 3:10' (1993), 220–21, comes quite close to this reading by noting that the question of 4.21, as a taunt about the negative results of the Law (i.e., curse), is 'satirical'.

[71] A number of textual, lexical and hermeneutical details will have to be left to one side, thus limiting this discussion to the question of whether an implicit warning about the curse of the Law is relevant to the basic line of thought in 4.22-30.

[72] Eastman, 'Evil Eye' (2001), 75.

[73] Jobes, 'Metalepsis' (1993), 306–9.

[74] E.g., Gen 20.18; Exod 23.26; Deut 7.14.

[75] Jobes, 'Metalepsis' (1993), 308–9. In the *Prot. Jas.* 3.1, Anna laments her barrenness with a prayer to God: 'I have become a curse in the opinion of the Israelites' (κατάρα ἐγενήθην ἐγὼ ἐνώπιον τῶν υἱῶν Ἰσραήλ; cited in McLean, *Cursed Christ* (1996), 124 n. 57.

point about the fate of those who seek to embrace the Sinai covenant and its works: they will come 'under a curse' (cf. 3.10).

This leads, however, to Paul's main point in this section: those who belong to the Sinai covenant have no part in the inheritance promised to Abraham. This is the function of the citation from Gen 21.10 in 4.30: 'But what does the Scripture say: "Cast out the slave and her son, for the son of the slave woman will not inherit with the son of the free woman"'. Interpreters are right to underscore the importance of the imperative in 4.30 (ἔκβαλε) and to see here an implicit charge to the Galatians to expel the Agitators from their midst.[76] As was noted earlier, Paul anticipates this when he invokes a curse/ban upon those heralding 'another gospel' (1.8-9), and he returns to the same point in 5.7-11 after a further warning in 5.2-4 (cf. 5.9, 12).[77] Those who insist that Gentiles must embrace the Sinai covenant are for Paul under a curse and should be 'cast out'.

But with this exhortation also comes the rationale: 'for the son of the slave woman will not inherit with the son of the free woman' (γάρ, 4.30b). While Abraham had two sons, who allegorically represent two covenants, only one son is an heir, the one born not according to the flesh, but through the promise (4.28-29; cf. Rom 9.6-12). The one born according to the flesh stands outside the line of promise and thus remains in the sphere of the curse, a point Paul expounds and applies again to the Galatians (and the Agitators) with tremendous force in 5.19-21: 'I warn you, as I warned you before, that those who do such things [i.e., the 'works of the flesh'] will not *inherit* the kingdom of God' (5.21; cf. 6.7-8). Moreover, this link may explain the connection between the (implicit) command to expel the Agitators in 5.7-12 and the Galatians' own call to 'freedom' expounded in 5.13-15 (cf. γάρ, 5.13).

As a warning about the curse of the Law, Paul's rhetorical question in 4.21 prepares for what follows in 4.22-30. This passage serves a dual purpose within the flow of the letter. Not only does it function as a warning to the Galatians to avoid embracing the Sinai covenant, which will only result in their coming under the curse of the Law, it also serves as an implicit exhortation to expel the Agitators, who themselves are under a curse (cf. 1.8-9; 3.10), because they have no part in the inheritance. For the Law itself says that those who come under its curse will have no share in the inheritance promised to Abraham.[78]

---

[76] Hansen, *Abraham in Galatians* (1989), 145–6. There he provides six reasons for taking the exhortation of 4.30 to be the focal point of the passage. Horbury, 'Excommunication' (1985), 24–25, notes that ἐκβάλλω was used 'for expulsion from the synagogue at the beginning of the Christian era' (cf. Josephus, *B.J.* 2.143).

[77] Cf. Betz, *Galatians* (1979), 250–1; Hansen, *Abraham in Galatians* (1989), 146.

[78] We shall consider Paul's fifth and final use of 'under Law' in 5.18 in Chapter 6.

'Under Law' elsewhere in Paul

While we have seen strong evidence to suggest that 'under Law' serves as shorthand for 'under the curse of the Law' in Galatians, it has not been my intention to argue that this phrase functions as a technical term for Paul with a uniform meaning everywhere else it occurs. Paul's use of 'under Law' as shorthand for 'under the curse of the Law' may very well have been an *ad hoc* device used only in Galatians to address the particular situation in Galatia. There is no reason why this could not have been the case, nor why Paul might not have used the expression 'under Law' (or any other phrase) one way in Galatians and another way in some other letter.

This is not intended to sidestep the issue of Paul's other uses of 'under Law' in Rom 6.14-15 or 1 Cor 9.20-21. I am less confident, however, about how to understand Paul's use of the expression in those contexts, even though a reference to the curse of the Law is not impossible in either one, particularly not in Romans.[79] My only point is that Paul may have coined the expression 'under Law' specifically in response to the polemical situation in Galatia, where the threat of a curse for failing to observe circumcision may have been an issue (see Chapters 3–4 below), and yet chose to employ the same phrase with slightly different nuances when addressing, perhaps several months or years later, the situations in Corinth or Rome. Alternatively, Paul may have tended to use the phrase as a prosaic way to refer to Jewish observance, but chose to give the phrase a particular polemical nuance to meet the situation of crisis in Galatia. Either way, this would not alter the basic thesis of this chapter, since the argument does not ultimately depend upon the claim that 'under Law' is shorthand for 'under the curse of the Law'. It only requires there to be a *reference* to the curse of the Law in the expression 'under Law'.

Conclusion

We have discovered that the rhetoric of cursing is a more prominent and indeed a more pervasive feature of Galatians than is generally assumed.[80] Paul refers to the curse of the Law in the letter opening (1.8-9), several times in one of its central passages (3.10-14), and throughout the remainder of the letter *via* the shorthand expression 'under Law' (3.23; 4.4, 5, 21; 5.18). Moreover, Paul has framed Galatians with a conditional curse (1.8-9) and blessing (6.16), indicating that the letter as a whole is intended to confront his apostatising converts with a stark choice between these two alternatives.

---

[79] Cf. Cranfield, *Romans* (1975–79), 1.319-20.

[80] Morland, *Curse* (1995), 139–233 (especially 226-33), similarly concludes: 'The reinterpretation of curse and blessing is thus more than minor arguments in the letter. It is rather organically related both to its main theme and to most of its main parts' (233).

Conclusion

While my aim in this chapter has been to demonstrate the prominence of the rhetoric of cursing in Galatians, a few other observations have surfaced along the way. First, if 'under Law' refers back to and thereby invokes the notion of the curse of the Law in 3.10-14, it implies that the motif of the curse of the Law extends even into the ethical section of the letter. Scholars seldom consider whether the issue of the curse of the Law has any bearing on 5.13–6.10. One of the chief contributions of this study will be to explore this possibility more fully and to suggest that this provides not only a fresh approach to this section, but also an alternative way to explain the thematic coherence between 5.13–6.10 and the rest of the letter.

Given the prominence of the rhetoric of cursing in Galatians, we also have reason to wonder whether the curse of the Law contributed to the crisis in Galatia. Of course, we cannot simply assume that Paul's priorities in the letter correspond exactly to the needs of the Galatians. Even if Paul was well-informed about their situation, he may have construed the whole thing in his own terms, rather than in a way more directly applicable to the concerns of his hearers. Moreover, we must allow for the possibility that when addressing the issue of the curse of the Law, Paul was only trying to forestall potential misunderstandings, not trying to redress the actual confusions or anxieties of the Galatians. For these reasons, then, and before turning to the exegesis of 5.13–6.10, we need to explore the relevance of the curse of the Law for the Galatian crisis.

Chapter 3

The Curse of the Law and the Message of the Agitators

> The argument of Galatians is a sequence of preposterous sophistries.
> The countermission has the Bible, the Church, and reason entirely on its side.[1]

In the previous chapter we discovered that the rhetoric of cursing is a more prominent and indeed a more pervasive feature of Galatians than has generally been assumed. This has several important implications for the present study, one of which is to provide justification for probing into the historical situation to ask how the curse of the Law may have contributed to the developing crisis in Galatia over circumcision. The next two chapters will address this question from two complementary angles. In this chapter we shall explore whether the threat of a curse played a part in the Agitators' appeal for circumcision and, in the next, whether the threat of a curse played a part in the Galatians' attraction to circumcision.

'Paul's opponents could have drawn on a powerful battery of arguments to commend the law to the Galatian Christians'.[2] This was almost certainly the case, even if the situation was not as lopsided as the above epigram suggests. The Agitators could have pointed to a number of advantages to circumcision, which would have made it a more attractive option for the Galatians: sharing in the blessing of Abraham (3.6-18), securing their identity as the 'sons of God' (3.23-4.7), even finding assistance in the battle against the 'desire of the flesh' (5.16).

But did the Agitators also confront the Galatians with the *consequences* of failing to embrace circumcision? This question has received less attention in recent discussions. While we can hardly doubt that the Agitators drew attention to the benefits of embracing circumcision, did they not also *warn* the Galatians of what would happen if they failed to do so? My aim in this chapter will be to explore whether the Agitators appealed to a curse in order to encourage the Galatians to embrace circumcision. Following a discussion of method, I shall consider Paul's portrayal of the Agitators' tactics and then inquire into their appeal to Scripture.

---

[1] Goulder, 'Pauline Epistles' (1987), 489.
[2] Barclay, *Obeying* (1988), 68.

A Word on Method

'Work on the opponents of Galatians has produced more discussion of method than any other Pauline letter'.[3] Ironically, however, increased sensitivity to methodology has done little to generate increased consensus.[4] The provenance, ethnicity and tactics of the Agitators are still hotly contested issues. In fact, proposals and counterproposals are proffered on an almost daily basis.[5] This underscores the fact that while methodological controls are certainly necessary, they are not a panacea for interpretative disagreement and do not enable one simply to circumvent the difficult task of exegesis. The continual proliferation of views of the identity of the Agitators (if this is even the right terminology)[6] also accentuates the fact that this task will always be two-thirds science, one-third art. An element of 'poetic fantasy' is simply endemic to the enterprise.[7]

My aim in this chapter is to explore whether the Agitators invoked the threat of a curse as part of their appeal for circumcision in Galatia. I am primarily interested, then, in their *activity* rather than their *identity*. Even though these are ultimately inseparable, the supposition that the Agitators appealed to the threat of a curse does not depend upon one particular understanding of their identity. Whether the Agitators hailed from Jerusalem, Antioch, or were indigenous to Galatia;[8] whether they were Christ-believers or non-Christ believers;[9] or whether they were Jews, Gentiles, or a mixed group;[10] these do not decisively impact the question under discussion in this chapter.

---

[3] Sumney, *False Brothers* (1999), 13 n. 2.

[4] See, for example, the recent *Forschungsbericht* presented by Mitternacht, *Sprachlose* (1999), 26–38, who concludes: 'die Identifikation der Gegner im Gal noch immer unentschieden ist' (58).

[5] Compare the recent proposals of Mitternacht, *Sprachlose* (1999); Nanos, *Irony* (2002); Elliott, *Cutting too Close* (2003); Wiley, *Reframing Galatians* (2005).

[6] See the discussion in Nanos, *Irony* (2002), 110–92 (especially 115–31), who prefers the label 'influencers'. While virtually any label has certain drawbacks, I have nonetheless opted to use the conventional designation 'Agitators' throughout. The capitalisation of the term is simply stylistic.

[7] Martyn, 'Law-Observant' (1985), 313.

[8] Cf. Longenecker, *Galatians* (1990), lxxxix; Dunn, *Galatians* (1993), 14–17; Nanos, *Irony* (2002), 159–83 (respectively).

[9] The vast majority of scholars continue to hold that the Agitators were Christ-believers (cf. 1.6-7; 6.12-13). This has been challenged recently by Nanos, *Irony* (2002), 137–59, 284–316. Cf. Walter, 'Gegner' (1986), 351–56.

[10] While the traditional view has been that the Agitators were Jewish, a number of recent interpreters have argued that they were Gentiles; see Segal, *Paul the Convert* (1990), 206–08; Murray, *Judaizing* (2004), 34–36 (allows for a mixed group); Schäfer, *Apostelkonzil* (2004),

The same can be said about the much-debated issue of whether the Agitators advocated complete Law observance or adopted a more lenient approach by focusing primarily on circumcision, calendar observance and perhaps a few ethical commands.[11] Either way, the Agitators could have still appealed to the threat of a curse for failing to be circumcised, whether they understood this as the first (or last) step in embracing the whole Law, as some want to argue,[12] or whether this was conceived of, for whatever reason, as an *ad hoc* measure for Gentile converts. In this chapter (and throughout this work), I shall speak primarily about the Agitators advocating circumcision, since circumcision is clearly the *immediate* issue at stake in the Galatian crisis (6.12; 5.1-12), though without necessarily excluding the possibility that their advocacy of circumcision was indicative of a desire to see the Galatians embrace the whole Law.[13]

While there are various ways we might shed light on the question of whether the Agitators appealed to the threat of a curse, I shall give priority to the internal evidence of Galatians itself as the most reliable source of information.[14] Recognising this fact, however, does not solve all the problems since Galatians itself contains different kinds of information about the Agitators. There are (1) direct references or allusions to their teaching or activity, and (2) various affirmations, assertions or points of emphasis intended to counter their teaching or influence. Utilising either one of these strands of evidence for the purpose of historical reconstruction is somewhat hazardous and needs to be approached cautiously and judiciously.

First, with regard to references or allusions, one cannot simply assume a direct correspondence between Paul's portrait of the Agitators and their actual profile. It is possible that Paul lacked solid information about the precise identity and activity of the Agitators.[15] More to the point, Galatians itself is a

---

35–36; Cornu and Shulam, *Galatians* (2005), lv–lxvi (Gentile non-believers, a far less likely supposition).

[11] Barclay, *Obeying* (1988), 60–65, has presented a strong case for thinking that the Agitators urged full Law observance; for various arguments that the Agitators advocated a more lenient 'halakha', see Söding, 'Gegner' (1997), 136–38; Sanders, *Jewish People* (1983), 29; Jewett, 'Agitators' (1971), 201; Sumney, *False Brothers* (1999), 142. Cf. Kwon, *Eschatology* (2004), 207–11.

[12] Cf. Justin, *Dial.* 8.3, where Trypho admonishes Justin: 'first be circumcised, then observe the precepts concerning the Sabbath, the feasts, and God's new moons; in brief, fulfil the whole written law, and then, probably, you will experience the mercy of God'.

[13] For an attempt to explore the implications of this for the Galatian women, see Wiley, *Reframing Galatians* (2005), 67–91; see also Lieu, 'Circumcision' (1994), 358–70.

[14] See the discussion in Sumney, *Opponents* (1990), 77–94.

[15] Schmithals, *Gnostics* (1972), 18, assumed that 'Paul was only meagrely informed about goings-on in Galatia', contending that if Paul had received a detailed report or an official embassy, he would have certainly referred to it in the letter. Stirewalt, *Letter Writer* (2003), 94–106, may have answered this objection, however, by arguing on the basis of a comparison

highly polemical and thus selective portrayal of the situation in Galatia, one obviously intended for maximum rhetorical effect. Galatians is, in other words, a value-laden description of the crisis, not an unbiased depiction of the facts. This, of course, has significant implications for what we make of Paul's presentation of the various *dramatis personae* in the Galatian crisis, not least the Agitators themselves. If Galatians is to be used as a way to gain insight into the historical situation in Galatia, one must reckon with the various rhetorical strategies at work in the letter.[16] This will, in turn, go some way to correcting the 'distorting' influence of the text for the purpose of historical reconstruction.

Secondly, treating the various affirmations, assertions or points of emphasis of the letter as reflective of the teaching or influence of the Agitators, a technique known as mirror-reading, presents us with perhaps even greater challenges. In fact, some think the difficulties with this method are so great and the payoff so minimal that it would be best to issue a moratorium on the whole exercise. Most are more optimistic, however, and recognise that while mirror-reading is not without its own limitations, it is an indispensable tool for seeking to understand historical events on the basis of literary artefacts.[17]

Often when discussing mirror-reading scholars will overlook the fact that the viability of the method depends largely upon how it is defined. Some work with a definition so broad as to encompass virtually any form of historical reconstruction, with the result that only the most ardent sceptic of historical inquiry would want to call the technique into question.[18] Others operate with a more constricted definition: 'the practice of reading statements or assertions in Paul's letters and *assuming* that Paul's adversaries were arguing just the opposite'.[19] This narrower understanding of mirror-reading,

---

of Galatians with official letters in antiquity that the reference to 'all the brothers who are with me' in the salutation (1.2) probably refers to a delegation from Galatia sent to Paul, indeed one which may even have included some of the Agitators themselves (cf. 106). For those who think Paul was well informed about the situation, see Söding, 'Gegner' (1997), 133 n. 5 and the references cited there.

[16] For example, part of Paul's strategy is to vilify the (perceived) opposition, a familiar tactic in the ancient world, no less than in the modern. On vilification as a conventional *topos* in Hellenistic and early Jewish polemical writings, see du Toit, 'Vilification' (1994), 403–12; Johnson, 'Ancient Polemic' (1989), 419–44; Mitternacht, *Sprachlose* (1999), 286–99.

[17] Longenecker, *Galatians* (1990), lxxxix: 'despite its difficulties, dangers, and frequent abuse, mirror-reading is the only method here available to us'.

[18] Hong, *Law* (1993), 98, seems to equate it with 'reconstructing the context'. Cf. Longenecker, *Galatians* (1990), lxxxix.

[19] Witherington, *Galatians* (1998), 21 (emphasis original).

however, tends to produce the kind of abuses and inconsistencies critics of the method enjoy stockpiling for the purpose of illustration.[20]

A slightly broader definition, like the one proposed by Barclay, is much less objectionable. '[W]e must use the text which answers the opponents as a *mirror* in which we can see reflected the people and the arguments under attack'.[21] On this understanding, mirror-reading is something slightly more specific than using the text to reflect the historical context, yet it is not restricted *solely* to Paul's defensive statements. Allusions, affirmations, prominent themes or emphases may all reflect points of contention between Paul and his 'opponents' and thus (at least, in principle) provide insight into the historical situation.

Debate about mirror-reading, however, is not simply about definitions. For some it is a question of whether mirror-reading is a valid technique *per se*; or at least whether it can be consistently and thus usefully employed. There are two issues here: one concerns the *validity* of the method itself, the other concerns the *viability* of its application. In response to the first issue, one must remember that mirror-reading is only a metaphorical description of a certain kind of inference and thus in principle no different from other kinds of inferences based upon literary evidence. The only difference is that mirror-reading is based upon what the text *reflects*, rather than what it states. This means, of course, that mirror-reading necessarily provides a lower degree of certitude and increases the potential for over-interpretation, but this does not necessarily undercut the integrity of the method itself.[22]

As to the issue of the viability of mirror-reading, several things should be said. First, the value of mirror-reading depends upon the degree of certainty of results one wants to obtain. Insistence upon a high degree of certainty will inevitably preclude the use of the method, since conclusions based upon a mirror-reading of the text can never garner that kind of certitude. If one is content, however, to work with a sliding scale of certainty, where evidence is placed on a spectrum of greater or lesser probabilities, then mirror-reading becomes more viable.[23]

Secondly, one must be clear on the relative value of the results of mirror-reading vis-à-vis evidence gained by other means (e.g., from explicit references or allusions). Several guidelines may prove useful. First, the information garnered from mirror-reading is necessarily less certain than

---

[20] Tyson, 'Opponents' (1968), exemplified this approach, the weaknesses of which, particularly as it was applied to Gal 1–2, have been underscored sufficiently enough by Lyons, *Pauline Autobiography* (1985), 75–121.

[21] Barclay, 'Mirror-Reading' (1987), 73–74 (emphasis original).

[22] See the level-headed discussion of mirror-reading by Silva, *Interpreting Galatians* (2001), 104–08.

[23] This is one of the strengths of Barclay's approach; see Barclay, 'Mirror-Reading' (1987), 85–86.

information gathered from passages which refer explicitly to the Agitators.[24] Secondly, the results of mirror-reading must be compatible with the evidence drawn from more certain passages. Thirdly, evidence gained from mirror-reading should not be used to overturn evidence gathered about the Agitators from more certain and reliable passages. Fourthly, the results of mirror-reading are best used to clarify certain aspects of the Agitators' identity or tactics which can be identified from more explicit passages.[25]

What is needed is not a disavowal of mirror-reading, but, as Barclay suggests, 'a carefully controlled method of working which uses logical criteria and proceeds with suitable caution'.[26] His classic essay on the subject has rendered a great service in this regard. After identifying several 'pitfalls' with the method, which include being unduly selective in gathering evidence, over-interpreting affirmations or denials, mishandling the polemical nature of the text and focusing on particular words or phrases as coming from the opponents,[27] he outlines seven criteria which ought to guide a responsible use of the mirror-reading technique: (i) type of utterance; (ii) tone; (iii) frequency; (iv) clarity; (v) unfamiliarity; (vi) consistency; (vii) historical plausibility.[28] One may want to quibble with these at certain points, or perhaps add one or two others. On the whole, however, this seems to be a reasonable and reliable way to proceed.

My approach in this chapter will be to begin with Paul's direct references or allusions to the Agitators to see whether they might shed light on the question of whether the Agitators were threatening the Galatians with a curse. In light of these preliminary findings I shall then turn to consider the information to be garnered through a judicious mirror-reading of certain features of the letter.

---

[24] Sumney, *Opponents* (1990), 98.

[25] Cf. Sumney, *Opponents* (1990), 98–100. There is, however, some ambiguity in stating that mirror-reading should be used to clarify what is already known of the Agitators' identity or tactics. This begs the question: when does clarifying an already known position become proffering new information? In the end this is a value judgement. The guideline for this chapter will be to allow mirror-reading to help to answer the question of how it is that the Agitators were doing what they were doing.

[26] Barclay, 'Mirror-Reading' (1987), 84.

[27] Barclay, 'Mirror-Reading' (1987), 79–83. Berger, 'Gegner' (1980), 373–400, is similarly cautious.

[28] Barclay, 'Mirror-Reading' (1987), 84–86.

Compelling Circumcision: Paul's Portrayal of the Tactics of the Agitators

Although Paul does not explicitly accuse the Agitators of threatening the Galatians with a curse, several indications may point in that direction. First, the Agitators were evidently exerting significant pressure on the Galatians to embrace circumcision. The sheer fact that the Galatians appear to have been ready to submit to the knife is confirmation enough of this fact, especially given the widespread antipathy to circumcision among pagans and the inherent undesirability and risks of the procedure for adult males.[29] But Paul actually uses the language of compulsion. 'It is those who want to make a good showing in the flesh who compel (ἀναγκάζουσιν) you to be circumcised (περιτέμνεσθαι)' (6.12; cf. 2.3, 14). This is a striking accusation, since the only other contemporaneous examples of compelling circumcision, which use this same terminology, involve cases of forced Jewish proselytism (Josephus, *A.J.* 13.318; 13.257-58; *Vita* 112–13).[30] That the Agitators were using physical coercion or legal pressure, however, is highly unlikely. Paul must, then, be describing an intense *moral pressure*, which, as far as he was concerned, amounted to a kind of militant proselytism. Whatever the Agitators were saying and doing, it evidently provided the Galatians with no other viable options; they were left with a singular choice: circumcision. This highly stylised depiction of the Agitators' method of persuasion probably reflects the fact that they were holding out circumcision as the *sine qua non* of inclusion into the people of God and/or entrance into final salvation (cf. 5.2-6; 3.3), perhaps together with warnings about the consequences of failing to embrace circumcision.

That the Agitators were using various warnings and threats to convince the Galatians of the necessity of circumcision is suggested by the fact that Paul describes the Agitators' influence as deeply unsettling or even frightening to the Galatians. On two occasions, Paul refers to the Agitators as those who 'trouble' (ταράσσω) the Galatians (1.7; 5.10). These are the only two occurrences of this terminology in Paul's letters. While Paul may simply want to suggest that the Agitators have created some amount of mental 'confusion' or 'bewilderment' for his converts, in certain contexts the use of this term carries slightly stronger connotations, including causing 'acute emotional distress or turbulence'.[31] In fact, in a number of places the term is closely associated with the notion of fearing something or someone:

---

[29] See the evidence in Hall, 'Arguing' (1996), 440–41.

[30] See also Stern, *Greek and Latin Authors* (1976), § 146; and the discussion in Borgen, *Early Christianity* (1996), 45–69.

[31] Louw and Nida, *Greek Lexicon* (1988), 315 (25.244); BDAG 'ταράσσω', 2: 'to cause inward turmoil'; Martyn, *Galatians* (1997), 112: 'mental anguish'.

> And Zechariah was troubled (ἐταράχθη) when he saw him, and fear (φόβος) gripped him (Luke 1.12).
>
> Let not your heart be troubled (ταρασσέσθω), nor let it be fearful (δειλιάτω) (John 14.27).
>
> And do not fear (φοβηθῆτε) their intimidation, and do not be troubled (ταραχθῆτε) (1 Pet 3.14; cf. LXX Isa 8.12).
>
> And the whole righteous nation was troubled (ἐταράχθη), fearing (φοβούμενοι) the evils that threatened them (LXX Esth 11.9).
>
> When the unrighteous see them, they will be shaken (ταραχθήσοντα) with dreadful fear (φόβῳ δεινῷ) (Wis 5.2).[32]

A particularly intriguing use of this term can be found in Acts 15, which recounts how certain persons from Judea were 'troubling' (ἐτάραξαν) the Gentiles in Antioch, Syria and Cilicia (15.24) by teaching that unless they were circumcised, they could not be saved (15.1). Without suggesting that there is any link between this episode and the situation Paul describes in Galatia, the overlap in terminology is indeed suggestive. In fact, it may not be over-reaching the evidence to claim, as does Martyn, that with the language of troubling:

> Paul is not identifying the Teachers as persons who confuse the Galatians. He is saying that they are frightening the Galatians out of their wits, intimidating them with the threat of damnation if they do not follow the path prescribed in the Teachers' message![33]

From Paul's perspective, the Agitators appear to have introduced not just a state of confusion among his converts, but an atmosphere of fear. This tallies nicely with the idea of the Agitators compelling circumcision: the Galatians were ready to embrace circumcision at least in part because they feared the consequences of *not* being circumcised.

This may, in turn, shed some fresh light on Paul's curious remark in 3.1: 'O foolish Galatians! Who has bewitched (ἐβάσκανεν) you?' S. Eastman has recently argued that there may be an echo of the Deuteronomic curse here. She thus translates the verse: 'You foolish Galatians! Who has put you under the curse, you before whose eyes Jesus Christ was publicly portrayed as crucified?'[34] She has several reasons for doing so. First, the verb βασκαίνω appears in only four places in the LXX, two of which can be found at the climactic point of the curses section in Deut 27-28 (Deut 28.53-57). Secondly, just a few verses later Paul cites from this same passage of Scripture (3.10; Deut 27.26; 28.58). Thirdly, an allusion to the Deuteronomic curse at the beginning of this section would suit the context; the following paragraph is

---

[32] Cf. Matt 14.26; Mark 6.50; Deut 2.25; 15.13; Tob 12.16; Prov 12.25; Wis 8.5; Hab 3.2; Jer 5.22.

[33] Martyn, *Galatians* (1997), 112.

[34] Eastman, 'Evil Eye' (2001), 72.

framed in terms of blessing and curse (3.6-14). Moreover, an allusion to the Galatians being put under a curse (or threatened with a curse) would fit well with Paul's emphasis upon the fact that they saw 'before their very eyes Jesus Christ publicly portrayed as crucified' (3.1b). Paul has just referred to 'Christ who loved me and gave himself for me' (2.20), and he will bring the present argument to a ringing climax with the affirmation that the crucified Christ endured the 'curse of the Law' in order to redeem those under a curse (3.13, 10). Thus, by succumbing to the threat of a curse, the Galatians are acting foolishly (ἀνόητοι) indeed, since they themselves have seen a public portrayal of the crucified, cursed Christ who himself dealt with the Law's curse (3.1b).

It should also come as no surprise that Paul immediately turns to the question of the Galatians' reception of the Spirit. This again parallels the same sequence in 3.13-14: 'Christ redeemed us from the curse of the Law by becoming for us a curse . . . in order that the Gentiles might receive the blessing of Abraham in Christ Jesus, in order that we might *receive* the promised Spirit through faith'. Thus, in 3.1-2 we find a reference to a curse (3.1a) remedied by the crucified Christ (3.1b), which points to the reception of the Spirit by the Galatians (3.2); 3.13-14 repeats this same sequence of a reference to a curse (3.13a) followed by a reference to the crucified Christ (3.13b), which is then followed by a reference to the reception of the Spirit by the Gentiles (3.14). This pair of verses may in fact form an *inclusio* around 3.1-14 and summarise the thrust of the whole passage: redemption from the curse and the reception of the Spirit come not from the 'works of the Law' (3.2, 3, 5, 10, 12), but from faith (3.2, 5, 14).

We find another important clue in 4.17. There Paul seeks to demonise the opposition by exposing their fraudulent designs; he accuses them of having spurious motives and of wanting to 'exclude' (ἐκκλεῖσαι) the Galatians (4.17). This is a puzzling remark, compounded by the fact that Paul does not state from whom or what the Galatians were to be excluded: from Christ (5.4), from God (1.6; 5.8), from the gospel (1.6; 2.5; 5.7), from the church (4.30), or from Paul himself (4.16)? Another possibility, one to my knowledge not heretofore proposed, would be to view this comment within the larger context of Gal 3–4, where the issue of who are the rightful heirs of the inheritance is paramount. Paul would then have in mind exclusion from the *inheritance* (3.29; 4.7, 30). Did this involve interposing the threat of a curse between the Galatians and their entering into the 'kingdom of God' (5.21b)?[35] In any event, by insisting on the necessity of circumcision, the Agitators were in effect excluding the Galatians from the eschatological inheritance (cf. 4.21-31; Acts 15.1).

---

[35] Longenecker, *Triumph* (1998), 156, thinks that in 4.17 Paul may be likening the Agitators to those who place a separation curse on others.

We have seen that while Paul nowhere explicitly accuses the Agitators of threatening the Galatians with a curse, there are several hints in that direction.[36] Not only were the Agitators holding out the benefits of circumcision, they were probably also warning the Galatians of the *consequences* of not being circumcised. This aspect of their polemical appeal has been somewhat overshadowed in recent scholarship, concerned as many are to explain the various reasons why pagan converts might have been attracted to the Law or circumcision. We have some indication, however, that the Agitators probably told the Galatians of the dangers of failing to follow their advice: they may find themselves under a curse!

The Threat of a Curse as Part of the Agitators' Use of Scripture

The Agitators were therefore exerting significant pressure on the Galatians to embrace circumcision (6.13; 4.17); and their effort was not only highly effective (5.2-4; 4.21), but also deeply unsettling to the Galatians (1.7; 5.10). But can we say anything more specific about how they were exerting such intense pressure? Given that circumcision is the point at issue in the Galatian crisis and given the prominence of Scripture as part of Paul's response in Galatians (cf. 3.6–4.31), there is very good *prima facie* support for thinking that the Agitators were using the Jewish Scriptures to convince the Galatians of the need for circumcision.[37] In fact, it is difficult to envisage a scenario in which Gentile Christ-believers would be urged to embrace circumcision without at least some appeal to the scriptural sanction and rationale for the practice.

This initial impression finds further support from even a cautious mirror-reading of Galatians. First, the sheer *density* and *subtlety* of Paul's scriptural argumentation is most easily explained as his attempt to counter competing interpretations proffered by the Agitators, especially if the Galatians were largely illiterate pagans with minimal familiarity with the Scriptures and little or no independent access to them.[38] Secondly, the *tone* of at least some of

---

[36] Conversely, I might add, nothing in Galatians would seem to *preclude* the hypothesis that the Agitators threatened the Galatians with a curse as part of their appeal for circumcision.

[37] Barclay, 'Mirror-Reading' (1987), 87.

[38] This has sometimes been taken to suggest that Paul must have been writing to Gentiles who were well acquainted with the Jewish Scriptures through their involvement in the synagogue; Davies, 'Betz' (1981), 312; Ciampa, *Presence* (1998), 260–70. One should not, of course, simply assume that Paul is *responding to* Scripture every time he *argues from* Scripture; Stanley, *Arguing* (2004), 116 n. 5. This should caution one against needing to assume the presence of a competing interpretation behind *every* scriptural citation or allusion

Paul's appeals to Scripture suggest he is on the defensive; indeed, on several occasions he appears to be matching the Agitators' scriptural exegesis with his own (3.10-14; 4.21-31).[39] Thirdly, a few of Paul's citations appear to be in *tension* with the ostensible thrust of his own arguments, which suggests he may have been struggling to find a way to respond to a competing interpretation of these same texts.[40] Fourthly, closely related to this last point, several of Paul's citations presumably would have been *well suited* to the Agitators' own position.[41] Finally, a comparison of Paul's use of several scriptural passages in Galatians with his use of these same passages in his other writings (e.g., Romans) reveals certain *peculiarities* and points of emphasis, which reinforce the impression that he is engaging in scriptural repartee with the Agitators.[42]

For these reasons, then, we can confidently conclude that the Agitators used Scripture to bolster their case for circumcision. Regrettably, however, we cannot be as confident about *which* Scriptures they may have used. For the purposes of this chapter, I shall limit my investigation to those scriptural texts or traditions which may have been used to warn the Galatians of or perhaps threaten them with a curse. There are at least two likely candidates: Abrahamic traditions (3.6-29; 4.21-31) and Deuteronomic traditions (3.10-14; 1.8-9). In the remainder of this chapter, I shall argue that the Agitators probably appealed to both of these traditions to persuade the Galatians that their lack of circumcision was a breach of God's covenant and Law, and thus, in accordance with the witness of Scripture, brought them under the Law's curse (Gen 12.1-3; 17.10-14; Deut 27.26).[43] I shall also suggest (somewhat more tentatively) that the Agitators may have accused Paul of being a false prophet whose gospel, if it were not abandoned, would expose the Galatians to a curse (cf. 1.8-9; Deut 13).

---

in Galatians (e.g., Lev 19.18 in 5.14). On the literacy levels of Paul's churches and the Galatians in particular, see Stanley, *Arguing* (2004), 38–61 and 114–18 (respectively).

[39] So Bouwman, 'Sara-Perikope' (1987), 3146 (about 4.21-31).

[40] Cf. Matera, *Galatians* (1992), 9 (about 4.21-31); Barclay, *Obeying* (1988), 53.

[41] Stanley, *Arguing* (2004), 118 n. 12, observes that 'anyone capable of consulting the original context of the verses that Paul quotes in Gal 3:10-14 could have seen that some of the passages are actually more consistent with the position of Paul's "opponents"'.

[42] Barclay, *Obeying* (1988), 53 n. 52, observes that while Paul refers to Abraham in Rom 4 and 9, 'his treatment of them in Galatians is sufficiently peculiar to support the hypothesis that he is directly responding to his opponents at this point'. Note also the use of two passages referring to a curse (Deut 27.26 in 3.10; Deut. 21.23 in 3.13), which appear nowhere else in Paul's writings.

[43] On the inseparability of the Law and the covenant during the NT period see especially *Jub.* 30.21–22; 30.21; CD 1.20; 1QS 5.8; *4 Ezra* 4.23; 7.24; Sir 24.23; 39.8; 42.2; 1 Macc 1.57; 2.50: νῦν τέκνα ζηλώσατε τῷ νόμῳ καὶ δότε τὰς ψυχὰς ὑμῶν ὑπὲρ διαθήκης πατέρων ἡμῶν.

Curse and Covenant: The Agitators' use of Abrahamic traditions

The vast majority of scholars agree that the Agitators bolstered their case for circumcision with an appeal to Abrahamic traditions.[44] Paul's references to Abraham and Abrahamic themes (e.g., blessing, covenant, seed, inheritance) are distinctive in their tone and emphasis and appear with enough frequency, clarity and unfamiliarity in Galatians to make this a highly probable supposition.[45] Abraham's story, of course, would have been extremely well suited to promote circumcision among pagan converts: Abraham was the first and thus paradigmatic Gentile proselyte. Philo speaks of him as 'the standard of nobility for all proselytes' (LCL: *Virt.* 219; cf. *Jub.* 11.15-17; *Apoc. Ab.* 1-8; Josephus, *A.J.* 1.154-57; *Gen. Rab.* 46.2).[46] Indeed, one has little trouble imagining the Agitators telling the Galatians of the story of 'our father Abraham' (John 8.53; Acts 7.2; Rom 4.16; 2 Cor 11.22): his 'migration' from idolatry to the worship of the one true God, his embrace of the divine promises that in him all the nations would be blessed (Gen 12, 15, 17, 22), and his receiving circumcision (Gen 17), only to conclude with a rather pointed exhortation to the Galatians to go and do likewise. Indeed, the inextricable link between circumcision and God's covenant with Abraham reflected both in Scripture and in a whole range of early Jewish literature would have made such an appeal very natural and quite convincing.[47]

Some are less sanguine about our ability to know whether the Agitators appealed to Abraham and (rightly) remind us that certainty on this issue is impossible.[48] Paul does not explicitly link Abraham with the teaching of the Agitators, nor does Abraham's prominence in Galatians necessarily imply that he was part of the Agitators' own message. Paul may have had his own reasons for introducing him into the discussion. While these are certainly valid cautions, they would carry greater conviction if the Galatian situation was a *non-polemical* context in which a number of Abrahamic themes like circumcision, inheritance and blessing were not already at issue. In light of both the *context* and *content* of the letter, therefore, the weight of evidence

---

[44] See Hansen, *Abraham in Galatians* (1989), 262 n. 32, for a list of scholars. Also to be included are Barclay, *Obeying* (1988), 52–54; Martyn, 'Law-Observant' (1985), 317–23; Martyn, *Galatians* (1997), 294–306, 343–44, 432–57; Lührmann, *Galatians* (1992), 105; Lategan, 'Argumentative Situation' (1992), 261; Matera, *Galatians* (1992), 9; Stanton, 'Law of Moses' (1996), 106–07; Smiles, *Law in Galatia* (1998), 63–65; Kok, *Truth of Gospel* (2000), 83; Murray, *Judaizing* (2004), 38.

[45] Barclay, 'Mirror-Reading' (1987), 87; Barclay, *Obeying* (1988), 53.

[46] Cf. Birnbaum, *Philo's Thought* (1996), 202; Calvert, 'Abraham' (1993), 225–35; Calvert-Koyzis, *Significance of Abraham* (2004), 6–84.

[47] Hansen, *Abraham in Galatians* (1989), 170–72.

[48] Schlier, *Galater* (1962), 127; Eckstein, *Verheissung* (1996), 94–95; Sumney, *False Brothers* (1999), 154–55.

tilts decidedly in favour of supposing that various Abrahamic traditions played a part in the Agitators' message.

There are numerous ways in which Abrahamic traditions might have informed the teaching of the Agitators. But is there reason to think that the Agitators were specifically using Abrahamic traditions to threaten the Galatians with a curse? We have an initial clue in 3.6-14, where Paul begins his argument from Scripture somewhat abruptly by referring to Abraham (καθὼς 'Αβραάμ, 3.6).[49] This passage is probably intended as a *rejoinder* to the Agitators and thus likely reflects their handling of Abrahamic traditions. It is significant, therefore, that this paragraph contains an unusually high concentration of blessing and curse terminology, a feature absent from Paul's treatment of Abraham in Rom 4. The closing pair of verses are especially significant because of their close juxtaposition of ἡ κατάρα τοῦ νόμου and ἡ εὐλογία τοῦ 'Αβραάμ: 'Christ redeemed us from the *curse* of the Law ... in order that the *blessing* of Abraham might be to the Gentiles in Christ Jesus' (3.13-14). In all likelihood, then, Paul was not the only one speaking to the Galatians of a curse in one breath and a blessing in the next. As Martyn (albeit somewhat over-confidently) suggests: 'In their instruction of the Galatians the Teachers are certain to have balanced their comments about God's blessing of Abraham with reference to the threat of God's curse'.[50]

It is also likely that the Agitators enticed the Galatians with the prospect of sharing in the 'blessing of Abraham' (3.9, 14). The Agitators certainly would have spoken of *some positive benefit* to embracing circumcision; partaking of the blessing promised to Abraham seems to be a natural choice. But perhaps they also spoke just as earnestly, if not as frequently, of the shadow-side of Abraham's blessing: the curse threatened upon those who 'curse' Abraham.[51] The juxtaposition of blessing and curse is rooted in the primordial promise given to Abraham: 'I shall bless (εὐλογήσω) those who bless you, and those who curse you, I shall curse (καταράσομαι). And in you all the families of the earth will be blessed (ἐνευλογηθήσονται)' (Gen 12.3). Paul quotes the second half of Gen 12.3 in 3.8: 'And the Scripture, foreseeing that God would justify the Gentiles by faith, preached the gospel beforehand to Abraham, saying "In you will all the nations be blessed"'. For a variety of reasons, scholars have supposed that this citation was on the lips of the Agitators. The emphasis upon the 'blessing' as mediated *in Abraham* (ἐν σοί) would certainly lend itself to being interpreted in a way that makes physical circumcision the necessary means of affiliation with Abraham, particularly in

---

[49] Hansen, *Abraham in Galatians* (1989), 172.
[50] Martyn, *Galatians* (1997), 324.
[51] Haraguchi, 'Blessing and Curse' (2004), 40–42, suggests that the Agitators operated within 'the OT rhetorical tradition of blessing and curse'.

light of the rest of the Genesis narrative (cf. 4.21-31).⁵² One can hardly doubt that they would have also mentioned the preceding clause, especially since a warning about 'cursing' Abraham would have been a useful way of engendering seriousness about the necessity of circumcision.⁵³

It is also worth noting that Paul links Abrahamic and Deuteronomic traditions in this context, a move not uncommon in other strands of early Jewish literature. Perhaps the Agitators were interpreting the promise to Abraham (cf. Gen 12.3; 17.1-14) through the lens of Deuteronomy's blessings and curses, a conflation the book itself makes on a few occasions:

> I call heaven and earth to witness against you today, that I have set before you life and death, the *blessing* (τὴν εὐλογίαν) and the *curse* (τὴν κατάραν). Therefore choose life, that you and your offspring may live, loving the Lord your God, obeying his voice and holding fast to him, for he is your life and length of days, that you may dwell in *the land that the Lord swore to your fathers, to Abraham, to Isaac, and to Jacob*, to give them (Deut 30.19-20).

The Agitators may well have been refracting the Abrahamic promise that 'in you all the families of the earth will be blessed' (Gen 12.3b; 3.8) through the covenant theology of Deuteronomy, arguably the way in which the biblical tradition and some strands of early Judaism did (cf. *Jub.* 12.23; 25.22; 26.24; 31.17, 20; Tob 13.9-18).⁵⁴ Blessing and life come *via* incorporation into Abraham, the father of a multitude of nations (cf. 4.21-31).

It is hardly accidental that in Galatians Paul makes no explicit reference to Gen 17.⁵⁵ As E. P. Sanders notes, this is the Agitators' 'most forceful passage'.⁵⁶ It is indeed telling that Justin's Jewish interlocutor Trypho reaches first for a citation from this very passage (Gen 17.14) when he takes issue with the fact that Christians dispense with circumcision and the Law and yet

---

⁵² Martyn, *Galatians* (1997), 301. Stockhausen, 'Pauline Exegesis' (1993), 153, argues that the Agitators were compelling the Gentiles to be circumcised on the basis of a 'consistently linear and exclusive reading of the narrative of Abraham'. 'The opponents have a perfectly straightforward case, drawn from Scripture, for the procedure they advocate for the Gentile Christians of Galatia' (139).

⁵³ The author of *Jubilees*, for example, understands 'cursing' Abraham to consist of 'hating' or 'afflicting' Israel (31.20), being an enemy of Israel (31.17), or 'cursing' Israel (25.22). Cf. Tob 13.12, which appears to interpret Gen 12.3 with special reference to Jerusalem: 'Cursed are all who speak a harsh word against you [Jerusalem; cf. 13.9]; cursed are all who conquer you and pull down your walls, all who overthrow your towers and set your homes on fire. But blessed forever will be all who revere you'.

⁵⁴ Cf. Barrett, 'Allegory' (1982), 167.

⁵⁵ Stanley, *Arguing* (2004), 117 n. 9; cf. Stanton, 'Law of Moses' (1996), 107: 'a shock tactic, designed to set the Galatians thinking'. However, Sumney, *False Brothers* (1999), 144 n. 55, and, most recently, Watson, *Hermeneutics of Faith* (2004), 216 n. 63, insist that there is no evidence that Gen 17 was used by the Agitators. See below.

⁵⁶ Sanders, *Jewish People* (1983), 18; cf. Barclay, *Obeying* (1988), 53.

still expect divine favour (cf. *Dial.* 10.3).[57] An advocate of circumcision would be hard pressed to find a more unambiguous text in the whole of Scripture. The decisive verses run as follows:

> And God said to Abraham, 'As for you, you shall keep my covenant, you and your offspring after you throughout their generations (τὸ σπέρμα σου μετὰ σὲ εἰς τὰς γενεὰς αὐτῶν). This is my covenant, which you shall keep, between me and you and your offspring after you: Every male among you shall be circumcised (περιτμηθήσεται ὑμῶν πᾶν ἀρσενικόν). You shall be circumcised in the flesh of your foreskin (τὴν σάρκα τῆς ἀκροβυστίας ὑμῶν), and it shall be a sign of the covenant between me and you. He who is eight days old among you shall be circumcised. Every male throughout your generations, whether born in your house or bought with your money from any foreigner who is not of your offspring (ὃς οὐκ ἔστιν ἐκ τοῦ σπέρματός σου), both he who is born in your house and he who is bought with your money, shall surely be circumcised. So shall my covenant be in your flesh an everlasting covenant (ἡ διαθήκη μου ἐπὶ τῆς σαρκὸς ὑμῶν εἰς διαθήκην αἰώνιον). Any uncircumcised male who is not circumcised in the flesh of his foreskin shall be cut off (ἐξολεθρευθήσεται) from his people; he has broken my covenant' (Gen 17.9-14).

We cannot, of course, be certain that the Agitators cited this passage.[58] Several observations, however, strengthen the likelihood that they did. First, these verses appear within a context in which God reaffirms his designs to make Abraham 'the father of a multitude of nations' (Gen 17.4) and to give to him and to his offspring the inheritance of the land (Gen 17.8). Secondly, it is clear from the context that the necessary means of receiving the promise of the land (inheritance) is by observing the covenant stipulations outlined in Gen 17.9-14: the circumcision of all the males of one's household, whether natural born or slave. Thirdly, this chapter concludes with Abraham's immediate response of circumcising his son Ishmael (Gen 17.22-27), which may stand behind the allegory in 4.21-31. Fourthly, this particular chapter of Genesis represents a significant turning point in the narrative of the book as a whole, since here both Abraham and Sarah receive new names. Fifthly, in addition to stating that circumcision is an everlasting covenant (Gen 17.13; cf. *Jub.* 15.25: 'an eternal ordinance'), central to this passage is the solemn warning that those who neglect the covenant obligation of circumcision will assuredly be 'cut off' from their people (Gen 17.14).[59] Worth noting are the covenantal associations of being 'cut off' (MT: כרת; LXX: ἐξολεθρεύω) within early Jewish literature, where it is linked with covenant curses and thus

---

[57] Cf. Stanton, 'Law of Moses' (1996), 107.

[58] Vos, *Argumentation* (2002), 87, however, insists that it is certain (*Sicherheit*) that the Agitators charged Paul with not preaching a complete gospel because of his failure to refer to Gen 17 and circumcision. Martyn, *Galatians* (1997), 423 n. 94, similarly claims: 'we can be confident that the Teachers made much of Genesis 17, emphasising the definition of God's covenant as circumcision'.

[59] There may be an echo of this in Paul's comment in 4.17: 'they want to shut you out'.

dispossession of the land (cf. Psa 37.22; Ps.-Philo 19.4; *Jub.* 15.14).[60] The author of *Jubilees*, in fact, expands upon this warning in Gen 17.14 with Deuteronomic language about being 'annihilated' and 'uprooted from the earth', thus interpreting being 'cut off' in terms of suffering the curses of the covenant described in Deuteronomy (Deut 15.26; cf. 15.28-20, 34).

Little wonder, then, that Paul appears to have passed over in silence Gen 17.[61] Evidently he opted to avoid a head-on collision with this *crux interpretum*, or at least he decided to frame his discussion in different terms and with different texts (e.g., Gen 12.3; 15.6), perhaps knowing that if the Galatians were at all interested in following the Scriptures, they would have been forced (compelled?) to admit that Gen 17 left them with very little room to negotiate around the necessity of circumcision.

There is good reason to suppose that the Agitators were using Abrahamic traditions as part of their polemical appeal to urge the Galatians to take on circumcision. This being the case, it is not difficult to imagine the Agitators also using these same traditions to threaten the Galatians with the prospect of coming under a curse, whether they argued that God would curse those who 'curse' Abraham (Gen 12.3) or that those who fail to observe the rite of circumcision would be 'cut off' from their people (Gen 17.14). Just as the Galatians were being lured by the prospect of sharing in Abraham's blessing, so too they were likely to hear of the deleterious consequences of failing to embrace the covenant of circumcision. In a word, the Agitators had probably warned the Galatians of or perhaps threatened them with the 'curses of the covenant' (αἱ ἀραὶ τῆς διαθήκης, LXX Deut 29.20).

Curse and Law: The Agitators' use of Deuteronomic traditions

A second important piece of evidence for the Agitators' use of the curse of the Law as part of their polemical strategy with the Galatians comes from Paul's citation of Deut 27.26 in 3.10: 'Cursed is everyone who does not abide by all things written in the book of the Law to do them'.[62] For obvious reasons scholars have often supposed this text to be part of the Agitators' own scriptural argumentation. Barrett had little doubt on this issue: 'The Old

---

[60] Cf. Horbury, 'Excommunication' (1985), 31–33.

[61] Martin, 'Circumcision' (2003), 111–25, has recently argued that 3.28 is a polemical inversion of the terms of the covenant as outlined in Gen 17.10-14. Paul's polemical use of σάρξ as a reference to circumcision may also stem from the language of the covenant being 'upon your flesh' (ἐπὶ τῆς σαρκὸς ὑμῶν) in Gen 17.13. If either one of these suggestions could stand, it would only strengthen the likelihood that the Agitators were appealing to Gen 17 and the 'covenant of circumcision'.

[62] Paul's citation appears, in fact, to be a conflation of Deut 27.26 and Deut 28.58. Cf. Stanley, *Language of Scripture* (1992), 238–43.

Testament quotation in 3.10 was almost certainly used by Paul's opponents'.[63] A number of scholars agree with this basic assessment, even if they express themselves in slightly less confident terms.[64]

As is widely recognised, the verse seems singularly ill-suited to Paul's line of thought; in fact, it seems to say precisely the opposite of what Paul wants to argue: that the curse falls upon those who *do* the 'works of the Law' – not upon those who *fail* to do so, which is the ostensible thrust of Deut 27.26. This awkwardness is perhaps most easily explained by supposing that the Agitators had already spoken of the curse falling upon those who fail to embrace the Law and its works, which would then explain Paul's seemingly tortuous counter-interpretation.[65] This becomes more likely in view of the fact that one or more of the other scriptural citations in this same paragraph could have easily been employed to support the opposing viewpoint.[66] Thus, many have thought it very likely that the Agitators were making some appeal to the curses of Deuteronomy, indeed to this very verse, as a means of warning the Galatians of the serious consequences of failing to comply with the demands of the Law.[67]

Even if one is not entirely persuaded of the need to smooth over Paul's handling of Deut 27.26 by supposing that he is responding to the Agitators,[68] there are still a number of good reasons for thinking that this was one of the Agitators' own texts. Martyn has recently identified four reasons in particular. First, Paul does not refer to Deut 27.26 anywhere else in his writings, which makes its appearance in Galatians particularly striking and in need of some explanation. Secondly, 3.10-14 contains an unusually high concentration of curse terminology; the language of 'curse' (κατάρα) and 'cursing' (ἐπικατάρατος) occurs only here. This is most easily explained on the

---

[63] Barrett, 'Allegory' (1982), 159. Hengel, *Pre-Christian Paul* (1991), 84, suggests that the pre-Christian Paul may have used Deut 27.26 against the 'Hellenists'.

[64] Longenecker, *Galatians* (1990), 117; Smiles, *Law in Galatia* (1998), 201–02; Martyn, *Galatians* (1997), 309; Young, 'Cursed' (1998), 86 n. 37. Sumney, *False Brothers* (1999), 152, denies that 3.10 can tell us anything about the Agitators' teaching without an unjustifiable use of mirror-reading, since the context is primarily didactic rather than polemical or apologetic. However, Paul's allusion to the Agitators as those who are 'of the works of the Law' in 3.10 suggests that while this passage may be primarily didactic, it is also highly polemical.

[65] See especially Barrett, 'Allegory' (1982), 158.

[66] Cf. Jervis, *Galatians* (1999), 90: 'It is easy to see how at least three of the four Scriptural quotations (Deut 27:26; Lev 18:5; Deut 21:23) could have been put to good use by the rival evangelists'.

[67] Barclay, *Obeying* (1988), 67, commenting on this passage, writes: 'In these and many other places Scripture unambiguously declares a blessing on those who keep the law and a curse on those who neglect to do so; if the Galatians took their Scriptures seriously they were doubtless urged to do what they say in this matter'.

[68] See the discussion in Wakefield, *Where to Live* (2003), 78–79.

assumption that the Teachers were threatening the Galatians with a curse. Thirdly, in Rom 4, where Paul similarly appeals to Abrahamic traditions and to those who derive their identity from the Law (cf. 4.14), he neither mentions blessing nor curse, probably because his audience was not faced with the threat of a curse. Fourthly, the curse threatened in Deut 27.26 'fits the Teachers' theology hand in glove'.[69] How could they *not* have appealed to a text so well suited for their own purposes?[70]

While these individual arguments are of varying degrees of persuasiveness, together they form a fairly strong cumulative case. We may reasonably infer, then, that when Paul speaks about the Agitators 'troubling' the Galatians (1.7; 5.10; cf. 4.17), he has in view the fact that the Agitators, as Martyn suggests, were actually 'frightening the Galatians out of their wits, intimidating them with the threat of damnation if they do not follow the path prescribed in the Teachers' message!'[71] Here one does well to remember that one of the characteristic features of the covenant theology of this period was the dualism of blessing and curse; and that this dualism was not infrequently invoked as a means of exhorting fidelity to the covenant.[72] Martyn's reconstruction of the message of the Agitators, then, sounds not altogether far-fetched:

> Walk in the way of Law observance, and, as the Law declares, God will bless you within the corpus of Abraham's descendants. Walk in the way of nonobservance, and, as the Law also declares, God will place his curse on you, excluding you from his people. God's holy Law speaks of these two ways, blessing and curse.[73]

The Threat of a Curse as Part of the Agitators' Polemic Against Paul

There is a third line of evidence which suggests that the Agitators were warning the Galatians of or perhaps threatening them with a curse. It cannot be affirmed with the same degree of confidence, however, since it rests upon the supposition that Paul was being accused by the Agitators of false prophecy. While the trend recently has been to downplay the apologetic

---

[69] Martyn, *Galatians* (1997), 309.

[70] Barrett, 'Allegory' (1982), 159: 'It requires no stretch of the imagination to see how naturally the passage could be used by Judaizers'.

[71] Martyn, *Galatians* (1997), 112 (see above p. 67). Martyn likewise thinks the Teachers' use of Deut 27.26 and the threat of the curse were part of their larger mode of instruction which concentrated on the duality of blessing and curse found in the Law itself. The Teachers' instruction was thus structurally similar to other Two Ways traditions know from ancient Jewish and Jewish-Christian sources, where blessing and curse are contingent upon one's conformity to God's Law.

[72] Elliot, *Survivors*, 280, 295 n. 131.

[73] Martyn, *Galatians* (1997), 325.

function of Gal 1–2, the defensive tone of these chapters cannot be wholly eliminated.[74] Paul's sharp antithetical contrasts (1.1, 10, 11), together with his carefully crafted travelogue vis-à-vis Jerusalem (1.17–2.10), is very difficult to explain apart from the supposition that his gospel and apostleship were somehow in question. Especially telling is the fact that Paul felt the need to guarantee the veracity of what he was saying with an oath: 'In what I am writing to you, before God, I do not lie!' (1.20; cf. 1 Thess 2.5, 10; 2 Cor 1.23; 11.31; 12.19; Rom 1.9; 9.1; Phil 1.8), which would otherwise appear 'dreadfully melodramatic' were he not faced with some kind of accusations.[75] Thus, Barclay, among others, thinks it is 'virtually certain' that Paul's gospel and apostleship were being called into question.[76]

The precise nature of the charges Paul suffered is difficult to discern. We must, therefore, proceed cautiously. Several general observations suggest that Paul may have been charged with false prophecy. Debate over true and false prophets was important at the time of the writing of the NT and, more importantly, often arose within contexts where competing interpretations of Scripture were at issue,[77] as would have probably been the case in the Galatian churches. Furthermore, an accusation of false prophecy would have been an effective means of *distancing* the Galatians from Paul, which evidently is precisely what has happened (cf. 4.17). Such accusations would have cast a shadow of doubt over Paul's character and thereby discredited the validity of his message. Reading Gal 1–2 against the backdrop of accusations of false prophecy also has the advantage of being able to correlate Paul's defence of his divine commission (1.1, 11-17), on the one hand, with the demonstration of his unswerving commitment to the 'truth of the gospel' (2.5; cf. 1.10; 2.11), on the other, without needing to choose one instead of the other, as is sometimes done. This dual emphasis may reflect, then, Paul's conviction that the prophet's *ethos* is inseparable from his message.

There are several more specific observations which suggest that Paul may have faced accusations of false prophecy. First, Paul's stress upon the divine, as opposed to merely human, origin of his apostleship (1.1) and gospel (1.11-12) is characteristic of contexts where prophetic legitimacy is at stake.[78] Luke's record of Gamaliel's advice to the council in Jerusalem deliberating over what is to be done to Peter and the other apostles, who they suspect are spreading a false teaching about Jesus of Nazareth, is indicative of this basic

---

[74] Similarly Longenecker, *Triumph* (1998), 29 n. 9.
[75] So Silva, *Interpreting Galatians* (2001), 105, who rightly criticises Lyons, *Pauline Autobiography* (1985), for downplaying 1.20.
[76] Barclay, 'Mirror-Reading' (1987), 88; cf. Martyn, *Galatians* (1997), 174.
[77] Horbury, 'False Prophecy' (1982), 438.
[78] Deut 18.20; Jer 23.16, 21, 32; 27.14-15; 29.9, 31; Mark 11.31-32; Acts 5.38-39 with Josephus, *A.J.* 20.97–99; Philo, *Spec.* 1.315.

outlook: 'if this plan or this undertaking is of human origin (ἐξ ἀνθρώπων) it will fail, but if it is of God (ἐκ θεοῦ), you will not be able to overthrow them' (Acts 5.38-39). The validity of the prophet's message depends upon the prophet having been sent by God (cf. Mark 11.31-32).[79] False prophets, on the other hand, can trace their calling only to a human source.

Secondly, Paul substantiates his claim to having received his gospel not 'from a human being' but 'through a revelation of Jesus Christ' (1.12) by recounting his calling in terms reminiscent of other OT prophetic callings (1.15-17). Whether this reflects Paul's own self-understanding is not my concern here.[80] It is sufficient simply to note that Paul clearly wants to bolster his claim to legitimacy by underscoring the divine origin of his calling and gospel. Paul's description of his own dramatic reversal from 'persecutor to preacher' (cf. γάρ, 1.13-24) is arguably intended to underscore this precise point.

Thirdly, Paul's contrast between 'pleasing human beings' and 'pleasing God' (1.10) is a stereotypical distinction to make when prophetic legitimacy is at stake. False prophets speak 'smooth things' and 'prophesy illusions' (Isa 30.10).[81] In various strands of early Jewish and Christian literature false prophets are portrayed as being religious charlatans with impure motives. They speak, in Paul's words, 'according to human standards' (κατὰ ἄνθρωπον, 1.11). Because they derive their message and authority ultimately from humans, they aim to please them. One of the hallmarks of genuine prophets, however, is their uncompromising moral integrity (cf. 1 Thess 2.3-6).[82]

But how might a charge of false prophecy against Paul be used to threaten the *Galatians* with a curse? Two things are worth bearing in mind here. First, various early Jewish and Christian traditions link the false prophet with a curse. The *locus classicus* on false prophecy is Deut 13, which calls explicitly for an anathema upon anyone who would lead the Israelites astray. This text is taken up, often in conjunction with other pertinent OT passages, in CD 12.3 (cf. 11QT 54.8-11),[83] Josephus (*A.J.* 4.310), Philo (*Spec.* 1.54-65), the NT (Matt 27.63-64; John 7.12, 47) and the Mishnah (*Sanh.* 7.4, 10-11).[84] If the Agitators judged Paul to be a false prophet, it would have been quite natural for them to treat him as an apostate who falls under the sanctions of Deut 13.

---

[79] Amos 7.14-15; Jer 1.8, 18; 14.14-15; 23.32; 28.15-16; 43.2; Ezek 13.6-9; Zech 2.8, 9, 11; 6.15.
[80] Cf. Sandnes, *One of the Prophets?* (1991), 48–76.
[81] Jer 6.14; 8.11; 23.17; Ezek 13.10-12, 16; 22.28; 1 Thess 5.3; Luke 6.26.
[82] Horbury, 'False Prophecy' (1982), 492–508.
[83] Wisdom, *Blessing* (2001), 106.
[84] Horbury, 'False Prophecy' (1982), 493.

Secondly, as this relates to the Galatians, various OT traditions link the punishment of the false prophet with the people. Deut 13 not only calls for the execution of the false prophet (13.5, 10), but also for an anathema upon the city and its inhabitants.

> If you hear in one of your cities, which the Lord your God has given you to inhabit, someone saying, 'Lawless persons (παράνομοι; MT בני־בליעל) have gone out from among us and have led astray all the inhabitants of their city, saying, "Let us go and serve other gods (θεοῖς ἑτέροις) whom you have not know"', then you must ask and inquire thoroughly into the matter. And if this abomination has actually happened among you, you must destroy all the inhabitants of that city by executing them with the sword; you must place it under an anathema (ἀναθέματι ἀναθεματιεῖτε αὐτήν) and all that is within it (Deut 13.13-16).

Perhaps the Agitators viewed Paul as a παράνομος (cf. 2.17), who was leading whole communities astray by failing to uphold the Law and the covenant. Barrett holds this view and offers the following reconstruction of the Agitators' polemic against Paul:

> Paul himself fails to observe all the things that are written in the law – he becomes all things to all men, and among the Gentiles lives as a Gentile: he is under a curse. He admits, or claims to admit, Gentiles to the people of God without requiring them to be circumcised and to keep the law: instead of enabling them to share in the blessing of Abraham he brings them under a curse. He would do better to leave them alone.[85]

The Agitators thus may have warned the Galatians that if they continue to follow Paul's teaching, they will also suffer Paul's fate.

Conclusion

In this chapter I have drawn attention to several strands of evidence which suggest that the Agitators warned the Galatians of or perhaps threatened them with a curse for failing to be circumcised. I began by arguing that while Paul does not explicitly accuse the Agitators of appealing to a curse, several indications point in that direction. It is highly likely that the Agitators not only appealed to the benefits of embracing circumcision, but also warned the Galatians of the consequences of failing to do so. The Agitators could have referred to several scriptural traditions which hold out a curse for failure to comply with the requirements of the covenant and the Law (Gen 17.10-14; 12.3; Deut 27.26).

That the Agitators appealed to a curse, however, does not necessarily imply that they were hostile towards either Paul or the Galatians, much less that they were religious charlatans. In fact, it may have been the case that they

---

[85] Barrett, 'Allegory' (1982), 159.

had the 'best interests of the Gentiles deeply at heart'.[86] And, if one rejects the idea that they charged Paul with being a false prophet, one need not suppose that they held any personal animosity towards him. It is certainly possible that they understood their role in Galatia as that of advisors to the Galatians, adopting a posture not entirely unlike the one we find reflected by the author of MMT:

> Consider all these things and ask Him that He strengthen your will and remove from you the plans of evil and the device of Belial so that you may rejoice at the end of time, finding that some of our practices are correct. And this will be counted as a virtuous deed of yours, since you will be doing what is righteous and good in His eyes, for your own welfare and for the welfare of Israel (DJD 10, 4Q398 14-17 ii [C28–32]).

Similarly, the Agitators may have been warning the Galatians of, rather than threatening them with, the possibility of coming under a curse, genuinely interested in helping these fledgling believers to avoid the dangers of a curse and thereby ensure that they obtain the 'hope of righteousness' (5.5; cf. 3.3).

In any event, the Agitators were successful in persuading the Galatians of the need to submit to circumcision. They evidently struck a cord with the Galatians, when they spoke of a curse coming upon 'everyone who does not abide by all things written in the book of the Law to do them' (3.10; Deut 27.26). But the Galatians' attraction to circumcision is not solely the result of the persuasive tactics of the Agitators. As we shall see in the next chapter, the Galatians themselves would have had very good reason to want to avert the possibility of a curse, even if this meant getting circumcised.

---

[86] Murphy-O'Connor, *Critical Life* (1996), 194.

Chapter 4

The Curse of the Law and the Galatian Converts

> In argumentation, the important thing is not knowing
> what the speaker regards as true or important,
> but knowing the views of those he is addressing.[1]

In the previous chapter we considered whether the curse of the Law played a part in the Agitators' appeal for circumcision. In this chapter we shall explore from a complementary angle whether the threat of a curse played a part in the Galatians' attraction to circumcision. Explaining why Paul's Gentile converts were even interested in circumcision is naturally a prerequisite for understanding the emergence of the crisis. This is a difficult question to answer, however, not only because divining intentions can be rather elusive, but also because our evidence is so limited.

It might be useful to employ the simple taxonomy of human behaviour suggested by the Greek satirist Lucian (c. 120–180 C.E.), who once observed that life's decisions are held under sway by two great tyrants: hope and fear (*Alex.* 8). Particularly recently, students of Galatians have tended to focus their attention on what the Galatians hoped to gain from circumcision: whether this is identified as justification (5.2-6), inclusion into the people of God (3.26–4.7), or help overcoming the 'desire of the flesh' (5.16-24). One or more of these probably played some part in their attraction to circumcision. In this chapter, however, I would like to draw attention to the somewhat overlooked issue of *fear* as a motivating factor in their decision to undergo circumcision.

'There is no one', observed Pliny the Elder (23–79 C.E.), 'who does not fear to be spell-bound by imprecations' (LCL: *Nat.* 28.4.19). My chief aim in this chapter is to suggest that this was also true of Paul's Galatian converts, who inhabited a world filled with tokens of divine vengeance and the workings of curses and, as a result, would have surely feared coming under the curse of a god. Hence, they would have been deeply unsettled by the threat of a curse and would have been quite keen to avert this possibility, even if it meant getting circumcised.

Following a brief description of the approach of this chapter, I shall argue, largely on the basis of epigraphic evidence from central Anatolia, that the

---

[1] Perelman and Olbrechts-Tyteca, *New Rhetoric* (1969), 23–24.

Galatians would have taken the threat of a curse very seriously indeed. I shall go on to suggest (albeit somewhat more tentatively) that the Galatians' encounter with suffering, both Paul's and their own, may have exacerbated their fears about the curse of the Law, since in a world dominated by the overseeing presence of the gods suffering could easily be interpreted as an expression of divine vengeance and the workings of a curse. Here I shall also suggest that the Agitators may have further provoked the Galatians' anxieties about the threat of a curse by interpreting the Galatians' suffering and Paul's own suffering as evidence of the fact that a curse had already overtaken them both.

The Galatian Audience

Traditionally, scholars have assumed that the primary context for interpreting Galatians is the controversy between Paul and the Agitators.[2] As a result, the Galatians' social context and religious outlook are sometimes neglected, with attention given, at times almost exclusively, to how the Jewish 'background' informs our understanding of the situation in Galatia and the content of the letter.[3] The advent of Greco-Roman rhetorical criticism, pioneered by Betz, has redressed this somewhat, as has the increased interest in the 'social world' of the ancient Mediterranean basin.[4] More recently, with the publication of S. Mitchell's magisterial two-volume, *Anatolia: Land, Men and Gods* (1993), there is growing interest in the Anatolian social and religious context of the Galatians. The ongoing work of the Paul and Politics Group of the Society of Biblical Literature, as well as S. Elliott's recent monograph, *Cutting too Close for Comfort: Paul's Letter to the Galatians in its Anatolian Cultic Context* (2003), typify this growing interest and may foreshadow new directions in Galatians research.[5]

Increased scholarly interest in the Galatian audience is a welcome development for a number of reasons. Consideration of the social and religious background of Paul's addressees will undoubtedly contribute

---

[2] Elliott, *Cutting too Close* (2003), 2–3; Kwon, *Eschatology* (2004), 20–23.

[3] Two notable exceptions are Ramsay, *Galatians* (1899) and Lightfoot, *Galatians* (1896).

[4] Cf. Malina, *New Testament World* (1993); Malina and Neyrey, *Portraits of Paul* (1996); Neyrey, *Paul, in Other Words* (1991). For the application of this line of approach to the interpretation of Galatians, see Neyrey, 'Bewitched' (1988), 72–100; Esler, 'Intergroup Conflict' (1996), 215–40; Esler, *Galatians* (1998); and, most recently, Asano, *Community-Identity* (2005).

[5] See also Elliott, 'Mother' (1999), 661–83; Elliott, 'Gentile Audiences' (1996), 117–36; Arnold, 'Anatolian Folk Belief' (2005), 429–49.

something useful to our understanding of the dynamics of the Galatian crisis, especially as we seek to understand why the Galatians were attracted to circumcision. We can reasonably assume that despite the profound reorientation that came as a result of their embrace of Paul's gospel (4.8-9), the Galatians would have nonetheless held on to some vestiges of their pre-conversion religious outlook, not least because these beliefs would have continued to be reinforced by their environment. This raises the possibility that the developments in Galatia are due at least in part to how the Galatians may have responded to their own circumstances and to the influence of the Agitators from an Anatolian perspective. In particular, one of the questions we shall explore in this chapter is whether the Agitators found such success in promoting circumcision in Galatia in part because their appeal resonated with the pre-conversion values and beliefs of the Galatians.

Within the scope of this present chapter we cannot, of course, even begin to consider all the ways in which the Anatolian social and religious environment might have come into play in the Galatian crisis. In keeping with our primary interest of trying to understand the relevance of the curse of the Law for the crisis in Galatia, this discussion will be limited to those features of the Anatolian context which have most relevance for elucidating this particular issue. Hence, building upon the results of the previous chapter, the aim of this chapter is to explore how the Galatians may have responded to the threat of a curse. Would this have been an effective means of persuasion? And how might the Galatians have responded to the threat of a curse, especially one already written down in the Scriptures of Israel and thus guaranteed by the God of the Jews? This should, in turn, provide us with a more well-rounded and balanced assessment of the situation in Galatia, at least as it concerns the issue of the curse of the Law.[6]

One obstacle to taking seriously the social and religious context of the Galatian audience is the problem of pinning down precisely where the Galatian churches were located.[7] While the so-called North-South Galatia debate does appear to be shifting slightly in favour of the South Galatian or provincial hypothesis,[8] the argument of this chapter does not depend upon a

---

[6] Elliott, *Cutting too Close* (2003), 349, suggests that attention to the world of the Galatian audience, as opposed to the Agitators, offers a 'different picture' of the situation. She may be faulted, however, for unnecessarily pitting these two angles of approach against each another, at least implying that the results from each are not all that compatible. One of the aims of this chapter is to demonstrate the opposite.

[7] Barclay, *Obeying* (1988), 45. Cf. Vouga, 'Kein Brief' (1996), 243–58, who advances the thesis that the there was no original audience to Galatians.

[8] Scott, *Paul and the Nations* (1995); Breytenbach, *Adressaten* (1996); Riesner, *Paul's Early Period* (1998), 286–91; Witulski, *Die Adressaten* (2000); Stanton, *Jesus and Gospel* (2004), 36–37. Note also the forthright (if somewhat overstated) comment by the ancient

decision either way. The Galatians were inhabitants of the west-central region of Anatolia, and the main epigraphic evidence here considered comes from that area. Furthermore, as Mitchell observes of the Anatolian region as a whole, 'the outlines of paganism were well defined and consistent from one city or region to another'.[9]

Anatolian Popular Religiosity and the Fear of Divine Vengeance

One of the leading features of Anatolian popular religiosity was a belief in the overseeing presence of the deities, what Mitchell refers to as 'the rule of the gods'.[10] Especially in rural areas, where legal sanctions were often more difficult to enforce, the task of maintaining cultic and social order fell to local enforcer deities. The rule of the gods thus functioned not only to ensure respect for local customs, order and authority, but also to guarantee some modicum of personal morality. Their overseeing presence provided a sense of juridical authority that might otherwise have been lacking outside urban contexts; and their ability to requite wrongdoers with personal afflictions served as an effective deterrent against wrongdoing. Consequently, as Mitchell points out, Anatolian popular religiosity was characterised by two things: (1) 'a preoccupation with a strict morality which was based on clearly defined notions of justice, proper behaviour, piety to the gods, a respect for divine authority', and (2) 'a well-developed fear of divine vengeance'.[11]

We gain some sense of popular Anatolian perceptions of divine retribution from the surviving epigraphic evidence, most of which hails from two spheres of life: religion and burial.[12] Funerary inscriptions are in particular abundance in Anatolia. Phrygia, for example, has been described as 'le domaine par excellence des imprécations funéraires'.[13] Funerary inscriptions provide very good (albeit limited) insight into the religious ethos of the region, particularly how beliefs about divine retribution and the workings of a curse would have functioned at a popular level.[14] These inscriptions are by their very nature

---

historian Mitchell, *Anatolia* (1993), 2.3: 'there is virtually nothing to be said for the north Galatian theory'.

[9] Mitchell, *Anatolia* (1993), 1.30.

[10] Mitchell, *Anatolia* (1993), 1.187–95.

[11] Mitchell, *Anatolia* (1993), 1.190–91.

[12] On the so-called 'epigraphic habit' in antiquity, see Bodel, *Epigraphic Evidence* (2001), 6–15, and the programmatic essay by MacMullen, 'Epigraphic Habit' (1982), 233–46.

[13] Robert, 'Malédictions funéraires' (1989), 253. Lattimore, *Themes* (1942), 109, suggests that the preponderance of funerary imprecations from Asia Minor evidences a 'special attitude' to death compared to the rest of the Greco-Roman world.

[14] See the numerous examples, with Greek and Latin texts and translation, in Lattimore, *Themes* (1942), 108–18, 121–23 (though not limited to Asia Minor). Strubbe, 'Jewish

future-oriented, threatening a curse upon anyone who would desecrate a tomb or unlawfully inter a body.[15] The following examples are illustrative, all taken from Asia Minor:

> If anyone does any harm to the statue, may he leave orphaned children, a bereaved estate and a desolate home behind him. May he lose all his goods by fire and die at the hands of evil men.[16]
>
> If anyone erases the dead image of this child, may he fall afoul of the curse of the untimely dead.[17]
>
> Whoever does anything counter to the injunctions set forth above, shall be held responsible to the authorities; and in addition, may he have no profit from children or goods, may he neither walk on land nor sail on sea, but may he die childless, penniless and ruined before death and all his seed perish with him, and after death may he find the underground gods to be angry avengers.[18]

The overlap in style between these inscriptions should be obvious: a condition is specified ('If anyone . . .'), which is then followed by a description of the consequences of meeting that condition in the form of a threat ('may he . . .'), usually in terms of some physical or psychological affliction, though not always using the language of a curse.[19]

There is a collection of funerary inscriptions that contain what has become known as the 'children's children's' curse because the would-be violator is threatened with a curse that is said to extend εἰς τέκνα τέκνων. There are sixteen attestations of this specific curse formula (or a slight variation thereof) found in the regions of Phrygia, Lydia, Caria, and Pisidia and dating mostly from the second and third centuries C.E.[20] They exhibit a number of interesting features, sometimes using curse terminology, other times specifying the content (or effect) of the curse. Two of the four examples considered below name specific deities who are expected to requite the

---

Epitaphs' (1994), 70 n. 3, has identified 365 pagan funerary curse inscriptions from Asia Minor. Cf. Strubbe, 'Cursed' (1991), 33–59; on Jewish funerary imprecations, see Horst, *Jewish Epitaphs* (1991), 54–60.

[15] Strubbe, 'Jewish Epitaphs' (1994), 102–03.

[16] Translation Gager, *Curse Tablets* (1992), 178 (from Iconium in Cilicia). For Greek text, see Lattimore, *Themes* (1942), 112.

[17] Translation Gager, *Curse Tablets* (1992), 178 (from Aezani, 250 Kilometers east of Pergamom). For Greek text, see Lattimore, *Themes* (1942), 112.

[18] Translation Gager, *Curse Tablets* (1992), 178 (from Hierapolis in Phrygia). For Greek text, see Lattimore, *Themes* (1942), 115–16.

[19] Cf. Lattimore, *Themes* (1942), 109: 'there must have been a widespread belief that such defensive curses would work, that the religious awe of the public in general would correspond to the intense concern felt by those who built the tomb'.

[20] For a complete listing of all attestations with Greek text, translation and discussion, see Strubbe, 'Jewish Epitaphs' (1994), 73–83.

offending party; especially noteworthy is the last of the four which calls upon the entire pantheon of Greece and Persia to protect the tomb from violators.

> There will be a curse (ἀρά) extending to his children's children (to prevent that) another corpse will be buried than my son Eutyches and his wife.[21]
>
> But whoever will do harm to this grave or will place a corpse in it other than that of my slave Kosmia, he will pay 2.500 denaria to the most sacred treasury and he will be cursed (ὑποκατάρατος), (to) his children's children.[22]
>
> Should anyone intend to desecrate this tomb, he will find enraged Apollo and Lady Anaeitis, to his children's children and grandchildren's grandchildren (ἔγονα ἐγόνων).[23]
>
> If someone will damage (the tomb), the gods of the Greeks and of the Persians will pay him back with blood and deaths (αἵματι καὶ θανάτοις ἀποδώσουσ[ι]), (to) his children's children.[24]

The scholarly consensus is that the phrase εἰς τέκνα τέκνων is Jewish, mainly because this exact phrase appears in a significant passage of the LXX (Exod 34.7; cf. Exod 10.2; Prov 17.6). It is also not insignificant that the curses of Deuteronomy (see below) are often said to extend to one's descendants, including one's children and grandchildren (cf. 28.18, 31, 35, 41, 45–46). P. Trebilco took this as evidence of the close relations between Jews and pagans in Asia Minor and as indicative of the esteem with which pagans regarded Jews.[25] J. Strubbe, however, has perhaps rightly cautioned against reading too much into the use of what from other literary and epigraphic evidence appears to have been a common Greek locution.[26] Thus, he concludes that these are all probably pagan rather than Jewish. In any event, these inscriptions, whether Jewish or pagan, illustrate assumptions about how curses were perceived to have functioned.

Also intriguing for our purposes, despite their relatively late date (third-century C.E.), are three inscriptions which appeal explicitly to the curses of Deuteronomy. There has been some debate as to whether these inscriptions are of a Jewish or Christian origin, though a Jewish origin is more likely. Either way, they provide good insight into what would have been, generally speaking, characteristic of the mentality of the region.

---

[21] Strubbe, 'Jewish Epitaphs' (1994), 74 (No. 1, from Akmonia, Phrygia, late Antonine period).
[22] Strubbe, 'Jewish Epitaphs' (1994), 75 (No. 7, from Prymnessos, Phrygia, 217–19 C.E.).
[23] Strubbe, 'Jewish Epitaphs' (1994), 76 (No. 9, near Kollyda, north-eastern Lydia, 261–62 C.E.).
[24] Strubbe, 'Jewish Epitaphs' (1994), 77 (No. 12, in the valley of Acipayam, Pisidia, Imperial period).
[25] Trebilco, *Jewish Communities* (1991), 69–74.
[26] Strubbe, 'Jewish Epitaphs' (1994), 79–83 (for the epigraphic evidence, see 81 n. 35–36).

In the year 333. Aur(elios) Phrougianos, son of Menokritos, and his wife, Aur(elia) Iuliane, have built (this grave) while alive for his (or her?) mother, Makaria, and for their very sweet daughter, Alexandria, in remembrance. If anyone, after they have been buried, if anyone will bury another corpse or will commit injustice (to the tomb) by way of purchase, he will get the curses that are written in Deuteronomy (αἱ ἀραὶ ἡ γεγραμμέναι ἐν τῷ Δευτερο– vac νομιῳ).[27]

... it will (not) be permitted to another person to open the lair, except only when it happens for his children Domne and Alexandria. But if they will marry, it will not be permitted to open (the grave). Who, however, will dare to put in it another (corpse), will pay to the most sacred treasury 1.000 Attic drachmae, and nonetheless he shall be liable for the accusation of grave robbery. Such a man will be accursed (ἐπικατάρατος) and may as many curses as are written in Deuteronomy (ὅσαι ἀραὶ ἐν τω Δευτερονομίῳ εἰσὶν γεγραμμέναι) befall him and his children and his descendants and his whole family.[28]

Made in the year 328. T(itus) Fl(avus) Alexandros built this tomb while alive for himself and for his wife Gaiane in remembrance. He has been a member of the city-council, an archon; he has lived nicely without causing grief to anybody. After I, Alexandros, and my wife Gaiane have been deposited, if someone opens the tomb, the curses, as many as are written (κατάραι ὅσε ἀνγεγραμμένα[ι ἰ]σιν), will befall him on his sight and on his whole body and on his children and on his life. If someone attempts to open (the grave), he will pay to the treasury as a fine 500 denaria.[29]

This third inscription is noteworthy for two reasons.[30] While the phrase 'curses which are written' (κατάραι ὅσε ἀνγεγραμμένα[ι ἰ]σιν) almost certainly refers to the curses in the book of Deuteronomy, both because of its close similarity to the other inscriptions and its approximation to the wording of the LXX (cf. Deut 29.19), the full phrase is not used, arguably because its author, T. Flavius Alexandros, wanted it to be effective in deterring Gentile pagans perhaps unfamiliar with Deuteronomy.[31] This is confirmed by the fact that, as Strubbe observes, the specific maledictions threatened in this inscription are neither the harshest nor the most common in Deuteronomy, which suggests that the author wanted to ward off would-be pagan tomb violators with maledictions which would have been familiar to them and thus effective as a deterrent.[32]

---

[27] For Greek text and translation, see Strubbe, 'Jewish Epitaphs' (1994), 116–17 (dated 248/9 C.E., from Acmonia in the province of Phrygia). Cf. Gager, *Curse Tablets*, 191; Trebilco, *Jewish Communities* (1991), 65–69.

[28] Strubbe, 'Jewish Epitaphs' (1994), 117–18 (No. 8, Akmonia, second or third-century C.E.). Cf. Trebilco, *Jewish Communities* (1991), 62–63, 65–69.

[29] Strubbe, 'Jewish Epitaphs' (1994), 119–20 (No. 9, reportedly brought from Ahat, Akmonia, 243–44 C.E.).

[30] Cf. Horst, *Jewish Epitaphs* (1991), 56–57.

[31] Trebilco, *Jewish Communities* (1991), 69–74, treats these inscriptions as further evidence of the close interaction between pagans and Jews in the region. For an alternative view, see Strubbe, 'Jewish Epitaphs' (1994), 100–05.

[32] Strubbe, 'Jewish Epitaphs' (1994), 92.

Another intriguing inscription comes from a second-century C.E. disciple of the Roman orator Herodes Atticus, who, despite being a pagan, sought to protect a bathhouse and statue he erected with a curse heavily indebted to the language of Deuteronomy:[33]

> I declare to those who will possess this property: there shall be a curse upon the owner of this property who does not spare this place and the statue which has been erected but who instead dishonors or moves the boundaries or insults terribly or injures or breaks – partially or in whole – or overturns on the ground or scatters or obscures it. May god strike this person with trouble and fever and chills and itch and drought and insanity and blindness and mental fits; and may his possessions disappear, may he not walk on land or sail at sea; may he (produce) no offspring. May his house not prosper; may he not enjoy crops, home, light, or the use and possession (of anything).[34]

J. Gager has perhaps rightly referred to the author of this inscription as a 'Judaizing' Gentile, who through his interactions with other Jews became convinced 'that the Bible could be used as a source book for potent curses'.[35] This corroborates the observation that Jews had a reputation in antiquity for being accomplished magicians.[36] In fact, as S. Cohen has observed, during this period some Gentiles were attracted to Judaism because of a reverence for the power of the God of the Jews.[37]

Anatolian fear of divine vengeance is perhaps nowhere more clearly illustrated than in the numerous confession inscriptions hailing from Lydia and Phrygia, most of which date from the second and third centuries C.E.[38] The basic sequence of events reflected in these inscriptions, allowing for minor variations, can be summarised as follows: personal wrongdoing provokes the wrath of the gods, who punish the wrongdoer with some bodily affliction or mental illness; this, in turn, compels the malefactor to confess his sin, usually in public and accompanied by the erection of a stele and the offering of praise for the deities demonstration of power (δύναμις), which is

---

[33] See the discussion in Robert, 'Malédictions funéraires' (1989), 249–52: 'l'influence de la Septante est indéniable' (250).

[34] Translation Gager, *Curse Tablets* (1992), 185 (Chalcis, Greece). For Greek text, see Lattimore, *Themes* (1942), 116. Cf. Mitchell, *Anatolia* (1993), 1.189 n. 217.

[35] Gager, *Curse Tablets* (1992), 185. Cf. Robert, 'Malédictions funéraires' (1989), 250: 'il était judaïsant'.

[36] Moses, for example, was sometimes regarded by pagans as a magician (cf. Pliny, *Nat.* 30.11). See further Graf, *Magic* (1997), 6–7; Gager, *Moses* (1972), 134–61. See also the extensive survey of material in Schürer, *Jewish People* (1986), 3.1.342–79.

[37] Cohen, 'Crossing the Boundary' (1989), 15–17, who refers to this same inscription.

[38] Cf. Versnel, 'Beyond Cursing' (1991), 75–79; Arnold, 'Anatolian Folk Belief' (2005), 429-49; Schnabel, 'Divine Tyranny' (2003), 182, notes that the earliest fully published inscription dates to 81/82 C.E. For a brief survey of the use of this evidence by NT scholars, see Klauck, 'Beichtinschriften' (1996), 63–87.

thought thereby to effect atonement.[39] Elliott nicely captures the religious ethos reflected in these inscriptions:

> The confession inscriptions were written from the point of view of someone who had committed an offence and experienced punishment from the deity in the form of disease or other calamity. The inscription stele itself served as expiation to release the individual from divine punishment and to confirm for all who would read it the effectiveness of the deities' power to administer justice. The confession steles show that the order of events for divinely administered justice differed from that of a human court system because the punishment was experienced before determination of guilt. Calamity, understood as punishment, was the first public indication of guilt and was prima facie evidence.[40]

A good example comes from the region of Lydia and is dated to 156/57 C.E.

> The 241st year, the month of Panemos, the 2nd day. Great Artemis, Anaeitis and Men of Tiamos. Because Loukoundos fell into a condition of insanity and it was noised abroad by all that he had been put under a spell [φάρμακον] by his mother-in-law Tatia, she set up a scepter and placed curses [ἀράς] in the temple in order to defend herself against what was being said about her, having suffered such a state of conscience. The gods sent punishment on her which she did not escape. Likewise also her son Sôkratês was passing the entrance that leads down to the sacred grove and carrying a vine-dressing sickle and it dropped on his foot and thus destruction came on him in a single day's punishment. Therefore great are the gods of Axiottenos! They set about to have removed/cancelled the scepter and the curses [τὰς ἀράς] that were in the temple, the ones the estate of Loukoundos and Moschios had sought to undo. The descendants of Tatia, Sôkrateia and Moschas along with Loukoundos and Menekratês, constantly propitiate the gods and praise them from now on, having inscribed on (this) stele the powers/deeds of the gods.[41]

This inscription illustrates several important features of the popular Anatolian religious mentality. First, it points to a robust belief in the overseeing presence of the gods and their ability to requite wrongdoers with suffering and personal misfortune. Secondly, it reflects the conviction, relatively widespread in antiquity, that suffering is often evidence of the workings of a curse. And, thirdly, the erection of this stele, as well as its wording, reflects the belief that further punishment can be avoided if proper restitution and homage is paid to the offended deity or deities.

---

[39] Pleket, 'Mentality' (1981), 156. Gordon, 'Confession-Narratives' (2004), 177–96, attempts to describe an underlying 'narrative system' presupposed (though with variations) in the confession *stelae*, which consists of four elements: (1) the provocation, (2) the punishment, (3) the recognition that punishment has come, and (4) the resolution (see especially 184–90).

[40] Elliott, *Cutting too Close* (2003), 71. Cf. Pleket, 'Mentality' (1981), 178: 'The subjection of the worshipper [through the erection of a confession stele] is suitably attended by the feeling that he is always running the risk of committing (material and/or spiritual) *sins* and that the almighty god and/or goddess of his village will then mete out suitable punishments (in the shape of illness or worse)' (emphasis original).

[41] Translation Gager, *Curse Tablets* (1992), 247–48. For Greek text, see Petzl, 'Beichtinschriften' (1994), No. 69.

Although the epigraphic evidence here surveyed is somewhat limited in scope and, on the whole, slightly post-dates the NT period,[42] it nevertheless provides a reliable portrait of the popular religious ethos of Anatolia, in particular the preoccupation with strict morality and well-developed fear of divine vengeance.[43] This religious mentality was sustained by the conviction that life was lived in full view of the overseeing presence of the gods, who always stood ready to punish sin with suffering. As Mitchell observes: 'When the gods' will was defied men suffered the discipline of summary and often violent punishment in the form of disease, destitution, or death'.[44]

We can reasonably assume that prior to their encounter with Paul, the Galatians would have operated with similar assumptions about the ruling presence of enforcer deities, beliefs probably not entirely jettisoned by their coming to 'know God' (4.8). For the Galatians continued to inhabit a world permeated with curses and cursing and would have understood what it meant to come under a curse and to endure the wrathful vengeance of a god.[45] As a result, they would have taken the threat of a curse very seriously indeed. We can safely infer, then, that the threat of a curse would have been deeply unsettling to the Galatians and provoked them to look to circumcision to avert the prospect of a curse.

One of the advantages of drawing attention to this aspect of the Galatians' pre-conversion religious outlook is that it throws light on why they would have been so susceptible to the Agitators' appeal to a curse to promote circumcision. There is, in other words, a considerable convergence between Jewish and pagan notions of divine retribution, not least in central Anatolia; or, as Mitchell points out with regard to this context: 'the pagan notion of exacting retribution from the wrongdoer fitted comfortably with Jewish ideas

---

[42] While the majority of the epigraphic evidence surveyed here dates from the second and third centuries C.E., we know that the protection of tombs with curses was an ancient practice across the Mediterranean world. Moreover, performing curses orally would have in most cases pre-dated the coming into existence of the epigraphic remains. Ricl, 'Forgotten Confession-Inscription' (1997), 36–37 n. 16. Pettazzoni, *History of Religions* (1954), 57, for example, claims that the confession inscriptions from Lydia and Phrygia represent 'the late survival and continuance *in situ* of a confessional practice of very ancient origin'; cited in Schnabel, 'Divine Tyranny' (2003), 179.

[43] Elliott, *Cutting too Close* (2003), 62–88: 'the Anatolians lived in constant awareness of the watchful eye of their deities, believing in their power to protect as well as punish by an active righteous rage. This is the ethos of Anatolian popular religiosity'.

[44] Mitchell, *Anatolia* (1993), 2.37.

[45] Here my argument could be substantially reinforced by giving attention to the very widespread use of curse tablets (*defixiones*) in antiquity. For a comprehensive collection of this material, see now Gager, *Curse Tablets* (1992); for general discussion, see Preisendanz, 'Fluchtafeln (Defixion)' (1972), cols. 1–29; Faraone, 'Binding Spells' (1991), 2–32; Graf, *Magic* (1997), 118–74. Davis, *Christ as Devotio* (2002), 147–66, utilises some of this material to illumine his reading of 3.10 and 3.13.

of divine justice and vengeance'.⁴⁶ Thus, it is not hard imagine why the threat of a curse, especially one written ἐν τῷ Δευτερονομίῳ, would have played powerfully upon the Galatians' own fears.⁴⁷

Suffering and the Situation in Galatia

The Anatolian belief in the rule of the gods has an important corollary. In a world dominated by the overseeing presence of the gods, calamity and personal misfortune can be easily interpreted as expressions of divine vengeance and as tokens of a curse.⁴⁸ We saw this mentality reflected in the range of epigraphic material just considered, particularly the confession inscriptions, where suppliants are moved to erect a stele to propitiate the offended deity and to avert further affliction as a result of an *ex post facto* interpretation of some misfortune or adversity. Hence, the experience of suffering would at least raise the possibility, if not suggest the likelihood, that an individual or individuals were experiencing divine retribution for some previous wrongdoing.

This religious outlook may have an important implication for our understanding of the situation in Galatia. In the remainder of this chapter, I would like to pursue the hypothesis, following a suggestion made by E. Baasland, that the Galatians' encounter with suffering may have precipitated or perhaps exacerbated their doubts about being under a curse.⁴⁹ As we have seen, it would have been tempting for them to treat their suffering, as well as Paul's own, as evidence of the fact that a curse had already overtaken them both. Furthermore, I shall tentatively suggest that the Agitators may have further provoked the Galatians' sense of unease about the curse of the Law by interpreting the Galatians' suffering as evidence that a curse had already come upon them as a result of their failure to embrace the Law in all that it enjoined.

This requires that we establish that suffering was an exigency of the Galatian crisis and, in particular, an issue for the Galatians themselves. A number of scholars have drawn attention to the various social factors which

---

⁴⁶ Mitchell, *Anatolia* (1993), 1.189. Cf. Mitchell, *Anatolia* (1993), 2.37: 'The Jews and the indigenous peoples of Lydia and Phrygia both worshipped a wrathful god of Justice, to be appeased not only by adhering to divine Law but by songs of praise'.

⁴⁷ Cf. Elliott, *Cutting too Close* (2003), 250, 354.

⁴⁸ This outlook was, of course, not peculiar to Anatolia, but was widespread within the ancient world. The *locus classicus* on divine retribution and suffering within the Greco-Roman tradition is found in a speech Livy attributes to Marcus Camillus: 'When we followed God's guidance, all was well; when we scorned it, all was ill'; cited by Trompf, *Retributive Justice* (2000), 52, who refers to this person as a 'pagan Deuteronomist'.

⁴⁹ Baasland, 'Persecution' (1984), 135–50.

may have contributed to the Galatian crisis, though the issue of suffering-persecution is usually overlooked. Over twenty years ago, Baasland drew attention to the neglect of the theme of suffering-persecution in Galatians in an article aptly entitled, 'Persecution: A Neglected Feature in the Letter to the Galatians' (1984). Ironically, however, his essay has been a neglected feature in the subsequent exegetical discussion, no doubt contributing to the continued neglect of this feature of the letter.[50] As a result, there appears to be at least some justification for dubbing suffering-persecution 'the much neglected aspect of the Galatian crisis'.[51]

Despite the scholarly neglect of the issue of suffering-persecution in the Galatian crisis, it is not difficult to demonstrate that it at least has a significant presence in the letter. Particularly noteworthy, though sometimes underplayed, is Paul's use of the strong semi-technical term for persecution throughout much of the letter (διώκω, 1.13, 23; 4.29; 5.11; 6.12). Galatians contains, in fact, an unusually high concentration of this use of the term: its five uses in Galatians match the number of comparable uses in the rest of Paul's writings.[52] This alone is enough to suggest the importance of the motif in the letter. In addition, Galatians contains other suffering-persecution terminology (πάσχω, 3.4; πορθέω, 1.13; συ/σταυρόω, 2.19; 3.1; 5.11, 24; 6.14, 17). When one combines this lexical data with a number of allusions to suffering-persecution in Galatians (1.16; 2.19-20; 3.1; 4.13-14, 19), the motif begins to appear with a surprising degree of prominence.

But Paul does more than simply refer to suffering-persecution; it contributes to several of the letter's basic rhetorical strategies. As Baasland observes, utilising Betz's rhetorical analysis, there is a reference to suffering-persecution in most of the epistle's major divisions: the *narratio* (1.13, 23), the beginning and end of the *probatio* (3.4; 4.29), the end of the transition period or the beginning of the *exhortatio* (5.11), and throughout the *peroratio* (6.12-17).[53] Similarly, though perhaps more importantly, a reference to suffering-persecution appears in most of the passages in which Paul directly addresses the Galatians or speaks to the situation in Galatia (3.1-5; 4.12-20;

---

[50] The following major commentaries lack any reference to Baasland's essay: Fung, *Galatians* (1988); Longenecker, *Galatians* (1990); Dunn, *Galatians* (1993); Matera, *Galatians* (1992); Martyn, *Galatians* (1997); Esler, *Galatians* (1998). Those who have taken up some aspect of his thesis include: Sandnes, *One of the Prophets?* (1991); Goddard and Cummins, 'Conflict and Persecution' (1993); Hafemann, 'Exile of Israel' (1997); Hafemann, 'Weakness' (2000); Cummins, *Crucified* (2001); Davis, 'Galatians 3:1' (1999); Davis, *Christ as Devotio* (2002).

[51] Cummins, *Crucified* (2001), 97. Cf. Riesner, *Paul's Early Period* (1998), 280–81 n. 3: 'In general, the theme of "persecution" has long been too neglected in the interpretation of the letter to the Galatians'.

[52] Rom 12.14; 1 Cor 4.12; 15.9; 2 Cor 4.9; Phil 3.6. Cf. 2 Tim 3.12.

[53] Baasland, 'Persecution' (1984), 142.

5.7-12; 6.11-18).⁵⁴ These observations alone provide strong *prima facie* support for thinking that suffering-persecution somehow played a part in the Galatian crisis.

One must also give due weight to the significant presence of suffering-persecution in the epistolary postscript (6.11-18), something commentators seldom do.⁵⁵ These verses provide 'the interpretive clues to the understanding of Paul's major concerns in the letter as a whole and should be employed as the hermeneutical key to the intentions of the Apostle'.⁵⁶ One might have expected this passage, then, to ring with affirmations of justification by faith and not by the 'works of the Law' (2.15–4.7; 4.21–5.12); instead, it appears shot through with allusions to suffering-persecution: the Agitators' desire to avoid persecution for the sake of the cross of Christ (6.12), Paul's boasting in his co-crucifixion with Christ and his crucifixion to the world (6.14; cf. 2.19-20), and especially his closing cryptic appeal: 'Finally, let no one cause me troubles, for I bear the marks of Jesus (στίγματα τοῦ Ἰησοῦ) on my body' (6.17). Although scholars continue to debate the exact significance of the στίγματα, there is widespread agreement that the phrase itself refers to the physical effects of Paul's own suffering-persecution (1 Cor 4.9-13; 2 Cor 4.8-11; 6.4-6; 11.23-30).⁵⁷ This final reference is thus as significant as it is intriguing: 'It is his final appeal, before which all opposition and controversy must give way'.⁵⁸ The implication is clear: Paul, at least, viewed his own suffering-persecution as somehow integral to the Galatian crisis.

Given the prominence of suffering-persecution within Galatians, particularly in the letter closing, there is very good reason to think that this issue probably contributed to the crisis in Galatia. But while some are willing to grant that suffering-persecution may have been an issue for Paul (5.11; 6.17) or for the Agitators (6.12-13), it is seldom argued that it was an issue for the Galatians. In fact, some doubt whether the Galatians were experiencing any suffering or persecution at all. 'There is in fact nothing in this letter to suggest that the Galatians themselves are being literally persecuted or are

---

⁵⁴ See Mitternacht, 'Foolish Galatians' (2002), 416–17, who contends that in reconstructing the situation one should give priority to discourse units with direct situational pertinence (i.e., 1.6-9; 3.1-5; 4.8-20; 5.2-12; 6.11-18). Cf. Mitternacht, *Sprachlose* (1999), 61–89; Nanos, *Irony* (2002), 62–72.

⁵⁵ Muddiman, 'Anatomy' (1994), 269: 'This theme of the threat of persecution in the codicil to the letter, and throughout, has often been ignored or dismissed'.

⁵⁶ Betz, *Galatians* (1979), 313. Cf. Lyons, *Pauline Autobiography* (1985), 168; Weima, 'Hermeneutical Key' (1993), 90–107.

⁵⁷ Lightfoot, *Galatians* (1896), 225; Burton, *Galatians* (1921), 360; Mussner, *Galaterbrief* (1974), 420; Ridderbos, *Galatians* (1953), 228; Pobee, *Persecution* (1985), 94–98; Matera, *Galatians* (1992), 232; Longenecker, *Galatians* (1990), 300; Dunn, *Galatians* (1993), 347; Martyn, *Galatians* (1997), 568–69; Hays, 'Galatians' (2000), 346.

⁵⁸ Lightfoot, *Galatians* (1896), 51.

literally suffering'.[59] However, there are at least four reasons for thinking that the Galatians were enduring some measure of suffering, if not persecution.

(1) There is, first of all, the sheer probability that their adherence to Paul's gospel would have entailed some measure of social fallout and perhaps outright persecution, whether from their own pagan associates, local Jewish authorities, or some combination of the two. On the one hand, by embracing Paul's gospel the Galatians had to relinquish the worship of other deities (4.8-9; cf. 1 Thess 1.9), which would have made continued participation in at least some of the cultic and civic activities of their communities much more difficult, if not impossible.[60] Their sitting loose to their ancestral traditions and social responsibilities would have inevitably raised a few eyebrows. Barclay explains why:

> Many sources, both within and without the NT, portray the surprise and resentment felt by non-Christian friends when Christian converts declined to take part in normal social and cultic activities. There was also a strong sense of betrayal. Family members who broke ancestral traditions on the basis of their new-found faith showed an appalling lack of concern for their familial responsibilities. Christians deserted ancestral practices, passed on since time immemorial, for a novel religion (if such it could be called) of recent manufacture. The exclusivity of the Christians' religion – their arrogant refusal to take part in, or to consider valid, the worship of any God but their own – deeply wounded public sensibilities. Such an unnatural and ungrateful attitude to the gods even branded them 'atheists'. Moreover, it was highly dangerous for even one segment of the community to slight the gods, whose wrath was ever to be feared. Civic peace, the success of agriculture, and freedom from earthquake or flood were regularly attributed to the benevolence of the gods. Both Christian and non-Christian sources testify that if anything went wrong the Christians could get the blame.[61]

On the other hand, Paul's gospel did not require (or perhaps permit) the assimilation of his Gentile converts into the larger Jewish communities. While the Galatians may, for example, have sought refuge through association with their local synagogue (if one was present), they were not yet circumcised and would therefore have not stopped, so to speak, being Gentiles, certainly to Jews and probably also to their own kinsmen. As a result, the Galatians would have found themselves in the awkward position of having abandoned at least some of their familial, social and religious affiliations, yet without simultaneously embracing the new status and identity which belongs to full-fledged Jewish proselytes. They would have thus found themselves in an extremely tenuous and delicate position vis-à-vis both the Jewish community and their (former) pagan co-religionists.

---

[59] Witherington, *Galatians* (1998), 338.

[60] A growing number of scholars point to the pressure that may have been exerted on the Galatians to participate in imperial cult worship. See the recent discussion in Stanton, *Jesus and Gospel* (2004), 35–49 (especially 42–45).

[61] Barclay, 'Conflict' (1993), 515.

Furthermore, we know that allegiance to this newfangled religion centred around a Jewish peasant executed as a criminal by the Romans was often a costly business, not least in Asia Minor, where it was apparently not uncommon for believers to suffer social dislocation and harassment (cf. 1 Pet 2.12-20; 3.1, 13-16; 4.3-5, 12-16).[62] We have little reason to doubt that the Galatians would have encountered similar sorts of reactions.[63] This may even have gone beyond verbal abuse, libel or slander to include actual physical mistreatment. Either way, it is very likely that the Galatians would have experienced some (perhaps significant) measure of suffering as a result of their adherence to Paul's gospel.

But were the Galatians also being *persecuted*? Some see evidence for this in 4.29, where, in what has the appearance of remarkable exegetical *tour de force*, Paul somehow relates Ishmael's 'persecution' of Isaac to his own present context: οὕτως καὶ νῦν.[64] Traditionally, this has been taken as a reference to the Jewish persecution of Christians, often understood in concrete terms as the synagogue's persecution of the church. Partly in response to the disastrous reception-history of this text for Jewish-Christian relations, however, many scholars have opted instead to treat this as a somewhat enigmatic reference to the persecution-like pressure exerted upon the Galatians by the Agitators (cf. 4.17; 6.12).[65] In other words, this was an *intra-Christian* affair.

Would Paul, however, call this persecution? He appears to reserve the term διώκω for cases of actual physical maltreatment or punishment; or, at least, this seems to be the case in Galatians (1.13, 23; 5.11; 6.12), if not elsewhere in his letters (Rom 12.14; 1 Cor 4.12; 15.9; 2 Cor 4.9; Phil 3.6).[66] Hence, a few scholars treat 4.29 as a reference to what Ishmael-like Jewish unbelievers were doing to Isaac-like believing Jews, Paul having either the Jerusalem

---

[62] Barclay, *Obeying* (1988), 58.

[63] Stanton, *Jesus and Gospel* (2004), 42: 'In principle, it is highly likely that the Galatian Christians did face strong social pressures'.

[64] This link, however, was not unprecedented within early Judaism; see Philo, *Sobr.* 8; *Congr.* 129–30; *Post.* 131.

[65] Söding, 'Verheißung' (2001), 157 n. 28: 'Fatal ist die christliche Rezeptionsgeschichte, die regelmäßig den Gegensatz von *ecclesia* und *synagoge* angesprochen findet' (emphasis original). See also Bachmann, *Antijudaismus* (1999), 127–58; Martyn, 'Hagar and Sarah' (1990), 160–92; and especially Martyn, *Galatians* (1997), 35–41, 431–466, whose reading of Galatians is significantly shaped by his concern to redress this problem; he asserts unambiguously, in fact, that 'the subject of church and synagogue lies beyond the letter's horizon' (40).

[66] Sanders, *Jewish People* (1983), 190–91. Cf. Niebuhr, *Heidenapostel* (1992), 67 n. 296 (cf. 66–78).

church (cf. 4.26) or himself especially in mind.[67] Given this ambiguity, it is not clear that Paul, at least, thinks of the Galatians' suffering as persecution, even though they themselves may have conceived of it as such.

(2) The second reason for thinking that the Galatians were encountering some measure of suffering comes from the tone and substance of Paul's references to suffering-persecution throughout the letter, together with his appeal to the Galatians to imitate him in his fidelity to the gospel in the face of opposition. Paul's polemical use of the motif of suffering-persecution in Galatians centres upon the cross. In fact, the letter is littered with references to the crucifixion (cf. 2.19-20, 21; 3.1, 13; 5.11, 24; 6.12, 14, 17; cf. 1.4; 4.4-5).[68] The cross obviously, then, serves as the christological centre of gravity in Galatians, so that Christ stands forth as the Crucified One, whose death was itself an example *par excellence* of suffering-persecution.[69] And while for modern readers historical and cultural distance may mute the force of Paul's repeated references to 'so horrible a deed' (Cicero, *Verr.* 2.5.66), 'the most wretched of deaths' (Josephus, *B.J.* 8.203), the impact of this steady refrain would not have been lost on the Galatians.

But suffering-persecution also plays an important part in Paul's own self-presentation in Galatians. On several occasions, he draws an inextricable link between his own fidelity to the gospel and his willingness to endure suffering-persecution for the sake of the cross (5.11; 6.14-17; cf. 2.1-15; 4.12-20). This is a crucial aspect of Paul's moral polemic in the letter, especially insofar as he on several occasions explicitly juxtaposes his *modus vivendi* with that of the Agitators (5.10-12; 6.12-17; cf. 2.1-14). He clearly wants to portray himself, in contrast to them, as 'an unfailing and divinely ordained follower and imitator of the suffering and persecuted Christ'.[70] He is, in a word, a 'slave of Christ' (1.10), whose own crucified existence is patterned after the paradigmatic self-giving of his Master (cf. 1.4; 3.13; 4.4-5).[71] As Paul boldly states in a passage that may constitute the hermeneutical centre of the letter: 'I have been crucified with Christ and I no longer live, but Christ lives in me' (2.19-20).[72]

---

[67] Muddiman, 'Anatomy' (1994), 260 (who prefers the variant reading of ἡμεῖς rather than ὑμεῖς in 4.28); Bockmuehl, '1 Thessalonians 2:14-16' (2001), 8, 24, 30; Söding, 'Verheißung' (2001), 160.

[68] Bryant, *Crucified Christ* (2000), 192: 'the Crucified Christ is a central and persistent theme throughout Galatians' (see 163–94).

[69] This emphasis is only partially mitigated by the strong emphasis upon the *self-giving* nature of Christ's death (cf. 1.4; 2.20; 4.4-5).

[70] Mitternacht, 'Foolish Galatians' (2002), 412. Cf. Dodd, 'Christ's Slave' (1996), 94–95; Lyons, *Pauline Autobiography* (1985), 149–50.

[71] Dodd, 'Christ's Slave' (1996), 94–95, relates 1.10 to the theme of suffering-persecution.

[72] Hays, 'Law of Christ' (1987), 280–83.

Paul's portrayal of the crucified Christ and his own self-presentation as Christ's crucified Apostle, in turn, provide warrant for and give shape to his call for imitation (4.12; cf. 2.19-20; 5.11; 6.17). Although imitation is less explicit in Galatians than in some of Paul's other writings, it is not difficult to discern a mimetic undercurrent in much of what he says. Regardless of whether one detects an apologetic note in Gal 1–2, Paul clearly presents himself as a courageous defender of the 'truth of the gospel' (2.5), one whose own *ethos* not only inspires admiration, but elicits imitation. At least, then, one of the purposes of Paul's autobiographical remarks becomes clear with the letter's first explicit imperative: Γίνεσθε ὡς ἐγώ (4.12).[73] As R. B. Hays rightly observes, this summons presupposes Paul's earlier narrative portrayal of himself: 'The basis for this exhortation would lie in Paul's belief that his own life manifested a conformity to the normative pattern of Christ's obedient self-sacrifice'.[74] The only refinement I would want to add is that within the context of the Galatian crisis, Paul conceives of conformity to Christ as an unwavering commitment to the truth of the gospel in the face of *opposition* (2.1-14) and even *suffering-persecution* (5.11; 6.17). The Galatians are thus called to imitate Paul's crucified commitment to Christ (2.19-20; 6.14), which suggests that they too were experiencing some degree of hardships themselves.[75]

(3) From Paul's recollection in 4.12-20 of his initial encounter with the Galatians, we have some indication that the Galatians were at present encountering suffering. Paul reminds them (albeit in a convoluted and enigmatic way) that he first preached the gospel to them on account of a 'weakness of the flesh' (ἀσθένεια τῆς σαρκός) and that this proved to be for the Galatians a 'trial' or 'temptation' (πειρασμός, 4.13-14). This is an intriguing comment worthy of some reflection. Most modern commentators treat Paul's 'weakness of the flesh' as a an illness of some kind, with numerous possibilities on offer.[76] Reviving a view more popular among Patristic and Reformation commentators, a few scholars have recently contended that the phrase should be taken as a reference to the debilitating or even disfiguring effects of Paul's persecution (cf. 6.17; 2.19-20; 3.1; 5.11).[77]

---

[73] On 4.12 as an (implicit) call for imitation, see de Boer, *Imitation* (1962), 188–96; Gaventa, 'Autobiography' (1986), 319–22; Hays, 'Law of Christ' (1987), 281–82; Goddard and Cummins, 'Conflict and Persecution' (1993), 94–100; Davis, *Christ as Devotio* (2002), 216–17.

[74] Hays, 'Law of Christ' (1987), 281.

[75] For further reflection on this motif in Paul, see Gorman, *Cruciformity* (2001), 178–213.

[76] The thesis put forward by Martin, 'Whose Flesh?' (1999), 65–91, that the 'weakness of the flesh' was the Galatians' and not Paul's own (cf. Rom 6.19), should be rejected given that Paul goes on to identify this 'weakness' as ἐν τῇ σαρκί μου (4.14). See Hafemann, 'Weakness' (2000), 142–43 n. 9.

[77] See especially Goddard and Cummins, 'Conflict and Persecution' (1993), 93–126.

Either way, Paul can commend them in the very next verse for 'neither despising nor rejecting' him in his suffering, but instead receiving him 'as an angel of God, as Christ Jesus himself' (4.14). Evidently, the Galatians valiantly embraced Paul in the midst of his affliction, even though, Paul implies, they would have had every reason to turn him away (cf. 4.12b: οὐδέν με ἠδικήσατε).

This then clarifies the rhetorical force of Paul's next remark: 'Where then is your blessing? For I testify concerning you that, if it were possible, you would have removed your own eyes and given them to me' (4.15). Obviously, Paul intends to contrast the Galatians' *former* willingness to embrace him in his suffering (4.13-14), even to the extent of being willing to gouge out their own eyes to remedy what afflicts him (4.15), with their *present* defection from him (4.16-17). Paul provocatively highlights this change of posture by implying that they have forfeited their original 'blessing' (ὁ μακαρισμὸς ὑμῶν, 4.15).[78] This seems like a slightly odd thing to say, but it may reflect the fact that Paul is here tapping into the well-attested early Jewish and Christian conviction that blessedness attends the righteous in their suffering (cf. Matt 5.11-12; 10.22; Luke 6.22; 1 Pet 3.14; 4.14; LXX Dan 12.12 Theo.). In James 1.12, for example, we see these two terms closely juxtaposed: 'Blessed (μακάριος) is the one who perseveres under trial (πειρασμόν)' (cf. Jas 5.11).[79] 1 Peter is perhaps more germane to Paul's comment here:

> Beloved, do not be surprised at the fiery trial (πειρασμόν) which has come upon you as though something strange were happening to you, but as you share in the sufferings (παθήμασιν) of Christ, rejoice, in order that you might also rejoice greatly at the revelation of his glory. If you are reproached for the name of Christ, you are blessed (μακάριοι), for the Spirit of glory and of God rests upon you' (4.12-15).

Paul may, then, intend this comment to serve as a subtle allusion to the Galatians' forfeiture of the Spirit, the source of eschatological joy in the midst of suffering (cf. 4.6),[80] which would, in turn, explain why he reaches for so dramatic a metaphor to describe the current situation in his churches: 'My little children, for whom I am in labour pains all over again until Christ is

---

[78] The genitive is objective, with God as the implied subject. Longenecker, 'Moral Character' (1999), 103–04, rightly sees this as 'an attestation of the Galatians' transformation in Christ by the power of God, a testimony to the working of the Spirit of the Son whose own life was marked out by love and self-giving. Their own actions were embodiments of the gospel, manifestations of the Spirit'.

[79] Cf. Baasland, 'Persecution' (1984), 145–46.

[80] Keesmaat, *Paul and his Story* (1999), 202–03 (cf. 74–77), suggests that the Spirit sent into the heart of the believer crying 'Abba, Father' is intended as a cry of desperation in the midst of trials or suffering (Rom 8.15-17; Mark 14.36; Matt 26.39; Luke 22.42). Cf. Bryant, *Crucified Christ* (2000), 181 n. 54.

formed in you!' (4.19). Apparently, the Galatians need nothing less than *rebirth* by the Spirit.[81]

(4) Finally, and perhaps most importantly, the letter itself contains a significant reference to the Galatians' own suffering. 'Have you suffered (ἐπάθετε) so much in vain?' (3.4).[82] It must be admitted, however, that this is not a wholly unambiguous remark. Commenting on this verse in his influential *TDNT* article on the verb πάσχω, W. Michaelis explains why: 'Neither the context nor the contents of the epistle support the idea of suffering under persecution'.[83] Instead, 3.1-5 is taken up with the reception of the Spirit in the Galatian churches (vv. 2-3, 5), while the rest of the letter appears to make relatively little of their suffering. As a result, a number of scholars and translators prefer to take this verse as a reference to how much the Galatians have experienced of the Spirit (cf. RSV).[84]

It must be said, however, that if lexicography alone determined exegesis, there would be no debate about this verse. Every other use of πάσχω in the NT (including Paul) and the LXX has a negative nuance.[85] This observation should carry more weight than it often does; instead, scholars opt to go against the preponderance of the lexical evidence (which, of course, is not always ill-advised) on the basis of what appears to be somewhat circular reasoning: neither the context nor the content of the letter refers to the Galatians suffering, therefore this verse cannot refer to their suffering. In fairness, Paul is undoubtedly referring in 3.1-5 to the Galatians' initial and ongoing experience of the Spirit. But even this observation points up a

---

[81] 4.19 thus constitutes more than Paul's desire for the Galatians to grow in Christian maturity; his assessment of the situation is much more radical. So Kwon, *Eschatology* (2004), 34–35. See also Gaventa, 'Maternity' (1990), 189–201.

[82] Taking 3.4 as a reference to the Galatians' suffering (and persecution) was evidently the consensus view among Patristic commentators: e.g., Chrysostom, Augustine, Victorinus, Ambrosiaster, Pelagius, Jerome, Theodore of Mopsuestia, Theodoret, John of Damascus, noted by Davis, *Christ as Devotio* (2002), 211. Among modern scholars and commentators, see Ridderbos, *Galatians* (1953), 115; Bruce, *Galatians* (1982), 150; Baasland, 'Persecution' (1984), 139–40; Cosgrove, *Cross and Spirit* (1988), 185–86; Goddard and Cummins, 'Conflict and Persecution' (1993), 119; Keesmaat, *Paul and his Story* (1999), 202; Nanos, *Irony* (2002), 189.

[83] Michaelis, *TDNT*, 5.912 n. 57.

[84] Burton, *Galatians* (1921), 149; Mussner, *Galaterbrief* (1974), 209; Betz, *Galatians* (1979), 134 (134 n. 64); Longenecker, *Galatians* (1990), 104; Fee, *Presence* (1994), 387; Martyn, *Galatians* (1997), 285.

[85] BDAG, 'πάσχω', identifies 3.4 as the only use of the verb with the sense of 'experience something', largely on the basis of its associations with ἐπιχορηγέω in 3.5. The negative sense to the verb is well attested in the Pseudepigrapha (cf. *T. Benj.* 7.4; *T. Jud.* 15.2; *T. Sim.* 4.3; *T. Reu.* 3.9; 4.1; *T. Gad* 5.11; *Sib. Or.* 3.529; 11.282; 4.209) and Josephus (*A.J.* 2.292; 4.270, 279; 5.166; 6.267; cf. 9.43; 13.268; 15.204; 17.83; *C. Ap.* 1.259; *Vita* 404; *B.J.* 1.35).

common fallacy when dealing with this verse. Why do commentators assume that either Paul is referring to the Galatians' experience of the Spirit or to their suffering? In other words, the interpretation of this verse is often framed in terms of a dichotomy that finds not only little support from Paul's other writings, but positive counterevidence. For Paul was quite happy to conceive of the Spirit as mediated in and through the experience of suffering:

> For our gospel did not come to you in word only, but also with power and with the Holy Spirit and with much conviction, just as you know what sort of persons we became among you for your sake. And you became imitators of us and of the Lord by receiving the word in the midst of much affliction (ἐν θλίψει πολλῇ) with the joy of the Holy Spirit' (1 Thess 1.5-6).

This may be quite close to what Paul has in mind in 3.1-5: the Galatians received Paul's gospel in the midst of much affliction with the joy of the Holy Spirit (cf. 4.12-15).[86]

Furthermore, while it is often asserted that the immediate context lacks any reference to the Galatians' suffering or persecution, Paul probably alludes to his own suffering-persecution, not insignificantly, in the paragraph's leading statement: 'O foolish Galatians! Who has bewitched you, before whose eyes Jesus Christ was publicly portrayed as having been crucified' (3.1). There is in this verse an unmistakable stress upon the *visible* nature of this portrayal (οἷς κατ' ὀφθαλμούς), which speaks against this language being taken simply metaphorically as a way to describe the rhetorical vividness of Paul's proclamation.[87] Instead, Paul wants to remind the Galatians that during his initial visit they actually saw something; they had a concrete encounter with the crucified Christ. Paul's reference to the crucifixion of Christ here should be viewed in light of the immediately preceding reference to his own co-crucifixion with Christ (2.19-20). Hence, the implication seems to be that the Galatians saw the living Christ in the dying Apostle, that is the life of Christ was manifest in Paul's suffering. This is probably what Paul envisages when he claims that God reveals his Son 'in me' (ἐν ἐμοί, 1.16; cf. 2 Cor 4.7-12). His own suffering has become 'paradoxically the locus of God's gift of life, being the present form of Jesus' own death-life pattern' (cf. Col 1.24).[88]

Paul's reference to his own suffering-persecution in 3.1 has important implications for the interpretation of the rest of the paragraph. That Paul immediately turns to the issue of how the Galatians received the Spirit, for

---

[86] Cf. Smith, *Suffering* (2002), 40.

[87] Davis, 'Galatians 3:1' (1999), 194–212; Davis, *Christ as Devotio* (2002), 207–210. Paul is, therefore, doing more then 'celebrating his rhetorical skills', Bryant, *Crucified Christ* (2000), 171.

[88] Martyn, *Galatians* (1997), 569. Cf. Hafemann, 'Weakness' (2000), 136–41, who draws upon the Corinthian correspondence for corroboration of this point (1 Cor 4.9; 2 Cor 1.9-10; 4.10-11; 6.3-10; 12.9-10; cf. 2 Cor 2.14).

example, suggests a link between their encounter with the Spirit and Paul's mediating the crucified Christ through his own apostolic sufferings.[89] Moreover, it is probably not coincidental that Paul's reference to the suffering of the Galatians should appear closely juxtaposed to two comments about the inability of the 'works of the Law' to supply them with the Spirit (3.2, 5). Little wonder that Paul upbraids them for so foolishly turning to the flesh: they have seen the crucified and cursed Christ, who became the very means of the blessing of the Spirit (cf. 3.13-14).

The Curse of the Law and the Interpretation of Suffering in Galatia

Having suggested, on the one hand, that the Galatians would have been very wary of coming under a curse and, on the other, that they were suffering as a result of their adherence to Paul's gospel, I would now like to explore how these two seemingly unrelated pieces of evidence may together, in fact, have made circumcision look to the Galatians like a rather attractive option.

As we observed earlier, in a world dominated by the overseeing presence of the gods, suffering could easily be interpreted as an expression of divine vengeance and the workings of a curse. Given the likelihood that the Galatians would have shared in this religious outlook, it stands to reason that their own suffering would have at least raised some doubts about their piety toward God, if not their relationship to the Law. Once Paul left Galatia and the Galatians continued to confront various hardships and difficulties, either as a consequence of their new religious allegiance or as an unavoidable feature of human existence, they may have begun to question whether their suffering was the result of their having made a misstep along the way and fallen out of favour with God.

These emerging anxieties may, in turn, have been further exacerbated by Paul's own suffering. From what Paul says about his initial encounter with the Galatians, they evidently could have had some trouble embracing him in his own affliction. As we have already noted, Paul refers to the fact that his 'weakness of the flesh' proved to be a 'trial' or 'temptation' to the Galatians (4.13-14). In fact, as he says, they had every reason to 'despise and reject' him in his suffering, even though, to their credit, they embraced him 'as an angel of God, as Christ Jesus himself' (4.15). What this suggests is that Paul recognises that the Galatians' own pre-conversion cultural and religious outlook could have inclined them to regard Paul in his suffering as a

---

[89] Note the same close connection between the cross and the Spirit in 3.13-14, which may form an *inclusio* with 3.1-2.

dangerous contagion, whose presence was to be avoided.[90] For he had the appearance of one suffering under the righteous rage of a god. Strubbe explains why:

> Punishments inflicted by the enraged gods were death, especially strange and cruel death like death by fire or lightning, and diseases, above all blindness, mental disorder and epidemics. All natural catastrophies [sic], like drought and flood, infertility of women and abnormal births were also considered divine punishments. Moreover a cursed person was avoided by his fellow citizens out of fear of being contaminated by the μίασμα, the pollution, and was banished from society.[91]

In other words, Paul gave every indication of being a marked man, one who was under the wrath of the gods, one who was under a curse.[92]

Now while Paul commends the Galatians for their courageous embrace of him during their initial encounter, he clearly believes things have changed in the interim. The natural implication of this passage, though perhaps not the whole story, is that the Galatians have recently succumbed to the very temptation they at first so successfully resisted: they have evidently begun to harbour suspicions about Paul's own suffering. This reconstruction would, of course, tally very nicely with Paul's repeated appeal to his own suffering-persecution, what he boldly and polemically explains as his own co-crucifixion with Christ, which he insists is the essence of his fidelity to the gospel, not the sign of his being out of step with God, much less with the Law (cf. 5.14; 6.2 with 6.12-13). At the very least, this passage suggests that the interpretation of suffering somehow was, and again now is, an issue for the Galatians.

We have seen, then, that the Galatians may have had some doubts about the curse of the Law given their encounter with suffering, both Paul's and their own. At this point, we should bring into the discussion the influence of the Agitators. As we discovered in the previous chapter, the Agitators were warning the Galatians of the danger of coming under a curse if they failed to follow the Law in all that it enjoins, particularly in the matter of circumcision (Gen 17.14; Deut 27.26). We also noted that the Agitators would have had

---

[90] Paul's use of the hapax ἐκπτύω may suggest that the Galatians were inclined to perform an apotropaic gesture to ward off possible demonic influence associated with Paul's 'weakness'. Oepke, *Galater* (1984), 142–43; Schlier, *Galater* (1962), 210–11; Schlier, 'ἐκπτύω' (1964), 448–49; Heckel, 'Dorn im Fleisch' (1993), 84–86. It is not impossible, however, that Paul intended this term as a synonym of ἐξουθενέω and thus as a way simply of expressing a strong sense of disdain or rejection (cf. *Jos. Asen.* 2.1). See Goddard and Cummins, 'Conflict and Persecution' (1993), 105–06.

[91] Strubbe, 'Jewish Epitaphs' (1994), 81 (emphasis added). Cf. Parker, *Miasma* (1996), especially 191–206; Strubbe, 'Cursed' (1991), 44.

[92] It is not impossible that prior to coming to Galatia, Paul had already received some form of synagogue discipline, perhaps even the thirty-nine lashes (cf. 2 Cor 11.24). Cf. Harvey, 'Forty Strokes' (1985), 83–88.

little trouble making a persuasive case to the Galatians of their need for circumcision, something which is at least partially confirmed by the sheer fact that the Galatians apparently accepted their line of argument and were ready to submit to the knife. Now we can explore yet another way in which the Agitators may have bolstered their case for circumcision: by interpreting the Galatians' suffering as evidence of the fact that a curse has already overtaken them.

In a recent essay on Anatolian confession inscriptions, E. Schnabel observes that Anatolian townspeople and villagers would have looked to local priests and other religious functionaries for an explanation of their own personal misfortune.[93] The Agitators may have been functioning in a similar capacity for the Galatians: as trusted and sympathetic interpreters of their suffering. It is not hard to imagine the Galatians eager for someone to make some sense of their rather precarious and no doubt confusing situation. To use the categories of the sociology of knowledge: in the face of the anomic experience of human suffering, the Galatians would have been wrestling with 'world-maintenance' and, as a result, looked to 'significant others' to help legitimate the chaos around them.[94]

Given the axiomatic (though not unquestioned) link between suffering and sin in a wide range of biblical and post-biblical traditions, it is reasonable to infer that the Agitators would have viewed the suffering of the Galatians as the divinely ordained consequence of their failure to uphold the Law.[95] In other words, the Galatians were experiencing the effects of the Law's curse, which, according to the two great curse catalogues of the OT (Lev 26; Deut 27–28), entailed all manner of human suffering and affliction, including fear, terror and horror (Lev 26.16, 17, 36; Deut 28.66; 32.25), oppression at the hands of one's enemies (Lev 26.16, 17, 32; Deut 28.31, 33, 48), agricultural disaster (Lev 26.19, 20; Deut 28.22, 23, 24), starvation and famine (Lev 26.26, 29; Deut 28.53-56; 32.24), illness, pestilence and contamination (Lev 26.14; Deut 28.21-22, 27, 28, 35, 59-61; Deut 29.22), desolation (Lev 26.31, 33, 43; Deut 28.51; 29.23), decimation and infertility (Lev 26.22; Deut 28.18,

---

[93] Schnabel, 'Divine Tyranny' (2003), 176.

[94] Berger, *Sacred Canopy* (1967), 3–101 (especially 53–80). Cf. Berger and Luckmann, *Social Construction* (1966).

[95] Josephus, for example, describes the moral lesson of his *Antiquitates judaicae* as follows: '[T]he main lesson to be learnt from this history by any who care to peruse it is that men who conform to the will of God, and do not venture to transgress laws that have been excellently laid down, prosper in all things beyond belief, and for their reward are offered by God felicity; whereas, in proportion as they depart from the strict observance of these laws, things (else) practicable become impracticable, and whatever imaginary good thing they strive to do ends in irretrievable disasters' (LCL: *A.J.* 1.14; cf. *A.J.* 1.20, 23–24; 2.293). See also Trompf, *Retributive Justice* (2000), 3–106, who surveys Greco-Roman, Jewish and early Christian notions of retributive justice.

59; 62; 32.36), loss of possessions and impoverishment (Deut 28.31), loss of family (Deut 28.30, 32, 41), helplessness and stumbling (Lev 26.36, 37; Deut 28.29, 32; 32.35-39), psychological afflictions (Deut 28.20, 28, 34, 65), lack of peace and rest (Deut 28.65), denial of burial (Deut 28.27), death and destruction (Lev 26.36, 39; Deut 4.26; 28.20; 30.15; 31.17), and various other general maledictions including distress, ruin, confusion, disaster, punishment and vengeance (Deut 4.30; 28.20, 45; 29.19, 22; 31.17, 21, 29; 32.41, 43).[96]

Moreover, it may not be insignificant that the curse catalogue of Deut 27–28 explicitly refers to these manifold afflictions as the *sign* of a curse:

> All these curses (κατάραι) shall come upon you and pursue you and overtake you till you are cut off and until you are destroyed, since you did not heed the voice of the Lord your God, to keep his commandments and his statutes that he commanded you. And they shall be a sign (σημεῖα) and a wonder against you and your offspring forever (Deut 28.45-46).

The Agitators would thus have had good reason to think that the Galatians suffer because they fail to embrace the Law and, therefore, come under its curse. In short, the Galatians' hardships are a sign that they are under the curse of the Law.

The Agitators may have applied a similar logic to Paul. Presumably, they would have known of Paul's many afflictions and of his attitude toward circumcision and the Law (2.15-17; 5.2-5; 6.15; cf. Rom 3.8; 6.1, 15). It would have been natural, then, for them to infer that Paul suffers as he does precisely because he fails to uphold the Law in all that it enjoins. In other words, Paul was an apostate suffering under the Law's curse.[97] The only difference may have been that while the Agitators would have viewed Paul as a renegade whose suffering was doubtless deserved, they probably would have taken a more lenient approach towards the Galatians. Paul was an outright apostate, whereas the Galatians were unwitting accomplices to an erroneous missionary enterprise. Hence, the Agitators may well have explained the suffering of Paul and the suffering of the Galatians (and, perhaps, their own suffering, cf. 6.12-13) in rather different terms. Paul's suffering was purely punitive, whereas the Galatians' was ultimately pedagogical. 'For the discipline of the righteous (for things done) in ignorance is not the same as the destruction of the sinners' (*Pss. Sol.* 13.7; cf. Jdt 8.27; *2 Bar.* 13.9-10).[98]

---

[96] Stuart, *Hosea-Jonah* (1987), xxxii–xl. For a fascinating first-century appropriation of the curse catalogues, one which thoroughly reinforces the notion of punitive suffering, see Philo, *De praemiis et poenis*. After describing the 'blessings invoked upon good men, men who fulfil the laws by their deeds', Philo then goes on to 'investigate the curses (ἀράς) delivered against the law-breakers and transgressors' (LCL: *Praem*. 126; cf. *Praem*. 1–2).

[97] Baasland, 'Persecution' (1984), 146.

[98] In a wide range of biblical and post-biblical literature afflictions are often interpreted as designed to bring about repentance, confession, prayer and self-examination among the

We can imagine, then, the Agitators inviting the Galatians to look upon their present suffering as divinely-ordained discipline (παιδεία), which serves as a sign not that God has ultimately abandoned them, but that he desires for them to open their hearts to his Law and his covenant:

> Now we urge those who hear our message not to be depressed by such calamities, but to recognise that these punishments were designed not to destroy but to discipline you. In fact, it is a sign (σημεῖον) of great kindness not to let the impious alone for long, but to punish them immediately. For in the case of the other nations the Lord waits patiently to punish them until they have reached the full measure of their sins; but he does not deal in this way with us, in order that he many not take vengeance on us afterward when our sins have reached their height. Therefore he never withdraws his mercy from us. Although he disciplines us with calamities, he does not forsake his own people. Let what we have said serve as a reminder.
>
> May God do good to you, and may he remember his covenant with Abraham and Isaac and Jacob, his faithful servants. May he give you all a heart to worship him and to do his will with a strong heart and a willing spirit. May he open your heart to his law and his commandments, and may he bring peace. May he hear your prayers and be reconciled to you, and may he not forsake you in time of evil. We shall be praying for you.[99]

Conclusion

In the previous chapter we discovered that the Agitators appealed to the curse of the Law in order to persuade the Galatians to embrace circumcision. My chief aim in this chapter has been to suggest that the Galatians would have taken such a warning very seriously indeed. For the Galatians inhabited a world filled with tokens of divine vengeance and the workings of a curse; they would have therefore feared coming under the curse of a god, not least the God of the Jews. As a result, we can safely infer that the Galatians would have been deeply unsettled by the threat of a curse and would have been quite keen to avert this possibility, even if it meant turning to circumcision.[100]

---

people of God (cf. Lam 3.40-42; Deut 30.1-3; Jer 2.19; 24.4-7; 29.12-13; 31.18-19; 1 Kgs 8.47; Psa 106.44). This was a common way to theologise suffering within early Judaism (2 Macc 6.12-16; 7.33; *Pss. Sol.* 3.3-4; 7.1-10; 10.2; 13.7-10), and it is a tendency not lost on the authors of the NT (Heb 5.8; 12.3-11; Jas 1.2-4; 1.12; 5.7-11; 1 Pet 1.6-7; 2.19-21; 4.1-2; 5.6-10), including Paul (1 Cor 5.1-5; 11.27-34).

[99] The first paragraph is adapted from 2 Macc 6.12-17a; the second from 2 Macc 1.2-6 (NRSV).

[100] While it seems likely that the Galatians would have viewed the observance of circumcision as a means of bringing their lives into alignment with the demands of the Law and thereby averting its curse, they may also have been partially influenced by viewing the rite, perhaps insofar as it involved the shedding of blood, as an apotropaic ritual or sacrifice, which could avert God's anger (cf. Exod 4.24-26). For this and other suggestions about the attraction of circumcision, see Elliott, *Cutting too Close* (2003), 249–53: 'Paul's language

I also suggested that the Galatians' knowledge of Paul's suffering-persecution and their encounter with their own suffering (and possibly persecution) may have exacerbated their anxieties about the curse of the Law. And I contended that the Agitators themselves may have further provoked these doubts by interpreting their suffering and Paul's own suffering as evidence of the fact that a curse had already overtaken them both. Of course, it goes without saying that this proposal was put forth as a tentative working hypothesis. Having said that, however, I would want to stress, and hope it has become apparent, that this (re)construction does have some explanatory power, especially when one tries to correlate the threat of a curse, on the one hand, with the reality of suffering as part of the exigency of the situation, on the other.

While the Galatians may have had a number of reasons for wanting to embrace circumcision, my aim has been to demonstrate how fear, doubt or anxiety about the prospect of a curse would probably have contributed to their desire. Appreciating this feature of the situation in Galatia prepares us to turn to the primary question of this study: the rationale for Paul's four references to the Law in 5.13–6.10.

---

suggests that by being circumcised the Galatians would hope to be blessed and to escape from being cursed. . . . Curse and blessing would clearly provide powerful constraints for an Anatolian audience. . . . to be under a curse would be a very serious threat. If circumcision had the effect of incorporating the circumcised in some form of blessing or protection from a curse, it would be a powerful incentive' (250).

Part 2

The Curse of the Law
and the Purpose of Galatians

Chapter 5

The Fulfilment of the Law and the Galatian Converts

> Then all human creation will come to the fire of testing,
> and many will fall away and perish, but those who endure in their faith
> will be saved by the Accursed one himself (*Did.* 16.5).[1]

In Part 1 we considered the relevance of the curse of the Law for understanding the crisis in Galatia. We discovered that the rhetoric of cursing is a more prominent and indeed a more pervasive feature in Galatians than is often assumed. We also found good reason to suppose that the threat of a curse played a key part in the Agitators' appeal for circumcision, and that such a threat would have had a considerable impact upon the Galatians, who would have been wary of coming under a curse, not least a curse from the God of the Jews.

The stage is now set for the primary task of this study: to consider the rationale for Paul's four references to the Law in 5.13–6.10. We begin in this chapter with Paul's two references to the fulfilment of the Law in 5.14 and 6.2. My aim will be to demonstrate that Paul's appeal to the fulfilment of the Law is intended at least in part to affirm that by serving one another in love the Galatians will fulfil the Law and thereby avoid its curse.

The Whole Law and the Law of Christ

It will be necessary first to establish whether Paul refers to the Law of Moses in 5.14 and 6.2. While no one would deny that the vast majority of Paul's uses of νόμος in Galatians (and elsewhere) refer to the Law of Moses, there is question about whether this is the case in 6.2 and, to a lesser extent, in 5.14.[2] In light of Paul's numerous negative references to the Law earlier in the letter, there is some *prima facie* support for thinking that Paul's two positive references to νόμος in 5.14 and 6.2 are ironic or polemical. Furthermore, in

---

[1] This translation reflects the majority view among scholars that the phrase ὑπ' αὐτοῦ τοῦ καταθέματος is a subtle allusion to Christ (cf. *Barn.* 7.6-12; Justin, *Dial.* 111.2.8-10).

[2] For general discussions of the Law in Galatians, see Winger, *What Law* (1992), 73–78; Hong, *Law* (1993), 122–24; Kuula, *Law* (1999), 46–57; Lémonon, 'La loi mosaïque' (1997), 243–70 (see 248–53); Esler, *Galatians* (1998), 178–204; Vouga, *Galater* (1998), 92–97; Smiles, *Law in Galatia* (1998), 219–30; Schnelle, *Paulus* (2003), 301–21.

both 5.14 and 6.2 νόμος is not used independently, but as part of expressions which are unique to Paul (ὁ πᾶς νόμος, ὁ νόμος τοῦ Χριστοῦ). This certainly leaves open the possibility that Paul is using these two unusual remarks to signal to his hearers that he has in mind something other than the Law of Moses.

The whole Law

'For you were called to freedom (ἐπ' ἐλευθερίᾳ), brothers and sisters, only do not allow your freedom to become an occasion for the flesh, but through love be slaves (δουλεύετε) of one another' (5.13).[3] Thus Paul marks his transition to the so-called ethical section of Galatians. Striking is not only the positive reference to slavery, but also its juxtaposition with freedom.[4] This is widely regarded as a paradox: 'freedom in the slavery of love'.[5] No doubt it was intentional on Paul's part, but what was his point? Betz suggests: 'It is the necessity of commitment and the difficulties of maintaining human relationships that cause Paul to describe the free exercise of love as a form of mutual enslavement'.[6] Taking a slightly different tack, Barclay proposes that Paul wanted to make clear that his understanding of freedom has 'stringent moral obligations' in order to allay fears that his preaching of freedom was morally vacuous.[7] In a recent article, I have argued that this paradox reflects an Exodus matrix of thought: having been redeemed from Egyptian-like bondage, the Galatians are called to enslave themselves to God (cf. 4.8-9) and therefore to one another.[8] Paul's call to be enslaved to one another in love thus constitutes more than a 'necessary nuance' to his notion of Christian freedom.[9] Instead, it provides freedom with its very *raison d'être*.

---

[3] On the translation of δουλεύετε, see the apposite comment of Perrot, 'Loi et son accomplissement' (1996), 133 n. 15: 'La traduction *asservissez-vous* les uns aux autres ... est assurément un peu violente; mais, *mettez-vous au service les uns des autres* paraît trop innocent' (emphasis original).

[4] 1.10 is the only other positive use of slavery terminology in Galatians. In 3.28 Paul refers to literal slavery, while every other use of slavery terminology in Galatians is negative (2.4; 4.1-9, 24-25; 5.1). Thus, Paul's positive use of slavery terminology here in 5.13, like his positive reference to νόμος in 5.14, provides counterpoise to his consistently negative use of the slavery metaphor elsewhere. Cf. Vouga, *Galater* (1998), 129; Perrot, 'Loi et son accomplissement' (1996), 133.

[5] Barclay, *Obeying* (1988), 109; cf. Eckert, *Verkündigung* (1971), 134; Betz, *Galatians* (1979), 274; Perrot, 'Loi et son accomplissement' (1996), 132; Witherington, *Galatians* (1998), 378. For some scholars the apparent paradox of Paul's juxtaposition of freedom in the slavery of love is but a subset of the broader issue of the paradox of Paul's ethics in general; see Barrett, *Freedom and Obligation* (1985), 53–70 ('Chapter 4 – The Paradox of Ethics').

[6] Betz, *Galatians* (1979), 274.

[7] Barclay, *Obeying* (1988), 109.

[8] Wilson, 'Wilderness Apostasy' (2004), 565–67.

[9] Westerholm, 'Fulfilling the Law' (1986–87), 231.

Paul also contrasts 'slavery in the service of love' with freedom being used as an 'occasion for the flesh' (ἀφορμὴν τῇ σαρκί, 5.13b). What does Paul have in mind here? An answer to this question turns on one's understanding of the use of the term σάρξ in this expression, unfortunately one of the most elusive terms in Paul's entire vocabulary. For most interpreters 5.13 represents a significant shift in Paul's use of the term in Galatians. According to Burton, for example, while Paul has been using σάρξ as 'a purely physical term' earlier in the letter, in 5.13–6.10 he uses it in a 'definitely ethical sense'.[10] As Martyn suggests: 'this is the first of a series in which Paul uses the word in a new way'.[11] And many scholars argue along similar lines.[12]

Often scholars will argue that this shift in the use of σάρξ coincides with a transition in the argument of the letter from the threat of nomism in 2.15–5.12 to libertinism in 5.13–6.10.[13] For those unconvinced of a threat of libertinism, Paul's warning is related to the 'fleshly' attitudes and communal infighting evidently already at work in the Galatian churches (cf. 5.15, 19-21, 26).[14] While there is doubtless something to this, Paul's charge not to allow freedom to become an 'occasion for the flesh' should not be entirely divorced from the issue of circumcision (cf. 5.1-2). For one thing, Paul uses σάρξ at several key points in Galatians to refer to circumcision (3.3; 4.23, 29; 6.12-13). Furthermore, 5.13–6.10 is bracketed by two sections which speak explicitly about taking on circumcision (5.1-12; 6.11-18).[15]

In any case, one is still struck by Paul's sudden positive appeal to νόμος in 5.14: 'For the whole Law (ὁ πᾶς νόμος) is fulfilled in one word: "You shall love your neighbour as yourself"' (5.14). His appeal to νόμος at this point is referred to as a 'striking paradox',[16] 'startling',[17] 'quite surprising',[18] a 'fateful moment',[19] or even 'the most unexpected development of Paul's thought in this letter'.[20] Little wonder that scholars draw wildly divergent implications

---

[10] Burton, *Galatians* (1921), 292. Cf. Witherington, *Galatians* (1998), 376.

[11] Martyn, *Galatians* (1997), 485.

[12] See, for example, Schlier, *Galater* (1962), 241–44; Jewett, *Anthropological Terms* (1971), 103; Betz, *Galatians* (1979), 272–74; Longenecker, *Galatians* (1990), 238–48.

[13] Jewett, 'Agitators' (1971), 209–212; Longenecker, *Galatians* (1990), 236–37; Williams, *Galatians* (1997), 144.

[14] Barclay, *Obeying* (1988), 219: '"fleshly" bickering and infighting'. Borgen, *New Perspectives* (1987), 242, translates the phrase: 'not as opportunity for pagan vices' and links it with the 'works of the flesh' (5.19-21), which he takes to be characteristically pagan.

[15] Matera, 'Culmination' (1988), 79–91.

[16] Burton, *Galatians* (1921), 294.

[17] Thielman, *Paul & the Law* (1994), 139; Barclay, *Obeying* (1988), 125.

[18] Hong, *Law* (1993), 171.

[19] Westerholm, 'Fulfilling the Law' (1986–87), 230.

[20] Shaw, *Cost of Authority* (1983), 50; cited in Barclay, *Obeying* (1988), 126. Cf. Mata, 'El ser amados' (1982), 100: 'La sorpresa es mayor cuando se percibe en este versículo una actitud positiva de Pablo respecto a la Ley'.

from this one verse: some insist that 5.14 provides proof of a lasting place for the Law in the life of the Christian,[21] while others think that it drives the last nail in the coffin of the Law.[22] Only slightly less problematic is how to understand the function of 5.14 within the immediate context. Most scholars agree that 5.13-15 sets forth the thesis Paul then expounds in 5.13–6.10,[23] but there is considerable debate about what this verse contributes to Paul's flow of thought and why he has chosen to refer to νόμος at this point in the letter.

Thankfully for our purposes things are far less controversial with regard to the referent of the expression ὁ πᾶς νόμος. In fact, ever since H. Hübner's largely failed attempt to persuade others of a distinction between this phrase and the one in 5.3 (ὅλος ὁ νόμος),[24] few have contested a reference to the Law of Moses in 5.14.[25] Scholars do continue to discuss the precise sense of this expression, particularly the implications of the attributive placement of πᾶς (see below), but there is very little doubt about whether the expression itself refers to the Law of Moses.[26]

The Law of Christ

On the whole, scholars are far less confident that the expression ὁ νόμος τοῦ Χριστοῦ in 6.2 refers to the Law of Moses.[27] Nearly three centuries ago J. A. Bengel referred to this phrase as a *rara appellatio*.[28] Recent interpreters, however, have been less discreet. They now refer to the Law of Christ as 'most remarkable',[29] 'arresting',[30] 'strange',[31] 'muy curiosa',[32] 'striking',[33]

---

[21] Dunn, *Galatians* (1993), 290.

[22] Esler, *Galatians* (1998), 204; Hamerton-Kelly, 'Sacred Violence' (1990), 64; see also Schnelle, *Paulus* (2003), 320.

[23] See, for example, Légasse, *Galates* (2000), 400.

[24] Hübner has found support from Hamerton-Kelly, 'Sacred Violence' (1990), 67–68.

[25] Part of the reason for this has been the general shift away from trying to resolve the (apparent?) tension between these two verses on the basis of the noun phrases (so Hübner), to explaining it on the basis of the different verbs used in each verse (ποιέω in 5.3 vs. πληρόω in 5.14).

[26] See the discussion in Barclay, *Obeying* (1988), 136–37. Cf. Martyn, *Galatians* (1997), 486.

[27] See further Wilson, 'Law of Christ' (2006), 129-50, where I also set this recent trend in interpretation within the exegetical and theological milieu in which it has arisen and draw out several of its implications for Pauline theology and exegesis.

[28] Bengel, *Gnomon* (1860; org. 1742), 738.

[29] Stoike, *Law of Christ* (1971), 237.

[30] Cole, *Galatians* (1989), 225.

[31] Betz, *Galatians* (1979), 299; Ebeling, *Gospel* (1985), 253: 'strange'; Brinsmead, *Galatians* (1982), 173: 'puzzling'.

[32] Ramos, *Libertad* (1977), 299.

[33] Stanton, 'Law of Moses' (1996), 116; Kim, *New Perspective* (2002), 267: 'the striking formulation'.

'extremely baffling',[34] 'doubly astonishing',[35] a 'breathtaking paradox',[36] a 'much-puzzled-over term',[37] an 'oxymoron étonnant',[38] indeed 'a phrase more likely to mislead than to instruct'.[39]

Given Paul's rather robust polemic against the Law in Galatians, which appears to climax in an outright antithesis between Christ and the Law (5.2-4), it is indeed striking to find him near the end of the letter refer to the Law of Christ (6.2).[40] 'Est-ce que Paul remplace simplement une loi par une autre, posant ainsi les fondations d'un nouveau légalisme?'[41] To avoid such implications some scholars appeal to the semantic range of νόμος to argue that Paul uses this expression as a circumlocution for 'the way of life fitting for a Christian'.[42] Others suggest that the expression does refer (albeit perhaps ironically) to some new law which is now binding for the Christian.

It is not altogether surprising to discover, then, that within the history of interpretation, the Law of Christ has seldom been taken as a direct reference to the Law of Moses. While it may not be entirely unprecedented, prior to the late twentieth century it would be difficult to find anyone stating explicitly and unambiguously that Paul refers to the Law of Moses with the Law of Christ. The near-universal view has been that with this expression Paul refers to that which *replaces* the Law of Moses. Particularly outside the Lutheran tradition, this has meant taking the Law of Christ as a reference to some kind of *nova lex* for Christians.[43] It was not at all uncommon, for example, for Patristic commentators to interpret the Law of Christ in terms of Jesus's 'new commandment' (cf. John 13.34-35).[44] The Law of Moses has thus been replaced by the love command as it was taught by Jesus himself. Taking a slightly different tack, though agreeing with this basic approach, F. Thielman has recently argued:

---

[34] Hong, *Law* (1993), 173.

[35] Barclay, *Obeying* (1988), 126.

[36] Hays, 'Law of Christ' (1987), 276; Bruce, *Galatians* (1982), 40: 'something of a paradox'; Esler, *Galatians* (1998), 181: 'the remarkable expression'.

[37] Stuhlmacher, 'Law' (1986), 123.

[38] Perrot, 'Loi et son accomplissement' (1996), 127.

[39] Winger, 'Law of Christ' (2000), 545. Cf. Bammel, 'Νόμος' (1997), 335-36.

[40] Hays, 'Law of Christ' (1987), 276: 'In view of the absolute opposition between "law" and "Christ" that Paul has deliberately established in the letter (see especially 5:4) the expression "law of Christ" must have fallen upon his readers' ears as a breathtaking paradox'.

[41] Pigeon, 'Loi du Christ' (2000), 431.

[42] Westerholm, *Israel's Law* (1988), 214 n. 38.

[43] Limbeck, *Das Gesetz* (1997), 126: 'So gesehen war Christus für Paulus zwar das Ende des *mosaischen* Gesetzes, zugleich aber auch der Ursprung eines *neuen* Gesetzes, des „Gesetzes Christi" (Gal 6,2)' (emphasis original).

[44] Theodoret of Cyrus, cited in Swete, *Theodori* (1880), 1.103-04 n. 22; Jerome, *Galatas* (1845), PL 24.423; Souter, *Pelagius's Expositions* (1926), 339. Cf. Aquinas, *Galatians* (1966), 190, and, more recently, Wenham, *Paul* (1995), 75-76.

... the law of the eschatological era turns out in Paul's understanding to be different from the law of Moses. Aspects of Moses' law such as the famous summary in Leviticus 19:18 are absorbed into this new law, but the covenant that God made with Moses at Mount Sinai is considered obsolete, and in its place Paul has substituted 'the law of Christ'.[45]

While the precise character or content of this new law has been understood in different ways by different interpreters in different traditions, the basic outlook appears to be the same: just as the Christian church has displaced Israel, so also the Law of Christ has displaced the Law of Moses. P. Esler makes this point quite explicit: 'the "law of Christ" represents Paul's most daring inversion of the position of the Israelite outgroup and the final nail hammered into his argument that the Mosaic law is quite irrelevant in the new dispensation. . . . Not only do [the Galatians] have Abraham as an ancestor, they also have their own equivalent to the law, albeit only metaphorically'.[46]

One may be somewhat more surprised, however, to learn that late nineteenth and twentieth-century developments in the study of the Jewish matrix of earliest Christianity appear to have done little to affect this approach to the Law of Christ. Increased sensitivity to early Jewish eschatological expectations has, of course, done something to colour the interpretative landscape by filling it with potential verbal or conceptual parallels to the Law of Christ. And this, in turn, has encouraged some at least to see in this expression a reference to a new law more akin to the Law of Moses, whether this was understood as a Messianic Torah, a transformed 'Zion Torah' or a new Torah comprised of the life and teachings of Jesus.[47] Nevertheless, the assumption that the Law of Christ refers to that which replaces the Law of Moses has gone largely unquestioned.

Recently, however, an increasing number of scholars are exploring the possibility that the Law of Christ in fact refers to the Law of Moses.[48] This conclusion is based on several observations. First, the close parallels between 6.2 and 5.13-14, where a reference to the Law of Moses is, as we have already seen, very well established, strongly suggests that Paul is also referring to the Law of Moses in 6.2. Both passages contain the language of 'fulfilment' (ἀνα/πληρόω), 'Law' (νόμος) and 'one another' (ἀλλήλων). The conceptual overlap is equally apparent: a call to mutual service (5.13; 6.2a)

---

[45] Thielman, *Paul & the Law* (1994), 142. Tellingly, Thielman, *Paul & the Law* (1994), 123, 134, captures the flow of Paul's argument in Galatians with the following two epigrams: 'Exit the Law of Moses'—'Enter the Law of Christ' (respectively). Cf. Thielman, *Law and New Testament* (1999), 18–20.

[46] Esler, *Galatians* (1998), 231–32.

[47] Davies, *Torah* (1952); Stuhlmacher, 'Law' (1986), 110–33; Dodd, '*Ennomos Christou*' (1968), 134–48 (respectively).

[48] Scholars do not necessarily agree on the precise implications of this phrase, however. Cf. Barclay, *Obeying* (1988), 131–35; Hong, *Law* (1993), 176–83; Longenecker, *Triumph* (1998), 86.

linked to an affirmation of the fulfilment of the Law (5.14; 6.2b). In fact, one could argue that 6.1-2 is simply a more concrete or perhaps situation-specific application of the exhortation, affirmation, and warning Paul issues in 5.13-15.[49]

Secondly, the close proximity of 5.13-14 to 6.2, together with the fact that 5.13-14 precedes and thus prepares for 6.2, makes it rather unlikely that Paul intended the Law of Christ to refer to something other than what he has just referred to with the whole Law in 5.14.[50] Could Paul have been able to justify this sudden shift in referent so close on the heels of 5.13-14?[51] One suspects that such a move would have been lost on his audience, who would have had a hard time not hearing in 6.2 an echo of 5.13-14 and therefore another reference to the fulfilment of the Law of Moses.[52] So if we allow audience reception to inform our understanding of an author's intention, we have good reason think that with the Law of Christ Paul meant to refer to the Law of Moses, albeit now related to Christ.

Thirdly, with the (possible) exception of 3.21b, every other use of νόμος in Galatians refers to the Law of Moses.[53] As Martyn has recently argued with some vigour: 'There is every reason, then, for taking Gal 6:2 to be the thirty-first juncture in this letter at which Paul refers to *the* Law'.[54] One response, of course, would be to insist that 6.2 marks an exception in Paul's normal pattern of usage, and that Paul signals this departure with the striking addition of the genitive τοῦ Χριστοῦ.[55] The difficulty with this is again the close parallel with 5.13-14, where the reference to the Law of Moses is clear. A more tenable position would be to argue that *neither 6.2 nor 5.14* refer to the Law of Moses, but as we have seen, very few are willing to go this direction with 5.14. This leaves many, then, in the somewhat awkward position of having to deny a reference to the Law of Moses in 6.2, while yet affirming a reference to it in the close parallel in 5.14.[56]

---

[49] Hong, *Law* (1993), 170.
[50] Barclay, *Obeying* (1988), 134 n. 89; Stanton, 'Law of Moses' (1996), 116. Cf. Lambrecht, 'Coherent Admonition' (1997), 45.
[51] Stanton, 'Law of Christ?' (2001), 55.
[52] Sanders, *Jewish People* (1983), 98.
[53] 3.21b is clearly marked in the form of a contrary to fact condition.
[54] Martyn, *Galatians* (1997), 555–56 n. 41. There he takes issue with those who want to gloss νόμος in 6.2 as 'principle' or 'structure of existence'. This would be unprecedented within the context of Galatians and can only succeed by appealing to Romans. See now especially Martyn, '*Nomos* Plus Genitive', 575–87.
[55] van Dulmen, *Gesetzes* (1968), 66; Esler, *Galatians* (1998), 231; Schnelle, *Paulus* (2003), 320.
[56] One further point could be mentioned. Doubtless part of the exegetical and theological motivation behind treating the Law of Christ as either a reference to some other law or as a circumlocution for Christian living is to avoid the problem of Paul making a positive appeal to the Law of Moses when enjoining Christian love. But this problem is already implicit in

Fourthly, though somewhat more speculatively, if Paul has taken over this expression from the Agitators, as some want to argue, it would perhaps further strengthen the likelihood that he would have intended it as a reference to the Law of Moses. For this is doubtless how it would have been understood by those who originally coined the expression. Furthermore, Paul's polemical purposes would have been greatly served by preserving the original referent of the expression (i.e., the Law of Moses), yet transposing the whole phrase into a new context and thereby reconfiguring its implications. This becomes a more plausible suggestion if one thinks that part of Paul's purpose with Galatians was to provide a proper perspective on the precise relationship between the Law and Christ, without entirely dismissing the former for the sake of the latter.[57]

This is admittedly not an unassailable case for taking the Law of Christ to be a reference to the Law of Moses. The strength of this argument comes from the cumulative effect of these several observations, particularly the close parallels in 5.14, which Barclay perhaps rightly thinks 'necessitate' viewing the Law of Christ as a reference to the Law of Moses.[58] Yet despite the strength of these observations, it is not impossible to understand the Law of Christ as a reference to some other law or perhaps as a polemical circumlocution for Christian living. Even if this were the case, however, it would not undermine my present thesis. Paul could still answer the threat of a curse directly in 5.14, with a clear statement about the fulfilment of the Law of Moses, and yet more indirectly in 6.2, with an assurance about the believer's fulfilment of a new law, the law of Christ. On the whole, however, it is more likely that Paul refers to the fulfilment of the Law of Moses in both verses. Therefore, in what follows I shall take this as my point of departure, and trust that the ensuing discussion will only further bolster the case for taking the Law of Christ as a reference to the Law of Moses.

The Fulfilment of the Law and the Threat of a Curse

We are now in a better position to explore the rationale for 5.14 and 6.2 within the context of the letter and the crisis in Galatia. Perhaps the first and most obvious thing to be noted about these two verses is Paul's rather dramatic change in tone; in both 5.14 and 6.2 he speaks in a positive and indeed an affirmative way about the Law, whereas elsewhere in the letter his portrait of the Law has on the whole been far less flattering. Because of this

---

5.13-14, hence little ground is gained by eschewing a reference to the Law of Moses in 6.2. The problem already exists in 5.13-14.

[57] Hong, *Law* (1993), 177; Longenecker, *Triumph* (1998), 86.
[58] Barclay, *Obeying* (1988), 134 n. 89; Stanton, 'Law of Moses' (1996), 116.

scholars will often suggest that 5.14 and 6.2 serve as counterpoise to Paul's earlier statements about the Law.[59] There is doubtless something to this observation, but one needs to probe a bit further by asking: counterpoise in what way? Is Paul simply being dialectical, balancing the negative and positive aspects of the Law; or is he trying to find a way to preserve some modicum of the Law within his understanding of the gospel?

In the Introduction we considered four different ways in which scholars explain the rationale for Paul's mention of the Law in 5.13–6.10, including his two references to the fulfilment of the Law in 5.14 and 6.2. What is clear from that survey is that insufficient attention has been given to the possibility that Paul's two references to the fulfilment of the Law were intended as counterpoise to the threat of the curse of the Law.[60] This approach has been largely overlooked, even though, as we discovered in the first part of this study, the issue of the curse of the Law was quite relevant to the situation in Galatia. The rhetoric of cursing is a prominent and indeed a pervasive feature of the letter. The threat of a curse was probably also a salient feature of the Agitators' case for circumcision. And the fear of a curse probably contributed to the Galatians' attraction to circumcision; they were eager to ensure that they would avoid the curse of the Law.

In light of this aspect of the Galatian crisis, we have good reason to wonder whether Paul's two references to the fulfilment of the Law were intended to answer the threat of the curse of the Law and thereby redress doubts about whether the Galatians were in fact under a curse. The remainder of this chapter is devoted to exploring several indications which suggest that both 5.14 and 6.2 (albeit in slightly different ways) were formulated by Paul in part as a way to answer the threat of the curse of the Law.

The expression ὁ πᾶς νόμος

In recent discussion of 5.14 scholars have focused their attention on the verb πληρόω. As a result, the expression ὁ πᾶς νόμος is sometimes neglected.[61] Its unusual syntax, however, merits attention. Although the established Pauline corpus contains more than three hundred uses of πᾶς, it occurs as an adjective in the attributive position with an articular substantive on only four other occasions (1.2; 1 Cor 12.19; 2 Cor 5.10; Rom 16.15).[62] There are, moreover, only a few other examples of syntactically similar uses of πᾶς in

---

[59] Cf. Stanton, 'Law of Moses' (1996), 116.

[60] Baasland, 'Persecution' (1984), 141, notes in passing that 5.14 may have been intended to answer the threat of a curse. See also Morland, *Curse* (1995), 232; Dunn, *Galatians* (1993), 291.

[61] Barclay, *Obeying* (1988), 135–41, rightly makes much of the verb πληρόω, but perhaps at the expense of attending to the significance of the noun phrase ὁ πᾶς νόμος. Many interpreters have followed Barclay in this regard.

[62] Stirewalt, *Letter Writer* (2003), 97 n. 64.

the entire NT (cf. Acts 19.7; 20.18; 27.37; 1 Tim 1.16), and none in the LXX. This is, then, an odd expression which probably has significance for Paul.[63]

It is sometimes claimed that the use of πᾶς in the attributive position underscores, as Burton suggests, 'the idea of totality, without reference to parts',[64] with the implication that Paul sidesteps the issue of the individual commandments of the Law.[65] Whether this is implied by the syntax itself is uncertain, though it is clear that Paul wants to underscore that love fulfils the *whole* Law. But here one does well to remember that 5.14 is not Paul's first reference to the notion of the whole Law in Galatians.[66] He refers to the comprehensive demand of the Law in 5.3 and 3.10. Of course, scholars often note the interplay between 5.14 and 5.3, yet for some reason they seem less inclined to detect any contact between 5.14 and 3.10.[67] This is curious, however, for the following reasons.

First, Paul juxtaposes πᾶς and νόμος in only two places in Galatians: 3.10 and 5.14.[68] This fact is often overlooked, even by those who stress the comprehensive demand of the Law in Galatians. For example, in his recent monograph, A. Das devotes an entire chapter to defending the view that 3.10 implies perfect obedience to the Law, yet in his discussion of '"All" the Law Elsewhere in Galatians', he fails even to mention 5.14.[69] This is a striking oversight which ironically only serves to underscore the potential link between these two verses.

Secondly, there is widespread agreement that 5.14 is closely related to 5.3, perhaps as polemical counterbalance. Many are also persuaded that 5.3 is closely related to 3.10, with 5.3 reiterating the thrust of 3.10.[70] Oddly enough,

---

[63] Burton, *Galatians* (1921), 296; Hübner, *Law* (1984), 37; Witherington, *Galatians* (1998), 380. Perrot, 'Loi et son accomplissement' (1996), 126, notes that 'la situation inhabituelle de πᾶς entre l'article et le substantif attire déjà l'attention'.

[64] Burton, *Galatians* (1921), 296.

[65] Cf. Mussner, *Galaterbrief* (1974), 370: 'das gesamte Gesetz, im Gegensatz zu seinen einzelnen Anordnungen'.

[66] Betz, *Galatians* (1979), 274.

[67] There are a few exceptions, though none draw the same implications as I do. See Hübner, 'Gesetz' (1975), 245; Hübner, *Theologie des Paulus* (1993), 103–05 (104 n. 191 for a brief response to critics of his thesis); Cranford, 'Perfect Obedience' (1994), 246–47; Dunn, *Galatians* (1993), 291.

[68] The other uses of πᾶς and νόμος in the same verse in Galatians are: 2.16 (πᾶσα σάρξ); 3.13 (πᾶς ὁ κρεμάμενος); 5.3 (παντὶ ἀνθρώπῳ).

[69] Das, *Covenant* (2001), 167–68. This is remedied somewhat by a fruitful discussion of both 5.14 and 6.2 in his more recent study, Das, *Jews* (2003), 166–86.

[70] Reasons for thinking that 5.3 refers back to 3.10 are, first, that Paul says that he is here repeating something he has already said ('But, I testify again') and, secondly, their shared use of ποιέω; cf. Eckert, *Verkündigung* (1971), 41; Howard, *Crisis* (1990), 16; Barclay, *Obeying* (1988), 64; and Martin, 'Apostasy' (1995), 87 n. 77, who rightly notes that this is 'the least problematic' explanation of 5.3.

however, scholars seldom relate 5.14 to 3.10 more directly. But if 5.14 serves as counterpoise to 5.3, and 5.3 reiterates the message of 3.10, then by implication 5.14 would also appear to be counterpoise to 3.10.

Thirdly, a number of interpreters stress the significance of the twofold appearance of πᾶς in Paul's citation of LXX Deut 27.26 in 3.10. Many understand this as Paul's way of stressing the comprehensive demand of the Law and its bearing upon the question of who is under the Law's curse.[71] While this feature of 3.10 is sometimes overplayed, it seldom encourages scholars to consider whether Paul intended the Galatians to hear his affirmation of the fulfilment of the whole Law (ὁ πᾶς νόμος) with the threat of the curse of Law upon 'everyone (πᾶς) who does not abide by all things written in the book of the Law (πᾶσιν τοῖς γεγραμμένοις ἐν τῷ βιβλίῳ τοῦ νόμου) to do them' (3.10) still ringing in their ears.[72]

These observations not only underscore the tendency among scholars to treat 5.14 somewhat in isolation from Paul's earlier references to the Law, except in a rather general way, they also provide some indication that Paul intended his affirmation of the fulfilment of the whole Law in 5.14 to provide counterpoise to the threat of the curse of the Law mentioned in 3.10.

The significance of the verb πληρόω

That Paul intended 5.14 to answer the threat of a curse and perhaps even to provide a specific response to the curse referred to in 3.10 is further suggested by his use of the verb πληρόω. While scholars sometimes used to treat the verbs πληρόω and ποιέω as essentially synonymous,[73] there has been a sea-change in opinion in recent years. Many now mark an important distinction

---

[71] Burton, *Galatians* (1921), 164–65; Schoeps, *Paul* (1961), 176–77; Mussner, *Galaterbrief* (1974), 224–26; Longenecker, *Galatians* (1990), 118; Fung, *Galatians* (1988), 141; Schreiner, 'Perfect Obedience' (1984), 256 n. 15. For a general discussion of the text form of this verse, see Koch, *Zeuge* (1986), 120–21, 163–65; Stanley, *Language of Scripture* (1992), 238–43. Sanders, *Jewish People* (1983), 21, argued that Paul did not intend to emphasize 'all' in this citation, though see the critique by Cranford, 'Perfect Obedience' (1994), 246. See also Reinbold, 'Erfüllbarkeit' (2000), 99–100.

[72] A comparison with the parallel statement in Rom 13.8, where πᾶς is conspicuously absent, may be instructive. In Galatians Paul does not say, as he does in Romans, that the Law is fulfilled in love, but that the *whole* Law is fulfilled, the inclusion of πᾶς in 5.14 perhaps underscoring the polemical function of the statement. This was rightly noted by Hübner, *Law* (1984), 83, though he drew different implications.

[73] Schlier, *Galater* (1962), 245; Mussner, *Galaterbrief* (1974), 370; Hübner, *Law* (1984), 36–37; Räisänen, *Paul and Law* (1987), 63–64 n. 104; Dunn, *Galatians* (1993), 290; Schnabel, *Law and Wisdom* (1985), 274–75; Thielman, *Plight to Solution* (1989), 52; Thielman, *Paul & the Law* (1994), 140.

between πληρόω and ποιέω and treat πληρόω as the hermeneutical key to 5.14.[74]

The attention given to the verb πληρόω is, however, well justified. The special significance of this verb can be demonstrated by the following two observations. First, Paul never uses πληρόω to speak of Jewish observance of the Law; and when he does use this verb in connection with the Law, it is with reference to what Christians do (Rom 8.4; 13.8-10; 5.14; 6.2). Furthermore, Paul never says that Christians 'do' the Law, only that they 'fulfil' it.[75] Secondly, πληρόω is never used in conjunction with νόμος in early Jewish literature written in Greek; Paul appears therefore to be using terminology unprecedented in the Jewish tradition.[76]

Although these observations are not altogether indisputable, they do provide rather impressive evidence for thinking that Paul is using special vocabulary in 5.14 (and 6.2). But what implications follow from his use of this unusual verb? Did Paul mean to contrast doing the Law with fulfilling it? If so, one might have expected an explicit statement contrasting the two, especially given Paul's penchant in Galatians for 'antinomies' of this kind (e.g., 'works of the Law' vs. 'faith', 'present evil age' vs. 'new creation', 'flesh' vs. 'Spirit').[77] In fact, what is missing in Galatians and elsewhere in Paul is an explicit rejection of doing the Law *per se*.[78] Of course, Paul insists that his Gentile converts should not be circumcised (5.2-4) and claims that the Law cannot mediate righteousness (2.15-21). But he nowhere insists that while fulfilling the Law is a good thing, doing the Law is a bad thing.

Some have argued that Paul saw a *qualitative* difference between doing the Law and fulfilling it. While doing the Law means punctiliously observing its individual commandments, fulfilling the Law implies something more spontaneous and Spirit-led.[79] Others suggest that it was Paul's intention to insist that the actual observance of the Law was unnecessary once the essence of the Law had been fulfilled through love and by the Spirit. Both of these alternatives, however, leave open the possibility of doing the Law within the

---

[74] Matera, *Galatians* (1992), 197; Vollenweider, *Freiheit* (1989), 313; Longenecker, *Galatians* (1990), 241–43; Hansen, 'Ethic of Freedom' (1997), 230; Lémonon, 'La loi mosaïque' (1997), 249; Witherington, *Galatians* (1998), 381; Weder, 'Normativität' (1998), 139; Hays, 'Galatians' (2000), 322; Légasse, *Galates* (2000), 404–05. Cf. Martyn, *Galatians* (1997), 486–90.

[75] Betz, *Galatians* (1979), 275; Westerholm, 'Fulfilling the Law' (1986–87), 233–34; Westerholm, *Israel's Law* (1988), 203–04.

[76] Barclay, *Obeying* (1988), 138. Cf. van de Sandt, 'An Explanation of Rom. 8,4a' (1976).

[77] Martyn, 'Apocalyptic Antinomies' (1985), 410–24.

[78] This is not to deny that Paul thinks of doing the Law as inadequate (or, perhaps, even wrong-headed) in the matter of justification or that he rejects the imposition of the Law upon Gentiles converts (cf. 5.1).

[79] Burton, *Galatians* (1921), 294; Betz, *Galatians* (1979), 275.

context of fulfilling it.[80] Furthermore, it is not hard to imagine the Galatians coming away with the impression that Paul's reference to fulfilling the Law implies, at least at some level, the actual *doing* of certain religious duties, especially within a context in which these questions were at issue.[81] This also casts doubt on whether Paul would have really put things in precisely the way he did, if his main point was to persuade the Galatians of the superfluity of Law observance.[82] For the notion of fulfilment does not obviously or even necessarily imply either replacement or superfluity.

Barclay's explanation of the language of the fulfilment of the Law has been particularly influential of late. He makes two points. First, he argues that Paul used the language of the fulfilment of the Law to describe 'the total realization of God's will in line with the eschatological fulness of time in the coming of Christ'; this was intended to give the Galatians the impression of completely satisfying the requirements of the Law and thereby allay doubts about the adequacy of Paul's prescription for ethics.[83] Secondly, Paul speaks of the fulfilment of the Law because of the inherent ambiguity of the notion of fulfilment. According to Barclay, to say that love fulfils the Law leaves unclear the status of the rest of the commandments; this allows Paul to avoid the implication that fulfilling the Law requires the same exactitude of observance inherent in doing the Law.[84]

What are we to make of these two suggestions? First of all, as I have already mentioned, it is not clear whether for the Galatians, at least, the language of fulfilling the Law would have lacked nuances of exactitude, as Barclay seems to assume.[85] This may have been the case, but unfortunately Barclay provides no lexical evidence to support this claim.[86] More problematic, however, is the supposition that Paul resorts to being *intentionally* ambiguous precisely when he would have had every reason to be especially clear: namely, when he affirms in a positive manner the Galatians' relationship to the Law. Given the nature of the crisis, such a remark could have easily been misunderstood by the Galatians or misapplied by the

---

[80] Longenecker, *Triumph* (1998), 84, acknowledges that Paul does not use the fulfilment of the Law to argue against doing its commandments, but insists that this is the 'effect' of his statement.

[81] Thielman, *Paul & the Law* (1994), 140; Thielman, *Plight to Solution* (1989), 51–52.

[82] Thielman, *Paul & the Law* (1994), 140.

[83] Barclay, *Obeying* (1988), 140.

[84] Barclay, *Obeying* (1988), 140. Perrot, 'Loi et son accomplissement' (1996), 126, speaks of 'une amplitude sémantique, voire une nébuleuse de sens, qui empêche de le ravaler au niveau d'une simple mise en pratique'.

[85] Barclay, *Obeying* (1988), 140.

[86] Thielman, *Paul & the Law* (1994), 140, in fact argues that the Galatians would have probably understood the language of the fulfilment of the Law in terms of 'completing' obligations.

Agitators, again leaving open the possibility of doing the Law within the context of fulfilling it. Well aware of this problem, Barclay insists that Paul had no other choice: he simply could not dismiss the Law altogether, which would have been of no help to the Galatians, so he had to resort to a certain 'looseness of speech'.[87] This portrayal of Paul papering over the cracks, however, stands in considerable tension with what Barclay identifies as perhaps Paul's chief aim in 5.13–6.10: to clarify the moral adequacy of his ethical policy as it relates to the Law. For Paul to have been intentionally ambiguous in 5.14 would be to undercut his own aims. We have reason to doubt, then, whether ambiguity was really a part of Paul's purpose in using the language of the fulfilment of the Law.

Barclay's first suggestion that the fulfilment of the Law carries an eschatological nuance seems to be on a more solid footing. As he rightly points out, this language dovetails nicely with the note of eschatological realisation sounded by the expression τὸ πλήρωμα τοῦ χρόνου in 4.4.[88] This link is all the more significant given that 4.3-5 may contain 'nothing less than the theological center of the entire letter'.[89] It is also worth noting that Paul links the fulfilment of the Law with love (5.13-14; 6.2; Rom 13.8-10), which is itself 'a wholly eschatological phenomenon' for Paul (2.20; 5.5-6; 5.23),[90] and with the agency of the 'promised Spirit' (3.14), whose presence marks the realisation of prophetic expectations for a future restoration of the people of God (Isa 32.15; 44.3; 59.12; Ezek 11.9; 36.26; 37.14; 39.29; Joel 2.28-32; Acts 2.33, 39; Eph 1.13).[91] In fact, when speaking of the fulfilment of the Law, Paul may well have in mind the 'new covenant' prophecy of Jeremiah about the Law being 'written on the heart' (Jer 31.33 [LXX 38.33]; cf. Ezek 36.26-27).[92]

---

[87] Barclay, *Obeying* (1988), 141–42.

[88] Barclay, *Obeying* (1988), 139; cf. Thielman, *Plight to Solution* (1989), 52; Witherington, *Galatians* (1998), 381.

[89] Martyn, *Galatians* (1997), 388.

[90] Longenecker, *Triumph* (1998), 71. Cf. Pedersen, 'Eschatologische Hauptbegriff' (1980), 159–86, with reference to 1 Cor 13; Kertelge, 'Freiheitsbotschaft' (1989), 337. Note the parallelism Paul creates between πίστις δι' ἀγάπης ἐνεργουμένη (5.6) and καινὴ κτίσις (6.15).

[91] Kwon, *Eschatology* (2004), 115–17, argues that the 'promised Spirit' in 3.14 should be identified not with the promise to Abraham, but with these prophetic expectations.

[92] Winger, 'Law of Christ' (2000), 541, though he draws rather different implications. This suggestion would be considerably strengthened if, as Martyn, *Galatians* (1997), 391–92, contends, there is an allusion to both Jer 31.31-34 and Ezek 36.26-27 in 4.6: 'God sent the Spirit of his Son into our hearts crying "Abba, Father"'. Cf. Söding, 'Verheißung' (2001), 147, who notes that the fulfilment of the Law is part of Paul's broader conception of promise and fulfilment, which includes reference to the fulfilment of the promise to Abraham that both Jew and Gentile would be justified by faith.

In addition to using the verb πληρόω to sound an eschatological note, Paul may also be using it with a more specific and indeed more polemical purpose in mind. As part of his interpretation of 3.10, D. Boyarin suggests, in passing, that the verb πληρόω in 5.14 is a rough equivalent of the verb ἐμμένω in the citation of LXX Deut 27.26 in 3.10.[93] Although he does not elaborate on or defend this claim, it could be argued that for Paul πληρόω and ἐμμένω are closely related by virtue of them both serving as viable translations of the Hebrew or Aramaic קוּם. Sometimes scholars object to the claim that πληρόω would have been used in the NT period as a translation of קוּם, particularly in relation to its use in Matt 5.17, on the basis that the LXX never translates πληρόω with קוּם; πληρόω is only used to translate the verb alm.[94] According to H. van de Sandt and D. Flusser, however, this objection 'will not wash'.[95] Three observations are worth bearing in mind. First, in LXX Jer 51.25 πληρόω, which translates מלא, and ἐμμένω, which translates קוּם, appear in close parallelism, indicating that there may have been some overlap between these two pairs of terms during the NT period. Secondly, as they point out, in the Targumim of the Tenach מלא is usually replaced with the pa'el of קוּם. Thirdly, in other rabbinic literature קוּם is sometimes used with the sense of 'to fulfil' (cf. *Mek. Amalek* on Exod 18.27; *b. Mak.* 24^b; *m. Sanh.* 7, 6; *m. Sukkah* 2, 7; *m. Menaḥ.* 10, 4; *m. Ḥul.* 7, 2; *m. 'Abot* 4, 9).[96] While these observations are by no means compelling, they do at least suggest that Paul may have viewed πληρόω and ἐμμένω as rough equivalents, and therefore open up the possibility that he intended his affirmation of the fulfilment (πληρόω) of the whole Law (5.14) *specifically* to counter the threat of failing to abide (ἐμμένω) by all that is written in the book of the Law (3.10).

While it is more difficult to determine whether the Galatians would have been able to grasp this latter point, we can be confident that they would have registered the eschatological nuance communicated by the language of the fulfilment of the Law. We have good reason to suspect that they would have heard in 5.14 a rather robust affirmation of the fulfilment of the Law and that they would have connected this with the coming of the 'fullness of time' (4.4). It would have also been difficult for them to miss the fact that the fulfilment of the Law coincides with Christ's coming to redeem 'us' from the

---

[93] Boyarin, *Radical Jew* (1994), 141. Boyarin sees a distinction between 'doing' (mere performance) and 'fulfilling' within 3.10 itself. He argues that the term ἐμμένω has the semantic component of 'completeness' (301 n. 10). Thus, he reads 3.10 as stating that those who 'do' the many material commands are not 'fulfilling' the one ideal logos: they are thus cursed 'because of their misunderstanding of the true import of the Law' (141).

[94] E.g., Davies and Allison, *Matthew* (1988), 485 n. 9.

[95] van de Sandt and Flusser, *Didache* (2002), 218 n. 74.

[96] See further van de Sandt and Flusser, *Didache* (2002), 218 n. 74, and van de Sandt, 'An Explanation of Rom. 8,4a' (1976), 361–78 (especially 368–70).

curse of the Law (3.13; cf. 4.4-5; 1.4). If, as I have argued, the threat of a curse was looming large in the background, Paul's affirmation of the total realisation of God's will would have been precisely what the Galatians needed to hear. While the Galatians may have had doubts about coming under a curse for failing to abide by all that the Law enjoins (3.10), they can nevertheless be confident of the fact that serving one another in love actually fulfils the whole Law (5.14).

The Crucified and Cursed Christ and the Law of Christ

We now turn to consider Paul's second reference to the fulfilment of the Law in 6.2: 'Bear one another's burdens and thus you will fulfil the Law of Christ'.[97] While this verse is sometimes thought to be disconnected from its surrounding context, there is good reason to suppose, first of all, that Paul understands burden-bearing to be closely related to the task of restoring the erring member of the community which he calls for in the previous verse (6.1). Since burden-bearing would have likely evoked the responsibilities of a slave (cf. 5.13),[98] it is also interesting to note that in the immediately following verses Paul appeals for a proper assessment of one's standing within the community, perhaps knowing that inflated egos only inhibit mutual service (6.3-5). But Paul's call to bear one another's burdens should not be entirely disconnected from his subsequent exhortation to 'share all good things with those who teach' (6.6-8), since financial support can easily be thought of as expression of burden-bearing within the life of the community.[99] Thus, one could argue that the whole of 6.1-10 serves as an exposition of bearing one another's burdens (cf. 6.9-10).[100]

Burden-bearing as cruciform, suffering love

While burden-bearing provides 6.1-10 with a certain thematic coherence and in turn is further explicated by the specific examples of burden-bearing mentioned there, if we restrict ourselves only to this section of the letter we will miss the full force of what Paul wants to say. When understood within the broader scope of the letter, Paul's call to bear one another's burdens implies

---

[97] On the text critical issues surrounding this verse, see Pigeon, 'Loi du Christ' (2000), 427, who notes that the two different readings (future or aorist) in the end make little difference.

[98] Barclay, *Obeying* (1988), 131.

[99] While Strelan, 'Burden-Bearing' (1975), 266–76, mistakenly tried to restrict the language of burden-bearing to this, he did underscore the fact that language comparable to that used here in 6.2a often occurs in Paul's letters within contexts that deal with meeting one another's financial needs.

[100] On 5.25–6.10 as whole, see especially Schrage, 'Probleme' (1996), 155–94.

nothing less than a call to a *cruciform, suffering love* which patterns itself after the example of the crucified Christ (3.13; cf. 1.4; 3.1; 4.4-5) and his crucified Apostle (2.19-20; 4.12; 5.11; 6.14-17).

In Galatians, Paul portrays Christ as the burden-bearer *par excellence*, the one who sacrificed himself to meet the needs of others (1.4; 2.20; 4.4-5). Hays thus rightly speaks of Christ's action in Galatians as 'a pattern of submission to God and of accepting suffering for the sake of others'.[101] This feature of Paul's portrayal of Christ is only further reinforced by Paul's own portrayal of himself as a 'slave of Christ' (1.10), who endures suffering for the sake of others (5.11; 6.14-17), and who for that reason can commend himself to the Galatians as 'a paradigm of Christian existence' (cf. 4.12).[102] Both Paul's portrayal of the crucified Christ and his own portrayal of himself as the crucified Apostle, then, inform and indeed support his call to the Galatians to 'serve one another in love' (5.13-14; cf. 2.20) and 'bear one another's burdens' (6.2). In their daily life together the Galatians are to exemplify the same kind of cruciform, suffering love they see reflected in the life of Christ and the life of Paul (4.12, 19).[103]

Although Paul's call to cruciform, suffering love runs like a thread through his letters, he does not always invoke the motif of cruciformity in the same way. The particular shape of the cruciformity to which Paul calls his churches depends upon the exigencies of their particular situation.[104] In Corinth, cruciformity is to manifest itself in the renouncing of individual rights and the proper exercise of spiritual gifts for the edification of the whole body. In Rome, cruciformity requires non-retaliation toward enemies and non-judgmental attitudes towards believers.[105] In Galatia, however, cruciformity means bearing one another's burdens by following Christ in accepting suffering for the sake of others in submission to God.

This points the way to part of the polemical function of this language within the Galatian crisis. Just as burden-bearing cannot ultimately be separated from the cross of Christ, nor can it be entirely divorced from the *curse* of the Law, since Christ has become a paradigm of cruciformity by taking on the curse of the Law on the cross in order to redeem those who were under the Law's curse (3.13; 4.4-5). Moreover, out of an allegiance to the 'truth of the gospel' (2.4), Paul himself endures suffering as a form of co-crucifixion with Christ (2.19-20; 5.11; 6.12-13), even though this leaves him open to the charge of being under the Law's curse as a transgressor of the

---

[101] Hays, 'Law of Christ' (1987), 278.
[102] Hays, 'Law of Christ' (1987), 281. Cf. Dodd, 'Christ's Slave' (1996), 90–104.
[103] Note that Paul combines a call for the Galatians to imitate him (4.12) with an expression of his desire that Christ be formed within their corporate life (4.19).
[104] Gorman, *Cruciformity* (2001), 214–67.
[105] Gorman, *Cruciformity* (2001), 222–53.

Law (cf. 2.17). In fact, it may not be fortuitous that Paul uses the same verb in 6.2 and 6.17, where he says: 'I bear (βαστάζω) on my body the marks of Jesus', almost certainly a reference to the physical scars resulting from his suffering-persecution, perhaps even the suffering (discipline) he has had to endure as a transgressor of the Law. Hence, like Christ, Paul too appears in his suffering as one cursed by the Law.

Within the rhetorical and polemical context of Galatians, then, Paul intentionally melds cruciformity and curse. But he does so in a way that is quite at odds with what the Agitators were suggesting. Suffering does not necessarily imply a curse. When suffering is endured for the sake of others, in dependence upon the Spirit and in submission to God's will, Paul insists it should not be understood as the evidence of a curse, but as the manifestation of love. The problem with a life of cruciformity, however, is that it often has the *appearance* of a cursed life, since the ignominy of suffering is so easily confused with the workings of a curse. As we saw in Chapter 4, this was probably a temptation that confronted the Galatians during their initial encounter with Paul (4.13); and it may well have been this precise temptation to which they have currently succumbed by listening to the Agitators' polemics about the curse of the Law and its relation to suffering.

Hence, although bearing one another's burdens will certainly expose the Galatians to further suffering and thereby possibly exacerbate their own sense of insecurity about the curse of the Law, Paul nevertheless assures them that this mode of existence can fully satisfy the Law's demands. Just as they need not submit to circumcision in order to fulfil the whole Law (5.13-14), so too they do not need to shy away from suffering for the sake of the cross for fear that this represents divine displeasure. If they will only return to the pattern of life with which they began, a life characterised by bearing burdens after the manner of Christ Jesus himself (cf. 3.1-5; 4.13-14), they do not need to fear the curse of the Law.

The Law of the crucified and cursed Christ

When Paul's call to bear one another's burdens is understood as a call to cruciform, suffering love, the fulfilment of the Law of Christ can be viewed from a fresh angle. *Who is the Christ of Galatians?* Any answer to this question can hardly overlook Paul's repeated reference to Christ's death by crucifixion. As we have seen, in fact, the letter is littered with references to the crucifixion (cf. 2.19-20, 21; 3.1, 13; 5.11, 24; 6.12, 14, 17; cf. 1.4; 4.4-5). Or as R. Bryant has observed: 'the Crucified Christ is a central and persistent theme throughout Galatians'.[106] But more than that: the crucified Christ is also the *cursed* Christ (3.13; 4.4-5).

---

[106] Bryant, *Crucified Christ* (2000), 192 (see 163–94).

By living a life of cruciform, suffering love, which to others may in fact look like a cursed life, the Galatians will thus fulfil the Law of the crucified and cursed Christ. The irony in all of this is simply brilliant: the Galatians must embrace the reality of cruciformity as the very means by which the Law is fulfilled and the Law's curse avoided. But so too is the polemical force of this formulation: within the context of the Galatian crisis, where the curse of the Law is probably being linked with suffering-persecution, Paul does not shrink from calling the Galatians to cruciform, suffering love for the sake of others. Even though the Agitators were probably raising doubts about the Galatians' own suffering, Paul nevertheless admonishes them to pattern their lives after the crucified and cursed Christ, who now provides the paradigmatic example of how to love (or bear burdens), which will fulfil the Law of Moses.

Conclusion

Before drawing this chapter to a close I should say that I have deliberately left as an open question how it is that Paul can say that by serving one another in love his uncircumcised Gentile converts will fulfil the whole Law of Moses (5.14; cf. 6.2). This is perhaps the perennial issue in the age-old debate about Paul and the Law, and I have no intention of proffering another solution at this point. To do so would be to move well beyond the scope of this study. However, the decision to bracket this issue, so to speak, is not merely a tactical move; it reflects the conviction that the conclusions reached in this chapter are amenable to a number of different proposed solutions to the problem of Paul and the Law. There are, of course, certain views that might tolerate the argument of this chapter (and the work as a whole) better than others; and some positions on Paul and the Law will no doubt put more stock by certain interpretations of 5.14 or 6.2 that I may have called into question in this chapter (e.g., that the Law of Christ refers to something other than the Law of Moses). Nevertheless, my basic claim that Paul's references to the fulfilment of the Law are intended at least in part to answer the threat of the curse of the Law can conceivably be integrated into a number of different working hypotheses on the much broader (and seemingly intractable) question of Paul and the Law, whether Lutheran, Reformed, New Perspective or other.

In this chapter we have explored the rationale for Paul's two references to the fulfilment of the Law in 5.13–6.10. My findings agree in at least one important respect with the consensus: both references to the fulfilment of the Law are highly relevant to the situation of crisis. Paul is not (merely) warding off potential misunderstandings or (simply) affirming the ethical implications of justification by faith in relation to the Law. Where I chart a different course, however, is in my understanding of the relevance of these two affirmations within the context of the Galatian crisis. I have tried to show that there is good reason to think that Paul uses the language of the fulfilment of the Law to answer the threat of the curse of the Law and to assure the Galatians that love fulfils the Law and thereby avoids the Law's curse.

Paul evidently believed that the only way to avoid the curse of the Law was to fulfil the Law. While Christ has redeemed us from the Law's curse (3.13), he has done so neither by eradicating any possible threat of a curse nor by circumventing the Law altogether. Instead, his death has allowed, as Paul says, the sending of the Spirit (3.14; cf. 4.5-6), who in turn enables believers to fulfil the Law and thereby avoid the Law's curse. Precisely what this entails Paul explains at greater length in 5.16-24, the passage to which we shall turn in the following chapter.

Chapter 6

The Curse of the Law and the Leading of the Spirit

> There is therefore now no condemnation for those who are in Christ Jesus.
> For the Law of the Spirit of life set me free from the Law of sin and of death (Rom 8.1-2).

While Paul's two references to the fulfilment of the Law in 5.14 and 6.2 have perhaps attracted more scholarly attention, the two references to the Law in 5.18 and 5.23 arguably have a greater impact upon how one understands the rationale for these four references to the Law in 5.13–6.10. Some scholars rely heavily, in fact, upon Paul's two references to Law in 5.18 and 5.23 for their understanding of his aims in the ethical section of the letter. Often these two verses are viewed as making essentially the same point: 'Where the Spirit is at work, the Law is superfluous'.[1]

Part of the purpose of this chapter is to scrutinise this way of reading of 5.18 and 5.23 and thereby call into question the understanding of 5.13–6.10 which it serves to support. The thesis of this chapter is that 5.18 and 5.23 serve, not as confirmation of the superfluity of the Law for Christian living, but as affirmations of the sufficiency of the Spirit to keep one from coming under the curse of the Law. I shall begin with a close exegesis of both 5.18 and 5.23 in context and demonstrate that both references to the Law refer to the curse of the Law. This has significant implications for how one understands the thrust of this passage and, in turn, the overall purpose of 5.13–6.10 within the letter. I shall then seek to bolster this reading and draw out further implications by showing that Paul is heavily indebted to OT wilderness narrative traditions in 5.16-24, which he uses to reinforce both his warning about the 'works of the flesh' (5.19-21) and his affirmation about the sufficiency of the Spirit (5.16-18, 22-23).

'If you are led by the Spirit, you are not under Law' (5.18)

In 5.16-24 Paul goes on to explain (λέγω δέ, 5.16) how it is that the Galatians can avoid allowing their freedom to become an 'occasion for the flesh' (5.13b) and, instead, serve one another in love, which thereby fulfils the Law

---

[1] Williams, *Galatians* (1997), 152. For some this implies that the Spirit *replaces* the Law; for others this entails the superfluity of *all* law.

(5.13c-14).² The basic thrust of Paul's explanation is captured in a single, opening remark: πνεύματι περιπατεῖτε (5.16a).³ This comes with a robust assurance of the fact that walking by the Spirit is effective for repelling the 'desire of the flesh' (5.16b). Paul then explains how this can be true in 5.17, though the precise point of this remark continues to elude interpreters. It is clear that Paul describes a mutual antagonism between the flesh and the Spirit (ταῦτα γὰρ ἀλλήλοις ἀντίκειται), but how this serves as an explanation of the assurance he provides in 5.16 is not entirely clear. Regardless, the thrust of the passage is clear enough: the Galatians should walk by the Spirit for only then will they be able to avoid fulfilling the 'desire of the flesh' (5.16b).

After the explanation of 5.17, Paul goes on in 5.18 to relate walking by the Spirit to the Law: 'And (δέ) if you are led by the Spirit [and, as a result do not carry out the 'desire of the flesh'], then you are not under Law (οὐκ ἐστὲ ὑπὸ νόμον)' (5.18).⁴ While the appearance of the Law in the discussion at this point often surprises interpreters, it is intended to support the exhortation of 5.16 by providing a rationale for *why* the Galatians would want to follow the leading of the Spirit. To be 'led by the Spirit' (5.18) is another way to describe the dynamic involved in 'walking by the Spirit' (5.16), perhaps highlighting the divine source or origin of this new obedience (cf. 5.22-23, 25).⁵ But what does Paul mean when he asserts that if the Galatians are led by the Spirit, they are not 'under Law'?⁶ Within this context, the phrase 'under Law' is usually understood to refer to: (1) the 'legalistic' system associated with the Law;⁷ (2) the condemnation or curse of the Law;⁸ or (3) the guiding, restraining influence of the Law.⁹

---

² The next two sections of this chapter are adapted from Wilson 'Under Law' (2006).

³ On the importance of this imperative not only for Galatians, but for Pauline ethics in general, see Betz, *Galatians* (1979), 277; Longenecker, *Galatians* (1990), 244; Fee, *Presence* (1994), 429.

⁴ Here taking δέ as consecutive; Longenecker, *Galatians* (1990), 246. If one reads 5.17 as suggesting behavioural failure, as does Martyn, *Galatians* (1997), 495, then there would be stronger grounds for seeing 5.18 as in contrast to 5.17.

⁵ Eckert, *Verkündigung* (1971), 136.

⁶ Wilder, *Echoes* (2001), 5–33, offers a more extended discussion of the history of the interpretation of 5.18 and a slightly different taxonomy of views.

⁷ Burton, *Galatians* (1921), 303: 'that legalistic system from which it is the apostle's aim to keep his readers free'. See also Oepke, *Galater* (1984), 176; Schlier, *Galater* (1962), 250; Cole, *Galatians* (1989), 209.

⁸ Borse, *Standort* (1972), 60–1; Ridderbos, *Galatians* (1953), 204–5; Hong, *Law* (1993), 175. Cf. Wilder, *Echoes* (2001), 25–7.

⁹ Betz, *Galatians* (1979), 281; Barclay, *Obeying* (1988), 116; Martyn, *Galatians* (1997), 496; Longenecker, *Galatians* (1990), 246; Dunn, *Galatians* (1993), 301. Williams, *Galatians* (1997), 149, speaks about not being under the authority of the Law, but the implication is that one need not look to the Law for guidance; it has become superfluous.

Recently, scholars have tended away from views (1) and (2), since, among other things, they are thought to fall foul of Paul's description of Christ as having come 'under Law' (4.4).[10] Many opt, instead, for view (3), which is not only free of this particular difficulty, but can also make sense of Paul's other four uses of the phrase in Galatians. On this reading, the point of 5.18 is that for those who are in possession of the Spirit, there is no need for the guiding, restraining influence of the Law. This is often related to 5.14, where love is said to fulfil the Law; hence, the leading of the Spirit replaces the Law because the Spirit itself achieves what the Law is intended to do: curb the flesh (5.16) and create a loving community (5.22-23; 5.14). According to Barclay: 'This amounts to saying that the Spirit will provide both moral safeguards and moral directives which render the law superfluous'.[11]

As I have already mentioned, this reading of 5.18 significantly shapes how many scholars understand the thrust of 5.13–6.10 as a whole. Paul needs to provide the Galatians with assurances of the sufficiency of the Spirit to enable them to live out the Christian life, especially in light of the Galatians' present interest in turning to the observance of the Jewish Law to help give them some moral directives for daily living. Paul insists, however, that the Law is no longer needed as an ethical resource since the Galatians have the Spirit. In short, Paul is saying: 'for those who are led by the Spirit, the Law is not necessary'.[12]

While this reading of 5.18 has a certain degree of plausibility, it also has a number of problems. Perhaps the most obvious weakness with this interpretation is that it depends upon softening the implicit logical relationship between 5.18a and 5.18b, the protasis and apodosis of Paul's conditional statement.[13] This was intimated in the previous citation from Barclay, but it finds its most telling and succinct expression in Betz's paraphrase of the verse: 'If they are driven by the Spirit, they *do not need to be* under the Torah'.[14] Rather than assuring the Galatians that if they are led by the Spirit, they *are not* under Law, for Betz this verse is an assertion about the superfluity of the Law for those who are led by the Spirit: they do not *need to be* under the Law. This, however, fails to do justice to the syntax of Paul's statement and the contours of his thought. First of all, the relationship between the protasis and apodosis of 5.18 implies the basic incompatibility

---

[10] Barclay, *Obeying* (1988), 116 n. 24; Dunn, *Galatians* (1993), 301.
[11] Barclay, *Obeying* (1988), 143. Cf. Barclay, *Obeying* (1988), 116: 'They do not need the law to marshal their behaviour: in the Spirit-led battle against the flesh they have all the direction they need'.
[12] Williams, *Galatians* (1997), 149 (emphasis original).
[13] Cf. Winger, 'Law of Christ' (2000), 542; Kwon, *Eschatology* (2004), 196.
[14] Betz, *Galatians* (1979), 281 (emphasis added).

between being led by the Spirit (5.18a) and being 'under Law' (5.18b).[15] In fact, Paul presses this very point throughout the letter: life lived in Christ and by the Spirit is incompatible with existence 'under Law' (3.23-29; 4.1-11, 21-31; 5.1-6).[16] These two situations – being led by the Spirit and being 'under Law' – are mutually exclusive.

Furthermore, softening the logical link between 5.18a and 5.18b undercuts the apparent rhetorical force of the statement. What looks like a ringing affirmation of the fact that the Spirit keeps one from coming 'under Law' comes out sounding, practically speaking, more like advice to dispense with the need to observe the Law. This softening of the link between 5.18a and 5.18b is necessary, however, if the reading proposed by Betz, Barclay and others is to succeed. For their reading of this verse, as well as their reconstruction of the situation, assumes the *compatibility* of the leading of the Spirit and existence 'under Law'. The whole problem in Galatia has arisen because the Galatians want to combine the leading of the Spirit with the observance of the Law.

But if 5.18 is not an affirmation of the superfluity of the Law for Christian ethics, what is it? This verse contains, of course, Paul's fifth and final use of 'under Law' in the letter, and we may reasonably assume (unless forced to conclude otherwise) that Paul uses the expression here as he has elsewhere in the letter. As we discovered in Chapter 2, there is good reason to think that 'under Law' serves in Galatians as shorthand for 'under the curse of the Law' (3.10, 13). We also discovered that Paul uses this expression as a way to allude back to 3.10-14 and thereby invoke the curse of the Law throughout the remainder of the letter.

This implies, somewhat surprisingly, not only that Paul continues to refer to the curse of the Law in the ethical section of the letter, but also that he wants to affirm the fact that if the Galatians follow the leading of the Spirit, then they are not under the Law's curse.[17] Paul's other use of νόμος in this same context (5.23b) provides a partial confirmation of this reading of 5.18.

'The Law is not against such things' (5.23b)

Following close on the heels of his enumeration of the 'fruit of the Spirit' in 5.22-23a, Paul adds the following curious remark: κατὰ τῶν τοιούτων οὐκ

---

[15] Bruce, *Galatians* (1982), 245: 'Here existence "under law" is antithetic to being "led by the Spirit"'.

[16] Finsterbusch, *Lebensweisung* (1996), 84–96.

[17] This is by no means a completely novel interpretation of this verse. See the numerous advocates of this approach in Wilder, *Echoes* (2001), 25–27, though most of whom talk about the 'condemnation' rather than the curse of the Law.

ἔστιν νόμος (5.23b). Scholars often puzzle over the unusual syntax of this expression and the anarthrous use of νόμος. As a result, some think that Paul is here echoing a well-known proverbial maxim about the virtuous life;[18] others argue that this comment is a deliberate understatement used to highlight (albeit ironically) the moral superiority of the Spirit vis-à-vis the Law.[19] As is sometimes confessed, however, neither of these readings have proven altogether satisfying.[20]

Clarifying several exegetical questions might help point the way to a more satisfactory solution. First, is the pronoun τῶν τοιούτων neuter ('such things') or masculine ('such persons')? While this may, in the end, make little difference, a slight edge should be given to the neuter reading ('such things') because of the parallelism with τὰ τοιαῦτα in 5.21b.[21] Secondly, is the verb εἰμί used as a copula or a predicate? In other words, is Paul denying the existence of a certain kind of law (i.e., 'there is no law against such things'), or is he simply denying a particular characteristic of the Law in question, the Law of Moses (i.e., 'the Law is not against such things')?[22]

This depends, thirdly, upon whether νόμος refers to 'law' in some general sense or specifically to the Law of Moses. Some commentators point to the absence of the article as suggestive of a more generic reference, though given the flexibility of the Greek language and Paul's varied usage of the article (cf. 5.17), it would be unwise to make too much of this fact. Besides, as C. F. D. Moule points out, 'the context is a surer guide to the meaning than is the use of the article'.[23] Certainly more decisive, then, is the fact that with only a few possible exceptions (cf. 3.21; 4.21b), Paul consistently uses νόμος in Galatians to refer to the Law of Moses, the covenant stipulations given to Moses on Sinai (cf. 3.17-18).[24] Furthermore, the close parallel with 5.18 and the link with 5.14, where in both cases νόμος clearly refers to the Law of

---

[18] Longenecker, *Galatians* (1990), 263–4; Witherington, *Galatians* (1998), 411–2. A few scholars have argued that Paul is citing Aristotle *Pol.* 3.13.1284A (κατὰ τῶν τοιούτων οὐκ ἔστι νόμος); see Robb, 'Galatians V. 23' (1944–45), 279–80 and, more recently, Rastoin, *Tarse et Jérusalem* (2003), 77.

[19] Bruce, *Galatians* (1982), 255; Deidun, *New Covenant Morality* (1981), 118; Esler, *Galatians* (1998), 229; Fee, *Presence* (1994), 453. Cf. Mussner, *Galaterbrief* (1974), 389.

[20] See Barclay, *Obeying* (1988), 122–24, for a candid discussion of this problem.

[21] Barclay, *Obeying* (1988), 123 n. 51: 'Since such qualities can only be displayed in the lives of individuals there is ultimately little difference between the two readings of gender'.

[22] Winger, *What Law* (1992), 76; Williams, *Galatians* (1997), 151.

[23] Moule, *Idiom Book* (1959), 113. Cf. Winger, *What Law* (1992), 76–77: 'The question may be put thus: for Paul and his audience, was the thought of different νόμοι so readily present that it could be suggested simply by the omission of the article? Or was the reference of νόμος to Jewish νόμος so ordinary that it would be presumed unless, as in Gal 3:21b, either Paul's expression or the context required another understanding?'.

[24] Hong, *Law* (1993), 122–3.

Moses, strongly suggest that this use of νόμος in 5.23b (albeit syntactically somewhat unusual) is another reference to that same Law, the Law of Moses.

It is best, then, to interpret this expression as a comment about the relationship between the Law of Moses and the 'fruit of the Spirit', and as such closely paralleling 5.18.[25] Paul is thus saying that the Law of Moses is not 'against' the 'fruit of the Spirit'.[26] But what does this mean? We find an initial clue from the fact that in both the NT and the LXX, the formula κατά + genitive is sometimes used in forensic contexts to identify the object of (quasi-)legal charges or accusations.[27] Similar ways of speaking can also be found in the legal speeches of Demosthenes.[28] Philo and Josephus may also provide a clue, since both authors occasionally use κατά + genitive to identify the recipients of a curse.[29] Josephus, for example, says of Joshua's cursing of Jericho: κατὰ τῶν οἰκισόντων . . . ἀρὰς ἔθετο ('upon those who would settle there . . . he pronounced imprecations', *A.J.* 5.31).

One should also note that the preposition κατά appears to have been particularly at home in the world of discourse associated with curses and cursing. Curse tablets were often referred to, sometimes within the texts themselves, as καταθέματα. Similarly, the verb καταγράφω was often used as a way to refer to the practice of cursing. Furthermore, a whole range of curse terminology appears, at some stage, to have come into contact with the preposition κατά: so, for example, καταθέματα, καταγράφω, κατατίθημι, κατάθεμα, καταθεματίζω. It may, in fact, have been the case that this terminology only came to be used for curses and cursing after the noun ἀνάθεμα had taken on particularly negative connotations, something which was signalled in the development of the term by the addition of the preposition κατά.[30]

---

[25] The close link between 5.18 and 5.23b is suggested by: (1) their shared use of νόμοβ, (2) their similar relating of 'law' and Spirit, and (3) their similar rhetorical functions (i.e., as affirmations or assurances). Dunn, *Galatians* (1993), 313, proposes an abccba pattern in 5.18–23, where 5.18 matches 5.23b. Cf. Thomson, *Chiasmus* (1995), 136–39; similarly, Bligh, *Galatians* (1969), 435, 446.

[26] Winger, 'Law of Christ' (2000), 543; Martyn, *Galatians* (1997), 499.

[27] Num 12.1; 21.5; Deut 19.15, 16; Acts 24.1; 25.2, 15, 27; Rom 8.33; Col 2.14; 1 Tim 5.19; Rev 2.4, 14, 20. Cf. Campbell, 'Against Such Things' (1996), 271.

[28] Demosthenes, *Naus.* 18–20; *Theocr.* 51–52: 'Against persons of this class [the law] ordains that there shall be a criminal information and other legal penalties' (ἀλλ' ἔνδειξιν κελεύει καὶ ἄλλας τιμωρίας κατὰ τούτων εἶναι).

[29] Philo, *Praem.* 126; Josephus, *A.J.* 7.39.

[30] Pardee, 'Curse that Saves' (1995), 169. As she notes, the association of κατά with cursing language may be due to the fact that curse tablets were often buried and thereby consigned to the underworld.

While these observations are admittedly only suggestive, they may point the way to a refined understanding of Paul's enigmatic remark in 5.23b: it is another reference to the curse of the Law.[31] Paul is therefore affirming the fact that the curse of the Law does not fall upon the kind of behaviour that is enabled by the Spirit and embodied in love (5.22; cf. 5.5-6; 5.14). This reading, of course, tallies nicely with the interpretation of 5.18 offered above. In fact, it reiterates basically the same point made in 5.18: those who are led by the Spirit (5.18), and whose lives are characterised by the 'fruit of the Spirit' (5.22-23), are not under the curse of the Law.

This reading also presupposes that those who are led by the Spirit actually satisfy the Law's demands. And as we saw in the previous chapter, this is one of the key points of Paul's two references to the fulfilment of the Law in 5.14 and 6.2. While a number of scholars note that walking by the Spirit (5.16) leads to the fulfilment of the Law (5.14), which in turn implies that the Galatians are not 'under Law' (5.18), they often interpret this as a statement about the superfluity of the Law, rather than as an affirmation of the fact that the leading of the Spirit enables one to avoid the curse of the Law. Those who are led by the Spirit fulfil the Law (5.14; 6.2) and thereby avoid its curse (5.18; 5.23). For when the empowering agency of the Spirit excludes the 'desire of the flesh' (5.16), believers are enabled to serve one another through love and thus fulfil the Law (5.13-14; 6.1-2; cf. 5.5-6).

Treating both 5.18 and 5.23b as references to the curse of the Law finds support from the concluding comment Paul appends to his list of the 'works of the flesh' in 5.19-21: οἱ τὰ τοιαῦτα πράσσοντες βασιλείαν θεοῦ οὐ κληρονομήσουσιν (5.21b). Here Paul repeats his earlier warning that those who practice the kinds of 'vices' mentioned in 5.19-21 will in no way share in the eschatological inheritance (6.7-8; 4.30). Given the future-orientation of the warning in 5.21b, one would expect Paul to balance this in 5.23b with a promise that those whose lives are characterised by the 'fruit of the Spirit' will assuredly enter into the 'kingdom of God'. Instead, we see Paul doing again in 5.23b what he has already done in 5.18: he assures the Galatians that the 'fruit of the Spirit' do not come under the censure of the Law, the Law's curse (5.23b). This pair of present-oriented assurances about the curse of the Law has obvious significance for our understanding of Paul's aims in 5.13–6.10. We shall return to this shortly. For now we should note the similarities between what Paul says in 5.19-21 and 5.22-23, as illustrated on the following page with the implied 'steps' in brackets.

---

[31] Ridderbos, *Galatians* (1953), 208; Westerholm, 'Fulfilling the Law' (1986–87), 236; Ebeling, *Gospel* (1985), 257; Eckstein, *Verheissung* (1996), 255-56.

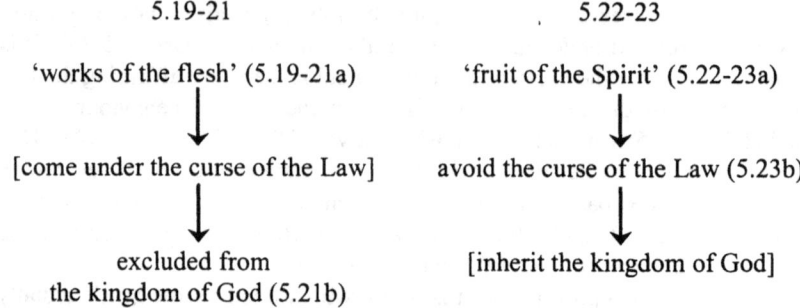

Paul's point, then, is that just as those who practice the works of the flesh are under a curse and will therefore not inherit the 'kingdom of God' (5.19-21), so too those who exhibit the 'fruit of the Spirit' are *not* under a curse and can therefore expect to inherit the 'kingdom of God' (5.22-23; cf. 5.5-6).[32] Hence, in 5.19-23 Paul elaborates the thesis-like statement of 5.18 that those who are led by the Spirit are not under the curse of the Law. He begins in 5.19-21 by explicating the converse of the conditional statement of 5.18: those who practice the works of the flesh are under a curse and will therefore not inherit the 'kingdom of God' (5.21b). In other words, if the Galatians do not follow the leading of the Spirit, they can expect a curse and, as a result, exclusion from the eschatological inheritance. Alternatively, in 5.22-23 Paul further explicates the conditional statement of 5.18 itself: those who are led by the Spirit (5.18) and exhibit the 'fruit of the Spirit' (5.22-23a) are not under a curse (5.23b) and will thus receive an eschatological reward (cf. 6.7-8).

We may now return to the implications of Paul's two references to the curse of the Law in 5.18 and 5.23b. Paul appears to want to assure the Galatians that the leading of the Spirit and love, which is the chief mark of the Spirit (cf. 5.22; 5.5-6), are sufficient to enable them to avoid the curse of the Law (5.18; 5.23b). If the Galatians follow the leading of the Spirit, they need not entertain any doubts about the Law's curse. If they succumb, however, to the 'desire of the flesh' (5.16) and manifest its works (5.19-21), which is what they appear to be doing (5.15, 26), Paul can only warn them that they will be excluded from the 'kingdom of God' (5.21b; cf. Matt 25.41).

While it is important to stress Paul's emphasis upon providing the Galatians with present assurances about the Spirit's ability to enable them to avoid the Law's curse, we should not let this overshadow Paul's equally strong interest in warning the Galatians about the consequences of succumbing to the flesh and its desire. The centralised warning in 5.21b

---

[32] Kamlah, *Paränese* (1964), 18: 'Wie der Lasterkatalog in V. 21 mit einer Verdammungsandrohung, so gipfelt der Tugendkatalog also in einer Verheißung der Freiheit vom Fluch des Gesetzes, oder positiv gesagt in einer Heilszusage'.

underscores this point,[33] as do a number of similar warnings elsewhere in 5.13–6.10 (cf. 5.13b, 15; 5.25-26; 6.7-8).[34]

There is an irony in this dual-aspect of warning and assurance in this passage. On the one hand, Paul assures the Galatians that the leading of the Spirit will enable them to avoid the curse of the Law (5.18; 5.23b). On the other hand, he warns them, at least implicitly, that the works of the flesh will only be met with the Law's curse and thus exclusion from the 'kingdom of God' (5.21b). Hence, while the Galatians were attracted to circumcision at least in part as a way to ensure that they avoid coming under a curse, Paul warns them that unless they get back on track with following the leading of the Spirit, that which they are trying to avoid will be the very thing that comes upon them: the curse of the Law. While the immediate aim, then, of this passage is to call the Galatians to 'walk by the Spirit' (5.16), this serves both to warn and to assure the Galatians about the curse of the Law: if they follow the leading of the Spirit, they are exempt from the Law's curse (5.18; 5.22-23), whereas if they succumb to the 'desire of the flesh' (5.16), they will come under a curse and face exclusion from the 'kingdom of God' (5.19-21).

Wilderness Topography in 5.16-24

Having argued that Paul's two references to the Law in 5.18 and 5.23 refer to the curse of the Law, I shall now bolster this interpretation by exploring how OT wilderness traditions appear to have at least partially informed what Paul says in 5.16-24. I shall argue, in fact, that Paul uses the wilderness narratives of the OT in order to reinforce the consequences of the two options now confronting the Galatians: either walking by the Spirit or submitting to the 'desire of the flesh' (5.16), both of which, as we have seen, Paul relates to the curse of the Law.

In a recent article, I have argued that part of Paul's rhetorical strategy to redress the developing crisis within the Galatian churches is to portray the Galatians, like Israel of old, as on the verge of apostatising in the wilderness.[35] After having been miraculously delivered from servitude through an Exodus-like redemption in Christ (1.1-4; 4.3-7; 4.21-5.1a; 5.13a), the Galatians are now contemplating a return to Egyptian-like bondage (1.6-7; 4.8-9; 5.1b). As a result, Paul tries to exercise whatever moral leverage he can over the situation, colouring his rebukes and warnings with language that

---

[33] Thomson, *Chiasmus* (1995), 142–44, supports this claim by contending that the warning of 5.21b is the central element of a well-developed chiasmus from 5.13–6.2 (see 116–51).

[34] Note my criticism of Barclay's handling of this passage in Chapter 1.

[35] Wilson, 'Wilderness Apostasy' (2004), 550–71.

evokes the Israelites' own tragic wilderness defection and ultimate disinheritance. He thus 'scripts' the Galatians into the role of wilderness wanderers, presumably because he thinks this will clarify for them the seriousness of their present situation and elicit from them the desired response: a return to the Pauline gospel (1.6-7; 5.7).

While we tend to think of the whole of 5.13-24 primarily as a piece of pastoral exhortation, Martyn correctly notes that this section is cast mostly in the indicative; Paul speaks in fundamentally descriptive terms.[36] Paul is concerned, then, according to Martyn, not so much to exhort the Galatians to follow a certain course of action as to provide them with a 'map' of the world in which they actually live, replete with topographical details of the apocalyptic battle in which they are engaged. But for Martyn it is quite important to realise that the topographic details of this map come *not from Scripture*, but from catalogues of vices and virtues circulating within the Greco-Roman and Jewish traditions – albeit significantly recast in view of Paul's apocalyptic convictions.[37] 'The result', writes Martyn, 'is a portrait of daily life that is appropriate to a group of soldiers who are on a field of apocalyptic battle, and who are led there not by a set of regulations, but rather by the power that is certain to be the victor on that battlefield, the Spirit of Christ'.[38]

While agreeing with Martyn that this section provides the Galatians with a particular topography, and without necessarily wanting to deny the apocalyptic cast of Paul's thought,[39] I shall argue in what follows, somewhat in contrast to Martyn, that because Paul conceives of (or at least portrays) the Galatians as occupying a 'narrative location' somewhere in the wilderness, he derives at least some of the topographical details for his map from the OT wilderness narratives. Hence, while Martyn may be right to question whether Paul is interested in providing the Galatians with a 'nomistic, moral discourse' centred around virtues and vices,[40] there is reason to question whether Paul sits as loosely to Scripture in this passage as Martyn wants to suggest. More importantly for the purposes of this chapter, appreciating Paul's debt to the wilderness narratives in this passage reinforces the fact that Paul here has in mind the consequences of the leading of the Spirit for the curse of the Law.

---

[36] Martyn, *Galatians* (1997), 482. Fee, *Presence* (1994), 424, likewise notes the 'general paucity of imperatives' in 5.13-26.
[37] Martyn, *Galatians* (1997), 483–84.
[38] Martyn, *Galatians* (1997), 483–84.
[39] For a useful overview and assessment of scholarly interest in apocalyptic in the twentieth century, see Matlock, *Apocalyptic Paul* (1996). For his interaction with Martyn in particular, see Matlock, *Apocalyptic Paul* (1996), 308–13.
[40] Martyn, *Galatians* (1997), 484.

The 'works of the flesh' and disinheritance (5.19-21)

Even though there are no obvious verbal links with the wilderness narratives in 5.13-26, one has reason to suspect they may still be in view.[41] In 5.13b Paul warns the Galatians: 'Only do not use your freedom as an occasion for the flesh',[42] a rather cryptic statement made more concrete by the vivid warning of 5.15: 'But if you bite and devour one another, take heed that you are not consumed by one another'.[43] Paul here likely follows the diatribe style of characterising undesirable behaviour as animalistic.[44] A key question is whether the warning in 5.15 implies actual or only potential developments within the Galatian churches.

A close inspection of the 'works of the flesh' enumerated in 5.19-21 suggests that communal infighting was a live issue for the Galatians. Paul's list focuses both structurally and numerically upon those vices naturally associated with situations of social discord. Eight of the fifteen vices mentioned (i.e., enmity, strife, jealousy, fits of anger, rivalries, dissension, divisions, envy) are social in orientation, and their centralised location gives them emphasis.[45] That communal infighting was a problem is also suggested by the parallel warning Paul issues in 5.26: 'Let us not become conceited, provoking one another, envying one another'. The Galatians, then, perhaps as a result of the influence of those heralding 'another gospel' (1.6-7; cf. 5.7), were beset by attitudes and actions that were destroying their social cohesion and loving service (cf. 5.13c-14, 6.1-10).

Now the relevance of the wilderness narratives for the pastoral situation in Galatia is not hard to find. Even a cursory reading of Exodus-Numbers reveals the fact that these same sorts of social vices characterised the wilderness generation: Miriam and Aaron's challenging of the authority of Moses (Num 12); Korah, Dathan, Abiram and the 250 chiefs instigating an uprising (Num 16–17); the rebellion of the congregation at the report of the spies (Num 13–14); the repeated episodes of grumbling and disaffection (Exod 16–17; Num 11). Perhaps Paul's warnings to the Galatians not to allow their freedom to become 'an occasion for the flesh' (5.13), to avoid 'biting and devouring one another' (5.15), to put away the 'works of the flesh' (5.19-21) and to stop

---

[41] Wilder, *Echoes* (2001), has tried to demonstrate that Paul's language of the leading of the Spirit in 5.18 is indebted to an Exodus matrix of thought. His thesis is indeed suggestive and, if correct, would considerably strengthen my argument.

[42] On the grammatical and lexical issues in 5.13, see Longenecker, *Galatians* (1990), 239.

[43] Intriguingly, the same terminology used in 5.15 is used of the 'biting' (δάκνω) of the serpents (Num 21.6, 8-9; cf. Lev 26.22, 38; Deut 8.15; Jer 8.17) and the 'devouring' (κατεσθίω) of the fire of judgement (Num 11.1; 16.35; 26.10) that came in response to the Israelites' rebellion in the wilderness.

[44] Betz, *Galatians* (1979), 276–77. For other possible examples, see Phil 3.2; Matt 7.15; Luke 13.32; 2 Pet 2.22.

[45] Barclay, *Obeying* (1988), 152–53.

'provoking and envying one another' (5.26) are intended to evoke the story of *Israel's own communal infighting* during her wilderness sojourn.[46]

This initial suggestion finds some support from a close inspection of the particular behaviours Paul specifies in 5.19-21. Unfortunately, there are no obvious verbal links between Paul's vice list and the language used to describe the failings of the wilderness generation in the LXX. Nonetheless, the conceptual parallels are rather striking. We have already noted the concentration on vices dealing with communal infighting and how this same sort of description might apply equally as well to the wilderness generation. What stands out, in particular, are the specific issues of rivalry and dissension within the camp and evidently within the Galatian churches (cf. 5.15, 26). Num 11.4-35, for example, describes how the so-called 'rabble' (אספסף, ὁ ἐπίμικτος) instigate a rebellion against Moses and challenge his provision for the people.[47] Num 12 continues along similar lines with the story of Miriam and Aaron, who question whether Moses is justified in his exclusive claim to serve as the mouthpiece for Yahweh (12.1-16). This then reaches a crescendo with Korah's rebellion (Num 16.1-35). Not insignificantly, the text says they 'became arrogant' (16.1b)[48] and 'rose up against Moses' (16.2) in order to challenge his exclusive claim to authority in light of their own purported equal sharing in the divine presence (16.3).

Early Jewish and Christian reception of these narratives may shed some light on the claim that Paul uses them to confront the situation in Galatia. For example, Psa 106.16 identifies 'envy' (קנא, παροργίζω) as the root cause of Korah's rebellion against Moses and Aaron. This was for Josephus also the reason for the debacle:

> Korah, one of the most eminent of the Hebrews by reason both of his birth and of his riches, a capable speaker and very effective in addressing a crowd, seeing Moses established in the highest honours, was sorely envious (εἶχεν ὑπὸ φθόνου); for he was of the same tribe and indeed his kinsman one of the most eminent of the Hebrews (LCL: *A.J.* 4.14).

Sirach 45.18 similarly explains the uprising against Aaron: 'Outsiders conspired against him, and envied (ἐζήλωσαν) him in the wilderness, Dathan and Abiram and their followers and the company of Korah, in wrath (θυμοῦ)

---

[46] One wonders whether Paul understood his relationship with the Galatians in terms of Moses' with the wilderness generation. On Paul's portrayal of himself as a 'second' Moses, primarily in relation to 2 Cor 3.4-18, see Bammel, 'Paulus' (1997), 205–14; note also the careful assessment of Hafemann, *History of Israel* (1995), especially 449–51.

[47] Ashley, *Numbers* (1993), 224, observes how Miriam and Aaron's complaint about Moses' foreign wife (11.1) only concealed 'the deeper problem of jealousy over their brother's unique status before God in the community (see v. 2)'.

[48] For the difficulties with this expression in Hebrew, see Ashley, *Numbers* (1993), 298 n. 2; the LXX does not translate this phrase, perhaps because it was implied in the following expression: 'And they rose up against Moses' (16.2).

and anger (ὀργή)'.[49] *1 Clement* invokes the rebellion of both Miriam and Aaron (Num 11) and Dathan and Abiram (Num 16) as a way to rebuke the Corinthians for their 'unholy sedition' (1.1), which is fraught with 'jealousy (ζῆλος) and envy (φθόνος), strife (ἔρις) and sedition (στάσις), persecution and disorder, war and captivity' (3.2). Evidently, then, these episodes from Israel's wilderness experience were paradigmatic within both early Jewish and Christian traditions, particularly inasmuch as they could be used to offer a polemical critique of infighting and rebellion (cf. *m. 'Abot.* 5.17).[50] Paul appears to be doing something similar with the wilderness traditions as he confronts the situation in Galatia.

Although there may be some suggestive conceptual overlap between Israel's wilderness rebellion and a number of the 'works of the flesh' which depict social discord and enmity, the remaining seven vices mentioned appear to deal with practices traditionally associated (at least by Jews) with pagan excess: fornication, impurity, licentiousness, idolatry, sorcery, drunkenness and carousing (5.19, 21). B. Witherington makes the interesting observation that these behaviours have to do with 'sins associated with the sort of κοινωνία that went on in pagan temples'.[51] It is intriguing to note that several of these 'vices' are conceptually quite closely related to that which went on during Israel's two great acts of wilderness apostasy: namely, during the sin with the Golden Calf (Exod 32.1-35) and the fornication with the daughters of Moab (Num 25.1-5). These two incidents are themselves closely related. The parallels include: (1) the worship of foreign gods (Exod 32.8; Num 25.2), (2) God's wrath being appeased by slaughter (Exod 32.26-28; Num 25.7-8), and (3) the tribe of Levi being singled out for special recognition (Exod 32.29; Num 25.11-13).[52] These two episodes may, in fact, form an *inclusio* around the whole of the wilderness narrative: the sin with the Golden Calf constituting the first and archetypal act of apostasy-idolatry, while Israel's whoring with the daughters of Moab represents their final, climactic act of covenant apostasy and defection. Indeed, the warning of Exod 34.15-16 against 'playing the harlot' with the foreign gods of the land into which Israel is about to enter is probably intended to link this narrative with the apostasy at Moab.

Moreover, both cases of wilderness apostasy involved cultic feasting, where the sacrifices offered were then consumed by the worshipers. In fact, one can detect several explicit verbal links between these two episodes, especially the common motif of eating (ἐσθίω). Exod 32.6 reads: 'So the next

---

[49] I owe this reference to Scott, *2 Corinthians* (1998), 247.
[50] For a survey of material relating to Korah in Rabbinic literature, see Draper, 'Korah' (1991), 150–74.
[51] Witherington, *Galatians* (1998), 397.
[52] Ashley, *Numbers* (1993), 515.

day they rose early and offered burnt offerings and brought peace offerings (προσήνεγκεν θυσίαν); and the people sat down to eat and to drink (ἐκάθισεν ὁ λαὸς φαγεῖν καὶ πιεῖν), and rose up to play'. No doubt intentionally alluding to the Golden Calf episode, Num 25.2 echoes this language and association of ideas: 'For they invited the people to the sacrifices of their gods, and the people ate their sacrifices (ἔφαγεν ὁ λαὸς τῶν θυσιῶν αὐτῶν and bowed down to their idols (προσεκύνησαν τοῖς εἰδώλοις αὐτῶν)'.

Furthermore, while the depiction of the idolatry with the daughters of Moab in Num 25 obviously involves πορνεία (cf. ἐκπορνεύω, Num 25.1), the LXX of Exod 32 probably also envisages a drunken orgy surrounding the incident with the Golden Calf. While it is difficult to determine exactly what is entailed by the phrase 'and the people sat down to eat and to drink and rose up to play' (32.6), at least some later Jewish interpreters understood this to refer to a drunken orgy, either on the basis of the verb 'to play' (צחק; παίζω),[53] or in conjunction with the mention of 'sounds of singing' coming from the camp in 32.18, which the LXX, at least, interprets as sounds of revelry and debauchery by linking it with drunkenness: 'the sound of those who begin with wine' (φωνὴν ἐξαρξόντων οἴνου).

Also, it may not be entirely fortuitous that Paul begins and ends his list in 5.19-21 with vices associated with pagan idolatry and excess. It is interesting to note that just as the wilderness narrative begins and ends with two paradigmatic episodes of idolatry-apostasy, while the central section recounts the continual disaffection of the people, so too Paul's list of the 'works of the flesh' begins and ends with vices associated with idolatry-apostasy, while the central section enumerates behaviours characteristic of an atmosphere of communal infighting and insubordination. A comparison brings this out:

The Wilderness Narratives:

    A Apostasy-Idolatry (Golden Calf, Exod 32:1-35)
       B Infighting (Num 11.1-35; 12.1-16; 13.1-14.45; 16.1-35; 21.4-9)
    A Apostasy-Idolatry (Plains of Moab, Num 25.1-5)[54]

The 'Works of the Flesh' (5.19-21):

    A Apostasy-Idolatry (πορνεία, ἀσέλγεια, εἰδωλολατρία)
       B Infighting (ἔρις, ζῆλος, θυμοί, διχοστασίαι, αἱρέσεις
    A Apostasy-Idolatry (μέθαι, κῶμοι, καὶ τὰ ὅμοια τούτοις)

---

[53] See the evidenced presented by Meeks, 'Rose Up to Play' (1982), 64–78.
[54] Budd, *Numbers* (1984), 162, provides a similar though more extensive analysis.

While the Galatians may not have actually indulged in the kinds of practices Paul mentions here, he perhaps saw their communal infighting as akin to Israel's own wilderness apostasy.

This suggestion may go some way to explain the curious warning Paul appends to the 'works of the flesh' enumerated in 5.19-21: 'I warn you, as I warned you before, that those who practice such things will not inherit the kingdom of God (οὐ κληρονομήσουσιν)' (5.21b). Interpreters often note that the language of 5.21b is unusual for Paul, particularly since elsewhere in Galatians inheritance terminology is used as 'reception of' rather than 'entrance into' (cf. 3.18, 29; 4.1, 7, 30).[55] But this peculiarity may be best explained by granting the influence of the wilderness narratives at this point, for they attest to the failure of the Israelites to *enter the Land* precisely because they 'practised' the very vices Paul *now* sees at work in the Galatian churches (cf. 1 Cor 10.1-13). Paul fears, then, that the Galatians are threatening to repeat the folly of the Israelites who turned their Exodus freedom into an 'occasion for the flesh' (5.13) by giving way to the dreaded 'works of the flesh' (5.19-21; cf. 5.15, 26), which in the end brought not the inheritance of what was promised, but divine judgement (cf. 5.21b; 6.7-8). He, too, fears that if the Galatians fail to follow the leading of the Spirit, they will, like the Israelites, come under the curse of the Law and be disinherited.

The 'fruit of the Spirit' and the transformation of the wilderness (5.22-23)

We have seen that there is good reason to think that Paul's description of the 'works of the flesh' and its consequences in terms of exclusion from the 'kingdom of God' (5.19-21) are intentionally framed in terms of the wilderness narratives. But can the influence of the wilderness be detected in Paul's language of the 'fruit of the Spirit' in 5.22-23?

Barclay is probably correct to draw attention to the OT background to Paul's use of fruit and Spirit language and imagery in 5.22-23.[56] In the OT Israel is often depicted as a fruit-bearing tree, or, at least, this is the ideal; the people are often upbraided for failing to produce the requisite fruit (i.e., moral qualities). But this failure is actually taken-up, transformed and becomes part of the eschatological aspirations of the prophets. For one day the Lord will revivify Israel so she becomes what she was always intended to be: an Eden-like plant whose fruitfulness stands in sharp contrast to the nation's present plight of barrenness and fruitlessness (cf. Isa 27.2-6; 37.30-32; Jer 31.27-28; 32.41; Ezek 17.22-24; Hos 14:5-8; Joel 2.18-32; Amos 9.13-15).[57] Several of these texts, moreover, ascribe this process of revivification to the agency of

---

[55] Betz, *Galatians* (1979), 285.

[56] Barclay, *Obeying* (1988), 120–21. See now especially by Beale, 'Fruit of the Spirit' (2005), 1–38.

[57] Barclay, *Obeying* (1988), 121.

the Spirit (e.g., Isa 32:15-16; Joel 2.18-32).[58] Barclay is thus right to observe: 'Paul's reference to the "fruit of the Spirit" may therefore be intended to evoke the prophetic statements on Israel and the promise for her future: such fruit is what God has always demanded of his people and what was promised for the "age to come"'.[59]

However, what should not be overlooked is the narrative location within which these prophetic depictions of eschatological restoration are said to take place. Consistently in the Prophets, especially Isa 40–66, Israel's future salvation is envisaged as a rejuvenation of their own *wilderness plight*, where the imagery of the wilderness serves as a metaphor for her own socio-political and/or moral and spiritual barrenness, which is itself often associated with the consequences of the nation coming under the curses of the covenant or the Law.[60] Hence, as LXX Isa 64.9 suggests, Jerusalem, here as a synecdoche for Israel, lies in a ruinous waste, a veritable uninhabitable wilderness, an accursed state: 'Your holy city has become a desert; Zion has become a wilderness, Jerusalem a curse (Ιερουσαλημ εἰς κατάραν)' (see also Isa 65.23). Similarly, as a result of their incessant whoring and adultery, the people of Israel have become 'like a wilderness' and 'like a parched land' (Hos 2.2-3).

In these and other texts, eschatological restoration entails socio-political and/or moral-spiritual rejuvenation, indeed regularly with the language and imagery of Eden-creation. Isa 27.6, for example, says: 'In days to come Jacob shall take root, Israel shall blossom and put forth shoots and fill the whole world with fruit'. Isa 11.1-2 couples this to the work of the Spirit: 'There shall come forth a shoot from the stump of Jesse, and a branch from his roots shall bear fruit. And the Spirit of the Lord shall rest upon him, the Spirit of wisdom and understanding, the Spirit of knowledge and the fear of the Lord' (cf. Isa 61.1-3, 11). Isa 32.14 describes Jerusalem, again as a metonymy for Israel, as a 'forsaken palace' and a 'populous city deserted'; this will persist, the prophet suggests:

> ... until the Spirit (πνεῦμα) is poured upon us from on high, and the wilderness becomes a fruitful field, and the fruitful field is deemed a forest. Then justice will dwell in the wilderness, and righteousness abide in the fruitful field. And the works of righteousness (τὰ ἔργα τῆς δικαιοσύνης) will be peace (εἰρήνη), and the result of righteousness, quietness and trust forever.

Few biblical passages rival the portrayal of the eschatological journey of the people of God found in Isa 35. In terms reminiscent of Israel's first Exodus-

---

[58] Barclay, *Obeying* (1988), 121.
[59] Barclay, *Obeying* (1988), 121.
[60] Wright, 'Wilderness' (1987), 286: 'The metaphor of the desert is applied to the people of Israel. The desert is a model of their inner state. It is also a symbol. Desert represents barrenness, lifelessness, chaos ...'.

wilderness pilgrimage, the author envisages a future trek in which the wilderness itself undergoes a miraculous transformation: 'The wilderness and the dry land shall be glad; the desert shall rejoice and blossom like crocus; it shall blossom abundantly and rejoice with joy and singing' (Isa 35.1-2); 'waters shall break forth in the wilderness, and streams in the desert' (Isa 35.6). So, too, therefore, will Israel's own experience of the wilderness be transformed and thus contrast markedly with their original wilderness sojourn: 'And the ransomed of the Lord shall return and come to Zion with singing; everlasting joy shall be upon their heads; they shall obtain gladness (ἀγαλλίαμα) and joy (εὐφροσύνη), and sorrow and sighing shall flee away' (Isa 35.10; cf. Isa 41.17-20; 55.10-13; 58.6-11).

Isa 44.1-4 provides similar hopeful assurances to Israel, though now the promise of blessing is said to extend even to Israel's descendants:

> But now hear, O Jacob my servant, Israel whom I have chosen! Thus says the Lord who made you, who formed you from the womb and will help you: Fear not, O Jacob my servant, Jeshurun whom I have chosen. For I will pour water on the thirsty land, and streams on the dry ground; I will pour out my Spirit (πνεῦμα) upon your offspring (σπέρμα), and my blessing (εὐλογίας) on your descendants. They shall spring up among the grass like willows by flowing streams.

Isa 51.1-3 is, in this regard, especially noteworthy:

> Listen to me, you who pursue righteousness, you who seek the Lord: look to the rock from which you were hewn, and to the quarry from which you were dug. Look to Abraham your father and to Sarah who bore you; for he was but one when I called him, that I might bless him (εὐλόγησα) and multiply him. For the Lord comforts Zion (Σιων); he comforts all her waste places and makes her wilderness like Eden, her desert like the garden of the Lord; joy (εὐφροσύνην) and gladness (ἀγαλλίαμα) will be found in her, thanksgiving and the voice of song.

The relevance of this passage for our discussion of Galatians should be obvious. First, it explicitly links Israel's eschatological redemption with the call of Abraham and the promise to 'bless him and multiply him' (Isa 51.2). Paul is also preoccupied with a similar link between Abraham, the promise and the pursuit of righteousness (cf. 3.6-29; 4.21-31). Secondly, this passage is closely related to Isa 54.1, which Paul cites in 4.29 to develop his allegory about Abraham's two wives and their offspring. Hays, in fact, argues that Paul's link between Sarah and a redeemed Jerusalem (Isa 54.1) presupposes Isa 51.2, even though Paul does not cite it explicitly.[61] Indeed, given the conceptual overlap between Isa 51.1-3 and Paul's allegory, one wonders whether Isa 51.1-3 was already part of the Agitators' scriptural arsenal. Thirdly, Isa 51.1-3 envisages future redemption in terms of the transformation of the wilderness into a fertile and fecund garden, where the resultant fruit is understood in terms of Israel's response of 'joy' and 'gladness' and

---

[61] Hays, *Echoes* (1989), 120.

'thanksgiving' (51.3), terms highly reminiscent of the three leading 'fruit of the Spirit': love, joy, and peace.[62] Fourthly, in describing Israel's end-time restoration with horticultural imagery, this text envisages her restoration as a return to the original situation in Eden: 'her wilderness [will be] like Eden, her desert like the garden of the Lord'. Thus, Israel's future restoration-redemption is explicitly conceived of in terms of 'new creation'; Paul's thought seems to move in a similar direction in Galatians (see 6.15 and 5.6 with the link to love in 5.22).

But Isaiah is not the only place where this matrix of ideas and images comes together. The prophet Hosea likewise understands Israel's future redemption in terms of her first redemption from Egypt. As in Isaiah, however, the motif of a recapitulation of the experience of the Exodus-wilderness is transformed; the success of Israel's second Exodus pilgrimage is now guaranteed by God's promise to create in the wilderness a faithful marriage partner for himself:

> Therefore, behold, I will allure her, and bring her into the wilderness, and speak tenderly to her. And there I will give her vineyards and make the Valley of Achor a door of hope. And there she shall answer as in the days of her youth, as at the time when she came out of the land of Egypt. And in that day, declares the Lord, you will call me 'My Husband', and no longer will you call me 'My Baal' . . . And I will betroth you to me forever. I will betroth you to me in righteousness (δικαιοσύνῃ) and in justice (κρίματι), in steadfast love (ἐλέει) and in mercy (οἰκτιρμοῖς). I will betroth you to me in faithfulness (πίστει). And you shall know the Lord (Hos 2.14-16, 19-20; LXX 2.16-18, 20-22; cf. 14.4-7).

Joel's prophetic vision of the future also contains several of these same images; he places heavy emphasis upon the revitalisation of the wilderness, here a symbol of Israel's exilic destitution as the result of the curse of the Law, through the agency of the Spirit:

> Fear not, O land: be glad and rejoice, for the Lord has done great things! Fear not, you beasts of the field, for the pastures of the wilderness are green; the tree bears its fruit; the fig tree and vine give their full yield . . . And it shall come to pass afterward, that I will pour out my Spirit on all flesh; your sons and your daughters shall prophesy, your old men shall dream dreams, and your young men shall see visions. Even on the male and female servants in those days I will pour out my Spirit (Joel 2.21-22, 28-29; LXX 2.21-22; 3.1-2; cf. Acts 2.17-21).

It is significant that many of these same texts and much of this same imagery was taken up and applied by the Dead Sea community to themselves

---

[62] In Isa 55.12-13 Israel's eschatological redemption is depicted thus: 'For you shall go out in joy (ἐν εὐφροσύνῃ; בשמחה) and be led forth in peace (ἐν χαρᾷ; בשלום); the mountains and the hills before you will break forth into singing, and all the trees of the field will clap their hands' (v.12). This text may have influenced the order in which Paul enumerates the 'fruit of the Spirit' in 5.22-23. Martyn, *Galatians* (1997), 498, has noted that the first three 'fruit of the Spirit' (love, joy, peace) are probably dependent upon Paul's 'Hebraic tradition' (cf. Deut 6.4-5; Lev 19.18).

as an eschatological outpost in the wilderness, a 'new covenant' community patiently awaiting God's final, cosmic redemption. F. Cross has described the group as 'an apocalyptic community, a *Heilsgemeinschaft*, imitating the ancient desert sojourn of Mosaic times in anticipation of the dawning Kingdom of God'.[63] Not surprisingly, then, one finds ample use of horticultural imagery by the community to depict themselves as heirs of the promises of restoration envisaged by the prophets. The community was especially fond of the self-designation, 'an everlasting planting' (1QS VIII, 5; CD I, 5–8), and saw themselves as re-planted by God in the wilderness just outside the Land, pinning and preparing for the full realisation of the restoration held forth in Israel's Scriptures, something they now experience only in part.[64]

In a recent Cambridge Ph.D. dissertation on the self-understanding of the Dead Sea community, P. N. W. Swarup has argued at length that the imagery of a plant/planting is 'one of the key metaphors which the sectarian community uses to express their self-identity'.[65] Thus, they freely appropriate fruit imagery as a way of describing their own obedience to God. 1QH^a XIV (VI), 13b–17a appears, in fact, to draw upon two of the above mentioned texts from Isaiah (27.6; 37.31-32; see 2 Kgs 19.30-31):

> he will [re]store its fruit because [...] and they will turn back according to your glorious word and they will be your princes in the lo[t of your holy ones. Their root] sprouts like the flo[wer of the field f]orever, to make a shoot grow up as the branches of the eternal plantation. And it shall cover the whole ea[rth] with its shade, [and] its [top] (shall go) up to the cloud[s], [and] its roots to the great deep. All the rivers of Eden [will water] its [bra]n[ch]es and it will be as [a great tree without] limit.[66]

Similarly, 1QH^a XVI (VIII), 4–8a says:

> I g[ive you thanks Lord] because you set me as a fountain of streams on dry ground, and a spring of water on the barren earth, and a well irrigated garden [in the desert. It will] be a planting of Cypress, Elm, with Box-tree together for your glory. Trees of life in a secret source hidden in the midst of all the tress of water and they will make a shoot grow up as the eternal planting, to take root before they sprout, and their roots they will send to a stre[am] and its stem opens to the living waters and it will be an eternal spring.[67]

Swarup rightly points out the influence of the new creation prophecy of Isa 41 on this particular passage. As he observes :

---

[63] Cross, *Ancient Library* (1995), 56; cited in Talmon, 'Desert' (1966), 62.

[64] 1QS IX, 19–20 and VIII, 13–14 describe the community's relocation into the wilderness/desert as a period of transition and preparation for the final, eschatological redemption and resettlement in the land; Talmon, 'Desert' (1966), 60. In the *War Scroll* the community is presented as 'exiles of the desert' (1QM II, 2); Talmon, 'Desert' (1966), 61.

[65] Swarup, 'Eternal Planting' (2002). See Swarup, *Eternal Planting* (2006).

[66] Translation Swarup, 'Eternal Planting' (2002), 12.

[67] Translation Swarup, 'Eternal Planting' (2002), 31.

The psalmist picks up there verses from Deutero-Isaiah and then reworks them to portray himself and his community as those through whom God had fulfilled what he had promised [cf. Isa 44.3; 49.10]. The New Creation motif is taken up by the psalmist. There is a making new of the old. The dry ground will become a fountain of streams; the barren earth will become a well-irrigated garden. There is a miraculous *transformation of the desert* as the DSS community continues to experience the transforming power of God.[68]

There are a number of suggestive implications here for what Paul may be doing in Galatians. Has Paul picked up and subtly reworked prophetic traditions for his own community as a way of reinforcing the transforming power of God that enables the miraculous rejuvenation of the desert as they follow the leading of the Spirit away from Egyptian-like bondage (3.22; 5.24; 4.8-9; 5.1; 1.4) and into the eschatological inheritance (5.5; 5.21; 6.8)?

If, as I have argued, the motif of the transformation of the accursed wilderness informs Paul's language of the 'fruit of the Spirit' in 5.22-23, it would reinforce his point that the Law does not pronounce a curse upon the 'fruit of the Spirit' (5.23b). This would in turn tally with Martyn's observation that by analogy to the pattern in 5.19-21, where the 'works of the flesh' are followed by an eschatological threat (5.21b), one might expect the same from Paul in 5.22-23: an eschatological promise attached to the 'fruit of the Spirit' as counterpoise to the threat attached to the 'works of the flesh'.[69] In fact, Paul's comment in 5.23b may serve as a counter-promise to the warning of 5.21b. Just as those who practice the 'works of the flesh' will, like Israel in the wilderness, come under the curse of the Law and thus be banned from inheriting/entering into the 'kingdom of God', so too those who now experience the leading of the Spirit and thus are producing its fruit need no longer fear the Law's dreaded curse upon disobedience; the Law's curse is silenced in the face of the leading of the Spirit. For the 'fruit of the Spirit', which consists summarily in love, is the fulfilment of the Law (cf. 5.13-14; 6.2).

We should pause for a moment to ask whether any of these allusions to the wilderness traditions in 5.16-24 would have been discernible by Paul's formerly pagan and perhaps largely illiterate audience in Galatia.[70] While this is not ultimately determinative for our understanding of Paul's communicative intent as he may well have communicated things not readily accessible to the 'average' member of his audience, it does have some bearing on what we may reasonably suppose about the rhetorical force and effectiveness of the communication. That the Galatians would have had some familiarity with the basic story-line of the OT seems fairly safe to assume. In a recent article

---

[68] Swarup, 'Eternal Planting' (2002), 35 (emphasis added).

[69] Martyn, *Galatians* (1997), 499, notes the possible parallel with 1QS IV, 6–8.

[70] On the 'biblical literacy' of the Galatians, see now Stanley, *Arguing* (2004), 114–18 (cf. 38–61). See also the salutary comments on ancient literacy and orality made by Esler, 'Sodom Tradition' (2004), 5–6.

devoted to the question of Paul's use of Scripture in his ethical instruction, C. Tuckett observes:

> With any society, the founding events that established the identity of that society will always play a key role in subsequent history. Thus in the case of the nation Israel, the events associated with the Exodus, including the giving of the Law at Sinai as well as the events of the wilderness wanderings as recounted in the Pentateuch, would be *easily recalled and evoked in different contexts*. So, for example, the failings of the Israelites at the time of the Exodus in the wilderness period could be, and were, used in various retellings of the story *to encourage repentance and a renewal of commitment* by later Jews (cf. Pss 78, 106; Neh 9; also the song of Moses in Deut 32). Paul's evoking of the same events in a similar way in 1 Cor 10.1-13 lies in the same tradition.[71]

That at least some of the Galatians would have known the basic outline of the wilderness story and perhaps have had some familiarity with the more paradigmatic episodes of wilderness disaffection seems likely. Nor is it hard to imagine some calling to mind these narrative traditions as they hear the admonition to use their (Exodus) freedom (5.13a, 24), not as an occasion for fleshly infighting and communal discord (5.13, 15, 19-21, 26), but as an opportunity to serve one another in love, which thereby fulfils the (Sinai) Law (5.14; cf. 5.18; 5.23b); perhaps all the more as Paul went on to encourage them to follow the leading of the Spirit (through the wilderness) in anticipation of inheriting the eschatological 'kingdom of God' (5.18-5.21).[72]

Conclusion

The aim of this chapter has been to demonstrate that Paul's two references to the Law in 5.18 and 5.23 are intended as affirmations of the fact that the Spirit is sufficient to enable the Galatians to fulfil the Law and thereby avoid its curse. First, I argued this by a close exegesis of 5.16-24. Secondly, I sought to bolster this reading by appeal to the narrative substructure, so to speak, of this section of the letter. This narrative backdrop reinforced the conclusion that

---

[71] Tuckett, 'Scripture and Ethics' (2000), 405 (emphasis added).

[72] See further Wilson, 'Wilderness Apostasy' (2004), 564–68. The argument of this chapter has some bearing on the important debate between W. D. Davies and E. P. Sanders as to whether Paul was a 'covenantal nomist'. See Davies, *Paul and Rabbinic Judaism* (1980), 147–76, and the response from Sanders, *Paul and Palestinian Judaism* (1977), 511–15, who demurs, in particular, that in Paul 'ethics are not derived from anything which could be considered a new exodus, as they would have to be if the exodus-Torah analogy is to hold'. See also the Preface to the 4th edition of Davies, *Paul and Rabbinic Judaism* (1980), xxix–xxxviii, where he responds to Sanders. A variation of this debate was taken up several years ago by J. D. G. Dunn and J. L. Martyn during a meeting of the Pauline Study Group of the Society of Biblical Literature. See Dunn, 'Covenantal Nomism' (1991), 125–46; Martyn, 'Events in Galatia' (1991), 160–79.

Paul is referring to the leading of the Spirit as the means by which the Galatians will avoid the curse of the Law.

For Paul Christ has redeemed us from the curse of the Law (3.13). But this redemption still awaits its final consummation. Just as Christ gave himself up to rescue the Galatians from this 'present evil age' (1.4), yet without eliminating the ongoing reality of that age, so too he has redeemed the Galatians from the curse of the Law without completely doing away with the possibility of coming under the Law's curse. In other words, redemption from the curse of the Law is *promised* redemption. And it will only be realised if the Galatians remain 'in Christ', which means if they continue to live 'by the Spirit from faith' (5.5). This is why Paul's emphasis upon the Spirit is so absolutely vital to the Galatians' own situation. Redemption from the curse of the Law is only mediated through the empowering agency of the Spirit, who will enable the Galatians, if followed, to fulfil the Law and thereby avoid its ultimate curse: exclusion from the 'kingdom of God' (5.21b).

Chapter 7

Conclusion

> Exegesis has both the right and the duty to experiment,
> because otherwise thinking is not possible.[1]

We have come to the end of this study and by way of conclusion I would like briefly to summarise my findings and then reflect upon several possible implications. We have been exploring the rationale for Paul's four references to the Law in the so-called ethical section of Galatians. While scholars have sought to answer this question in a number of ways, the current consensus is that these four references are intended to affirm the superfluity of the Law for Christian ethics in view of the sufficiency of the Spirit to effect moral transformation in the life of believers. This reading is often bolstered by presuming that the Galatians had found the moral guidelines of the Jewish Law particularly attractive and by supposing that the Agitators had claimed that only the Law can provide adequate guidance for daily living. Hence, Paul must respond by assuring the Galatians that if they are led by the Spirit, they do not need the Law as a moral resource. 'Where the Spirit is at work, the Law is superfluous'.[2]

While agreeing with the thrust of this reading that Paul emphasises the sufficiency of the Spirit (cf. 5.16-18; 3.3; 5.5; 6.8), I have taken issue with the idea that Paul's four references to the Law in 5.13–6.10 are intended to demonstrate the irrelevance of the Law for Christian living. Instead, as I have sought to show, Paul's aim is to assure the Galatians of the sufficiency of the Spirit to enable them to fulfil the Law and thereby avoid its curse. If the Galatians will allow themselves to be led by the Spirit, they will not come under the curse of the Law. Where the Spirit is at work, the Law's curse is suspended (cf. 5.18, 22-23).

In Part 1 we explored the relevance of the curse of the Law for the crisis in Galatia. Before we probed into the historical situation, however, we first considered how the issue of the curse of the Law informs Paul's response to the crisis by exploring the rhetoric of cursing in Galatians. We discovered that the rhetoric of cursing is a more prominent and indeed a more pervasive feature of the letter than is generally assumed. Crucial to the argument of this

---

[1] Käsemann, *Perspectives* (1969), 32–33.
[2] Williams, *Galatians* (1997), 152.

chapter is the claim that 'under Law' serves as shorthand for 'under the curse of the Law' (3.10, 13). This not only supports the view that the rhetoric of cursing is relatively widespread in Galatians, it also implies that with the fifth and final use of 'under Law' in 5.18 Paul extends his discussion of the curse of the Law into the ethical section of the letter.

In view of the importance of the curse of the Law to Paul's aims in Galatians, we were in a better position to ask about the relevance of the curse of the Law for the developing crisis over circumcision. In Chapters 3 and 4 we addressed this question from two complementary angles. We first considered whether the curse of the Law played a part in the Agitators' appeal for circumcision. We discovered that the Agitators probably referred to the curse of the Law, either as a warning or as a threat, in order to encourage the Galatians to embrace circumcision. This conclusion serves to counter-balance the tendency among scholars to explain the Galatians' interest in circumcision primarily or sometimes exclusively in terms of its perceived benefits. While the Agitators doubtless would have drawn attention to the advantages of circumcision, they probably also stressed the consequences of failing to be circumcised, among which, as I sought to show, would have been the possibility of coming under a curse.

In Chapter 4 we turned to explore whether the threat of a curse played a part in the Galatians' attraction to circumcision. Several important contributions surfaced as part of the argument of this chapter. Epigraphic evidence from central Anatolia has been largely underutilised for the interpretation of Galatians, yet we discovered that this material throws fresh light on the Galatians' own pre-conversion religious outlook concerning divine vengeance and the workings of a curse. This helped further elucidate why the Galatians would have been especially wary of coming under a curse and deeply unsettled by the threat of the curse of the Law. As part of the argument of this chapter, I also developed a hypothesis about the relevance of suffering-persecution to the situation in Galatia. Suffering-persecution has been a neglected feature of the letter and a largely ignored aspect of the situation for some time now. We discovered, however, that there may have been a link between the issue of the curse of the Law and the Galatians' encounter with suffering-persecution, both Paul's and their own. Thus, while the Galatians may have had a number of reasons for wanting to embrace circumcision, we concluded that the fear of a curse played some part. By embracing circumcision the Galatians could allay doubts about whether they were in danger of coming under the curse of the Law.

Although Chapters 3 and 4 were designed to demonstrate the relevance of the curse of the Law for understanding the crisis over circumcision, it was not my intention to use this evidence as the determinative basis for my exegesis of 5.13–6.10. Instead, my reconstruction of the circumstances in Galatia was intended to support and further elucidate my claim about the rationale for Paul's four references to the Law in 5.13–6.10. Hence, the basic argument of this study can stand even if the discussion in Chapters 3 and 4 is found to be less than fully convincing.

Part 2 was devoted to the primary task of this study: exploring the rationale for Paul's four references to the Law in 5.13–6.10. I argued that Paul's two mentions of the Law in 5.18 and 5.23 are references to the curse of the Law (Chapter 6) and that his two references to the fulfilment of the Law in 5.14 and 6.2 are intended to assure the Galatians that by serving one another in love they will fulfil the Law and thereby avoid its curse (Chapter 5). In addition to presenting a sensible case for taking each of the four uses of νόμος in 5.13–6.10 as a reference to the Law of Moses (including the Law of Christ in 6.2), I have also provided a *coherent explanation* of all four uses of νόμος in this section. Each of these references, in fact, addresses the same issue: the curse of the Law, either indirectly by affirming that love fulfils the Law (5.14; 6.2), or directly by affirming that the Spirit enables the Galatians to avoid coming under the curse of the Law (5.18, 23).

Implications

By demonstrating that Paul continues to address the issue of the curse of the Law in the ethical section of Galatians, I have shed new light on the question of the thematic relationship between 5.13–6.10 and the rest of the letter. As we have seen, addressing the question of the curse of the Law is *not only* an important issue earlier in the letter (3.10-14; 3.23-29; 4.1-7; 4.21-31), it also *continues* to be a central concern for Paul in 5.13–6.10. Thus, Paul's references to the Law in this section of the letter are not setting out on a new trajectory, addressing a second issue, or even taking-up another phase of the argument. Rather, they are dealing with the key question of how to obtain the blessing or inheritance and avoid the curse. In 5.13–6.10 Paul thus reinforces the necessity of finishing 'by the Spirit' (3.3), which he describes as 'walking by the Spirit' (5.16), following the 'leading of the Spirit' (5.18), or 'keeping in step with the Spirit' (5.25). In short, the Galatians will be blessed if they follow the leading of the Spirit (5.16-25 with 6.16) and cursed if they fail to do so (5.19-21).

Our discussion of the curse of the Law in Galatians has also exposed an apparent tension in Paul's presentation. On the one hand, he states in no uncertain terms that 'Christ has redeemed us from the curse of the Law' (3.13; 4.4-5; cf. 3.23-25). On the other hand, he seems to assume that coming under the curse of the Law continues to be a real possibility for the various persons involved in the Galatian crisis, not least himself (1.8-9; 3.10; 4.21-5.4; 5.18).

For Paul, then, redemption from the curse of the Law is not a *fait accompli*. Nor has the cursing voice of the Law been altogether silenced.[3] In fact, it will only be silenced *if* the Galatians walk by the Spirit and do not fulfil the 'desire of the flesh' (5.16-18). Otherwise, Paul insists, the Galatians will come under the Law's curse and be disinherited (5.19-21). In addition to suggesting that Paul's view of redemption in Galatians is both proleptic and dynamic, this also underscores the centrality of the Spirit to his whole response to the Galatian crisis. Redemption from the curse of the Law depends upon the empowering agency of the Spirit.

It should be clear from this that I conceive of Paul's approach to the Galatian crisis rather differently from scholars like Martyn, who strongly resist the idea that Paul is presenting the Galatians with a pair of human alternatives to follow: either the way of a blessing or the way of a curse. For Martyn, in fact, this is the approach of the Agitators – *not* Paul. 'In a word, blessing and curse are not for Paul two alternative paths between which the human being can make a choice'.[4] By way of contrast, on my reading perhaps Paul's chief aim in Galatians is to confront his apostatising converts with precisely this choice between blessing and curse, evidenced by the fact that he has framed the entire letter in terms of blessing (6.16) and curse (1.8-9) and by the fact that he devotes considerable attention to explaining precisely how it is that the Galatians can obtain the blessing and avoid a curse.

While it has not been my intention to provide a comprehensive analysis of the Law in Galatians, we have discovered that Paul places less emphasis upon the *superfluity* of the Law than is often assumed. This was one of the implications of our exegesis of 3.23-25 and 4.1-7, where the chronological nature of Paul's argument, which is often assumed to imply the idea of superfluity, actually revolves around the cessation of the Law's *curse* for those who participate in redemption in Christ (3.25; 4.4-5; cf. 3.13-14). Although Paul strongly opposes the circumcision of his Gentile converts (5.1-4), which may imply some element of superfluity in his understanding of the Law (cf. 5.6; 6.15), it has become clear nonetheless that the *basic thrust* of his polemic in Galatians centres upon the Law's inability to mediate righteousness (2.15-21; 3.21; 5.5-6), its contrast with faith (3.11-12), and its power to curse (1.8-9; 3.10, 13), rather than upon its irrelevance within a *post Christum* situation.

This has potentially far-reaching implications for how Galatians contributes to discussions about Christian supersessionism: the idea that the church has displaced the Jews as the elect people of God.[5] *For the superfluity*

---

[3] Cf. Martyn, *Galatians* (1997), 322, who argues that for Paul 'the cursing voice of the Law has been silenced'.

[4] Martyn, *Galatians* (1997), 327.

[5] Marshall, 'Jewish People' (1997), 82.

of the Law is closely related to supersessionist eschatology. Telling, for example, is F. F. Bruce's interpretative paraphrase of 5.18: 'With the coming of Christ and the completion of his redeeming work, the age of the law has been superseded by the age of the Spirit'.[6] Betz is also particularly clear on this point. 'If the validity of the Jewish Torah ends for the Jew when he becomes a Christian, there is no point or basis for Gentiles *as well as for Jews* to adhere to the Jewish religion'.[7] In other words, the superfluity of the Law is a corollary of the supersession of the Jews within God's redemptive purposes. What is more, some advocates of the New Perspective have only reinforced this basic assumption by reading the argument of 5.13–6.10 (and often the rest of the letter) in the following terms: this is what Paul finds wrong with the Law: it is not the Spirit. In other words, the Law is not a problem *per se*; it is simply superseded by the dawning of the Spirit.[8]

Having argued that Paul's aim in 5.13–6.10 is not to demonstrate the superfluity of the Law for Christian ethics, we are left with the perennial question of what *is* the role of the Law in the life of his Gentile congregations. This is still an unresolved issue in Pauline scholarship. As S. Westerholm observes: 'Exegetes cannot agree whether or not Paul thought Christians are subject to the law'.[9] Given my aims and the limitations of this study, I have of course not tried to engage directly in this discussion. In fact, I have intentionally tried to present the argument of this study in a way that does not wed my conclusions to a particular solution to this age-old problem. However, addressing this question more directly will be the focus of future research. What is needed is a synthetic, constructive and exegetically rigorous approach to the question of the Jewish Law in Paul's mixed congregations, a reading which takes seriously his negative polemic against the Law and yet does not assume its superfluity.

---

[6] Bruce, 'Spirit in Galatians' (1985), 44.

[7] Betz, *Galatians* (1979), 179 (emphasis added). Cf. Betz, *Galatians* (1979), 251: 'According to Galatians, Judaism is excluded from salvation altogether, so that the Galatians have to choose between Paul and Judaism'.

[8] I take this to be a fair characterisation of the argument of Barclay, *Obeying* (1988).

[9] Westerholm, *Israel's Law* (1988), 198.

Bibliography

Thomas Aquinas. *Commentary on Saint Paul's Epistle to the Galatians*. Translated by F. R. Larcher. Aquinas Scripture Series Vol. 1. Albany, N.Y.: Magi Books, 1966.

C. E. Arnold. '"I Am Astonished That You Are So Quickly Turning Away!" (Gal 1.6): Paul and Anatolian Folk Belief'. *NTS* 51/3 (2005): 429-449.

A. Asano. *Community-Identity Construction in Galatians: Exegetical, Social-Anthropological and Socio-Historical Studies*. JSNTSup 285. London: T & T Clark International, 2005.

T. R. Ashley. *The Book of Numbers*. NICOT. Grand Rapids: Eerdmans, 1993.

E. Baasland. 'Persecution: A Neglected Feature in the Letter to the Galatians'. *ST* 38 (1984): 135–50.

M. Bachmann. *Sünder oder Übertreter: Studien zur Argumentation in Gal 2,15ff.* WUNT 59. Tübingen: Mohr, 1992.

M. Bachmann. *Antijudaismus im Galaterbrief? Exegetische Studien zu einem polemischen Schreiben und zur Theologie des Apostels Paulus*. NTOA 40. Göttingen: Vandenhoeck and Ruprecht, 1999.

E. Bammel. 'Νόμος Χριστοῦ'. In *Judaica et Paulina: Kleine Schriften II*. WUNT 91. Tübingen: Mohr, 1997, 320–36.

E. Bammel. 'Paulus, der Moses des Neuen Bundes'. In *Judaica et Paulina: Kleine Schriften II*. WUNT 91. Tübingen: Mohr, 1997, 205–14.

J. M. G. Barclay. 'Mirror-Reading a Polemical Letter: Galatians as a Test Case'. *JSNT* 31 (1987): 73–93.

J. M. G. Barclay. *Obeying the Truth: A Study of Paul's Ethics in Galatians*. Edinburgh: T & T Clark, 1988.

J. M. G. Barclay. 'Conflict in Thessalonica'. *CBQ* 55 (1993): 512–530.

C. K. Barrett. 'The Allegory of Abraham, Sarah, and Hagar in the Argument of Galatians'. In *Essays on Paul*. London: SPCK, 1982, 118–31.

C. K. Barrett. *Freedom and Obligation. A Study of the Epistle to the Galatians*. London: SPCK, 1985.

R. Bauckham. *James: Wisdom of James, Disciple of Jesus the Sage*. New Testament Readings. London and New York: Routledge, 1999.

W. Bauer, F. W. Danker, W. F. Arndt and F. W. Gingrich. *A Greek-English Lexicon of the New Testament and Other Early Christian Literature*. Rev. and ed. by F. W. Danker. 3rd ed. Chicago: University of Chicago Press, 2000.

J. F. Bayes. *The Weakness of the Law: God's Law and the Christian in New Testament Perspective*. Paternoster Biblical and Theological Monographs. Cumbria: Paternoster, 2000.

G. K. Beale. 'The Old Testament Background of Paul's Reference to "the Fruit of the Spirit" in Galatians 5:22'. *BBR* 15.1 (2005): 1–38.

J. Becker. *Der Brief an die Galater*. NTD 8/1. Göttingen: Vandenhoeck & Ruprecht, 1998.

L. L. Belleville. '"Under Law": Structural Analysis and the Pauline Concept of Law in Galatians 3.21–4.11'. *JSNT* 26 (1986): 53–78.

J. A. Bengel. *Gnomon Novi Testamenti, in Quo ex Nativa Verborum VI*. 3rd ed.; Stuttgart: Steinkopf, 1860 (org. 1742).

K. Berger. 'Die impliziten Gegner: Zur Methode des Erschliessens von "Gegnern" in neutestamentlichen Texten'. In *Kirche: Festschrift für Günther Bornkamm zum 75. Geburtstag.* Ed. by D. Lührmann and G. Strecker. Tübingen: Mohr, 1980, 373–400.

P. L. Berger. *The Sacred Canopy: Elements of a Sociological Theory of Religion.* New York: Doubleday, 1967.

P. L. Berger and T. Luckmann. *The Social Construction of Reality: A Treatise in the Sociology of Knowledge.* New York: Doubleday, 1966.

H. D. Betz. *Galatians: A Commentary on Paul's Letter to the Churches in Galatia.* Hermenia. Philadelphia: Fortress, 1979.

E. Birnbaum. *The Place of Judaism in Philo's Thought: Israel, Jews, and Proselytes.* Studia Philonica Monographs 2. Atlanta: Scholars, 1996.

J. Bligh. *Galatians: A Discussion of St Paul's Epistle.* Household Commentaries 1. London: St Paul Publications, 1969.

M. N. A. Bockmuehl. *Jewish Law in Gentile Churches: Halakhah and the Beginning of Christian Public Ethics.* Edinburgh: T & T Clark, 2000.

M. N. A. Bockmuehl. '1 Thessalonians 2:14-16 and the Church in Jerusalem'. *TynBul* 52/1 (2001): 1–31.

J. Bodel, ed. *Epigraphic Evidence: Ancient History from Inscriptions.* Approaching the Ancient World; London and New York: Routledge, 2001

N. Bonneau. 'The Logic of Paul's Argument on the Curse of the Law in Galatians 3:10-14'. *NovT* 39/1 (1997): 60–80.

P. Borgen. *Philo, John and Paul: New Perspectives on Judaism and Early Christianity.* Brown Judaic Studies. 131. Atlanta: Scholars, 1987.

P. Borgen. *Early Christianity and Hellenistic Judaism.* Edinburgh: T & T Clark, 1996.

U. Borse. *Der Standort des Galaterbriefes.* Bonner Biblische Beiträge. Köln: Peter Hansten, 1972.

P. J. J. Botha. 'The Verbal Art of the Pauline Letters: Rhetoric, Performance and Presence'. In *Rhetoric and the New Testament: Essays from the 1992 Heidelberg Conference.* Ed. by S. E. Porter and T. H. Olbricht. JSNTSup 90. Sheffield: JSOT, 1993, 409–28.

G. Bouwman. 'Die Hagar- und Sara-Perikope (Gal 4,21-31): Exemplarische Interpretation zum Schriftbeweis bei Paulus'. In *ANRW.* Ed. by W. Haase. Part 2. *Principat*, 25.4. New York: de Gruyter, 1987, 3135–3155.

D. Boyarin. *A Radical Jew: Paul and the Politics of Identity.* Berkeley and Los Angeles: University of California Press, 1994.

C. Breytenbach. *Paulus und Barnabas in der Provinz Galatien: Studien zu Apostelgeschichte 13f.; 16,6; 18,23 und den Adressaten des Galaterbriefes.* AGJU 38. Leiden: Brill, 1996.

B. H. Brinsmead. *Galatians – Dialogical Response to Opponents.* SBLDS 65. Chico, Calif.: Scholars, 1982.

D. Brondos. 'The Cross and the Curse: Galatians 3.13 and Paul's Doctrine of Redemption'. *JSNT* 81 (2001): 3–32.

F. F. Bruce. *The Epistle of Paul to the Galatians: A Commentary on the Greek Text.* NIGTC 2. Exeter: Paternoster Press, 1982.

F. F. Bruce. 'The Spirit in the Letter to the Galatians'. In *Essays on Apostolic Themes: Studies in Honor of Howard M. Ervin Presented to him by Colleagues and Friends on his Sixty-Fifth Birthday.* Ed. by P. Elbert. Peabody, Mass: Hendrickson, 1985, 36–48.

R. A. Bryant. *The Risen and Crucified Christ in Galatians.* SBLDS 185. Atlanta: Society of Biblical Literature, 2000.

P. J. Budd. *Numbers.* WBC 5. Waco, Tex.: Word, 1984.

E. de W. Burton. *A Critical and Exegetical Commentary on the Epistle to the Galatians.* ICC. Edinburgh: T & T Clark, 1921.

Bibliography

N. L. Calvert. 'Abraham and Idolatry: Paul's Comparison of Obedience to the Law with Idolatry in Galatians 4:1-10'. In *Paul and the Scriptures of Israel*. Ed. by C. A. Evans and J. A. Sanders. JSNTSup 83. Sheffield: JSOT Press, 1993, 222–37.

N. Calvert-Koyzis. *Paul, Monotheism and the People of God: The Significance of Abraham Traditions for Early Judaism and Christianity*. JSNTSup 273. London: T & T Clark, 2004.

J. Calvin. *Institutes of the Christian Religion*. Translated by F. L. Battles. The Library of Christian Classics. 2 Vols. London: SCM Press, 1960.

J. Calvin. *Commentaries on the Epistles of Paul to the Galatians and Ephesians*. Translated by W. Pringle. Repr. ed.; Calvin's Commentaries. 22 Vols. Grand Rapids: Eerdmans, 1993.

R. A. Campbell. '"Against Such Things There is no Law"? Galatians 5:23b Again'. *ExpTim* 107 (1996): 271–72.

J. H. Charlesworth, ed. *The Old Testament Pseudepigrapha*. 2 Vols. New York: Doubleday, 1983–85.

R. E. Ciampa. *The Presence and Function of Scripture in Galatians 1 and 2*. WUNT 2/102. Tübingen: Mohr, 1998.

S. J. D. Cohen. 'Crossing the Boundary and Becoming a Jew'. *HTR* 82 (1989): 13–33.

R. A. Cole. *The Letter of Paul to the Galatians*. 2nd ed.; TNTC 9. Grand Rapids: Eerdmans, 1989.

F. H. Colson, G. H. Whitaker, J. W. Earp and R. Marcus, eds. *Philo: The Complete Works*. LCL. 12 Vols. Cambridge, Mass.: Harvard University Press, 1929–53.

H. L. Cornu and J. Shulam. *A Commentary on the Jewish Roots of Galatians*. Jerusalem: Netivyah Bible Instruction Ministry, 2005.

C. H. Cosgrove. *The Cross and the Spirit: A Study in the Argument and Theology of Galatians*. Macon, Ga.: Mercer, 1988.

C. E. B. Cranfield. 'St Paul and the Law'. *SJT* 17 (1964): 43–68.

C. E. B. Cranfield. *A Critical and Exegetical Commentary on the Epistle to the Romans*. ICC. 2 Vols. Edinburgh: T & T Clark, 1975–79.

M. Cranford. 'The Possibility of Perfect Obedience: Paul and an Implied Premise in Galatians 3:10 and 5:3'. *NovT* 36/3 (1994): 242–58.

F. M. Cross. *The Ancient Library of Qumran*. Biblical Seminar Series 27. Sheffield: Sheffield Academic, 1995.

S. A. Cummins. *Paul and the Crucified Christ in Antioch*. SNTSMS 114. Cambridge: Cambridge University Press, 2001.

H. Danby. *The Mishnah: Translated from the Hebrew with Introduction and Brief Explanatory Notes*. Oxford: Oxford University Press, 1933.

A. A. Das. *Paul, the Law, and the Covenant*. Peabody, Mass.: Hendrickson, 2001.

A. A. Das. *Paul and the Jews*. Library of Pauline Studies. Peabody, Mass.: Hendrickson, 2003.

W. D. Davies. *Torah in the Messianic Age and/or the Age to Come*. Philadelphia: Society of Biblical Literature, 1952.

W. D. Davies. *Paul and Rabbinic Judaism: Some Rabbinic Elements in Pauline Theology*. 4th ed.; Philadelphia: Fortress, 1980.

W. D. Davies. 'Review: *Galatians: A Commentary on Paul's Letter to the Churches of Galatia* by Hans Dieter Betz'. *RSR* 7/4 (1981): 310–318.

W. D. Davies and D. C. Allison. *A Critical and Exegetical Commentary on the Gospel According to Saint Matthew*. ICC. Vol. 1. Edinburgh: T & T Clark, 1988.

B. S. Davis. 'The Meaning of Προεγράφη in the Context of Galatians 3.1'. *NTS* 2 (1999): 194–212.

B. S. Davis. *Christ as Devotio: The Argument of Galatians 3:1-14*. Lanham, Md.: University Press of America, 2002.
W. P. de Boer. *The Imitation of Paul*. Kampen: J. H. Kok, 1962.
T. J. Deidun. *New Covenant Morality in Paul*. AnBib 89. Rome: Biblical Institute, 1981.
B. J. Dodd. 'Christ's Slave, People Pleasers and Galatians 1.10'. *NTS* 42 (1996): 90–104.
B. J. Dodd. *Paul's Paradigmatic "I": Personal Example as Literary Strategy*. JSNTSup 177. Sheffield: Sheffield Academic, 1999.
C. H. Dodd. '*Ennomos Christou*'. In *More New Testament Studies*. Manchester: Manchester University Press, 1968, 134–48.
T. L. Donaldson. 'The "Curse of the Law" and the Inclusion of the Gentiles: Galatians 3.13-14'. *NTS* 32 (1986): 94–112.
J. W. Drane. *Paul: Libertine or Legalist? A Study in the Major Pauline Epistles*. London: SPCK, 1975.
J. A. Draper. '"Korah" and the Second Temple'. In *Templum Amicitiae: Essays on the Second Temple presented to Ernst Bammel*. Ed. by W. Horbury. Sheffield: Sheffield Academic, 1991, 150–74.
A. du Toit. 'Vilification as a Pragmatic Device in Early Christian Epistolography'. *Bib* 75 (1994): 403–412.
J. D. G. Dunn. 'The Theology of Galatians: The Issue of Covenantal Nomism'. In *Pauline Theology, Volume 1: Thessalonians, Philippians, Galatians, Philemon*. Ed. by J. M. Bassler. Minneapolis, Minn.: Fortress, 1991, 125–46.
J. D. G. Dunn. *The Epistle to the Galatians*. BNTC. Peabody, Mass.: Hendrickson, 1993.
J. D. G. Dunn. *The Theology of Paul's Letter to the Galatians*. New Testament Theology. Cambridge: Cambridge University Press, 1993.
J. D. G. Dunn. *The Theology of Paul the Apostle*. Grand Rapids: Eerdmans, 1998.
S. Eastman. 'The Evil Eye and the Curse of the Law: Galatians 3.1 Revisited'. *JSNT* 83 (2001): 69–87.
G. Ebeling. 'On the Doctrine of the *Triplex Usus Legis* in the Theology of the Reformation'. In *Word and Faith*. London: SCM, 1963, 62–78.
G. Ebeling. *The Truth of the Gospel: An Exposition of Galatians*. Translated by D. Green. Philadelphia: Fortress, 1985.
J. Eckert. *Die urchristliche Verkündigung im Streit zwischen Paulus und seinen Gegnern nach dem Galaterbrief*. BU 6. Regensburg: Pustet, 1971.
H.-J. Eckstein. *Verheissung und Gesetz: Eine exegetische Untersuchung zu Galater 2,15-4,7*. WUNT 86. Tübingen: Mohr, 1996.
K. Elliger and W. Rudolph, eds. *Biblia Hebraica Stuttgartensia*. Stuttgart: Deutsche Bibelgesellschaft, 1977.
M. A. Elliot. *The Survivors of Israel: A Reconsideration of the Theology of Pre-Christian Judaism*. Grand Rapids: Eerdmans, 2000.
S. M. Elliott. 'Paul and his Gentile Audiences: Mystery Cults, Anatolian Popular Religiosity, and Paul's Claim of Divine Authority in Galatians'. *Listening* 31 (1996): 117–36.
S. M. Elliott. 'Choose Your Mother, Choose Your Master: Galatians 4:21–5:1 in the Shadow of the Anatolian Mother of the Gods'. *JBL* 118 (1999): 661–683.
S. M. Elliott. *Cutting too Close for Comfort: Paul's Letter to the Galatians in its Anatolian Cultic Context*. JSNTSup 248. London: T & T Clark, 2003.
T. Engberg-Pedersen. *Paul and the Stoics*. Edinburgh: T & T Clark, 2000.
A. Eriksson. *Traditions as Rhetorical Proof: Pauline Argumentation in 1 Corinthians*. CBNTS 29. Stockholm: Almqvist & Wiksell, 1998.

P. F. Esler. 'Group Boundaries and Intergroup Conflict in Galatians: A New Reading of Galatians 5:13–6:10'. In *Ethnicity and the Bible*. Ed. by M. G. Brett. Leiden: Brill, 1996, 215–40.
P. F. Esler. *Galatians*. New Testament Readings. London: Routledge, 1998.
P. F. Esler. 'The Sodom Tradition in Romans 1:18-32'. *BTB* 34 (2004): 4–16.
R. J. Evans. *In Defense of History*. London: Granata Publications, 1997.
C. A. Faraone. 'The Agonistic Context of Early Greek Binding Spells'. In *Magika Hiera: Ancient Greek Magic and Religion*. Ed. by C. A. Faraone and D. Obbink. New York: Oxford University Press, 1991, 2–32.
G. D. Fee. 'Freedom and the Life of Obedience (Galatians 5:1–6:18)'. *RevExp* 91 (1994): 201–17.
G. D. Fee. *God's Empowering Presence: The Holy Spirit in the Letters of Paul*. Peabody, Mass.: Hendrickson Publishers, 1994.
S. Finlan. *The Background and Content of Paul's Cultic Atonement Metaphors*. Academia Biblica 19. Atlanta: Society of Biblical Literature, 2004.
K. Finsterbusch. *Die Thora als Lebensweisung für Heidenchristen: Studien zur Bedeutung der Thora für die paulinische Ethik*. SNTSU 20. Göttingen: Vandenhoeck & Ruprecht, 1996.
R. Y. K. Fung. *The Epistle to the Galatians*. NICNT. Grand Rapids: Eerdmans, 1988.
J. G. Gager. *Moses in Graeco-Roman Paganism*. Nashville, Tenn.: Abingdon, 1972.
J. G. Gager, ed. *Curse Tablets and Binding Spells from the Ancient World*. New York and Oxford: Oxford University Press, 1992.
L. Gaston. *Paul and the Torah*. Vancouver: University of British Columbia Press, 1987.
S. J. Gathercole. *Where is Boasting? Early Jewish Soteriology and Paul's Response in Romans 1–5*. Grand Rapids: Eerdmans, 2002.
B. R. Gaventa. 'Galatians 1 and 2: Autobiography as Paradigm'. *NovT* 28/4 (1986): 309–326.
B. R. Gaventa. 'The Maternity of Paul: An Exegetical Study of Galatians 4:19'. In *The Conversation Continues: Studies in Paul and John in Honor of J. Louis Martyn*. Ed. by R. T. Fortna and B. R. Gaventa. Nashville, Tenn.: Abingdon, 1990, 189–201.
B. R. Gaventa. 'The Singularity of the Gospel: A Reading of Galatians'. In *Pauline Theology, Volume 1: Thessalonians, Philippians, Galatians, Philemon*. Ed. by J. M. Bassler. Minneapolis, Minn.: Fortress, 1991, 147–159.
T. George. *Galatians*. NAC 30. Nashville, Tenn.: Broadman & Holman, 1994.
A. J. Goddard and S. A. Cummins. 'Ill or Ill-Treated? Conflict and Persecution as the Context of Paul's Original Ministry in Galatia (Galatians 4.12-20)'. *JSNT* 52 (1993): 93–126.
R. Gordon. 'Raising a Sceptre: Confession-Narratives from Lydia and Phrygia'. *Journal of Roman Archaeology* 17 (2004): 177–96.
T. D. Gordon. 'A Note on Παιδαγωγός in Galatians 3.24-25'. *NTS* 35 (1989): 150–54.
M. J. Gorman. *Cruciformity: Paul's Narrative Spirituality of the Cross*. Grand Rapids: Eerdmans, 2001.
M. Goulder. 'The Pauline Epistles'. In *The Literary Guide to the Bible*. Ed. by R. Alter and F. Kermode. London: Collins, 1987, 479–502.
F. Graf. *Magic in the Ancient World*. Translated by F. Philip. Cambridge, Mass.: Harvard University Press, 1997.
L. H. G. Greenwood. *Cicero. The Verrine Orations*. LCL. 2 Vols. Cambridge, Mass.: Harvard University Press, 1953.
S. J. Hafemann. *Paul, Moses, and the History of Israel: The Letter/Spirit Contrast and The Argument from Scripture in 2 Corinthians 3*. WUNT 81. Tübingen: Mohr, 1995.
S. J. Hafemann. 'Paul and the Exile of Israel in Galatians 3–4'. In *Exile: Old Testament, Jewish, and Christian Conceptions*. Ed. by J. M. Scott. Leiden: Brill, 1997, 329–71.

S. J. Hafemann. '"Because of Weakness" (Galatians 4:13): The Role of Suffering in the Mission of Paul'. In *The Gospel to the Nations: Perspectives on Paul's Mission*. Ed. by P. Bolt and M. Thompson. Downers Grove: InterVarsity, 2000, 131–146.

R. G. Hall. 'The Rhetorical Outline for Galatians: A Reconsideration'. *JBL* 106 (1987): 277–287.

R. G. Hall. 'Arguing like an Apocalypse: Galatians and Ancient *Topos* outside the Greco-Roman Rhetorical Tradition'. *NTS* 42 (1996): 434–53.

R. G. Hamerton-Kelly. 'Sacred Violence and "Works of Law." "Is Christ then an Agent of Sin?" (Galatians 2:17)'. *CBQ* 52 (1990): 55–75.

R. G. Hamerton-Kelly. *Sacred Violence: Paul's Hermeneutic of the Cross*. Minneapolis: Augsburg Fortress, 1992.

G. W. Hansen. *Abraham in Galatians: Epistolary and Rhetorical Contexts*. JSNTSup 29. Sheffield: JSOT, 1989.

G. W. Hansen. 'Paul's Conversion and His Ethic of Freedom in Galatians'. In *The Road from Damascus: The Impact of Paul's Conversion on His Life, Thought, and Ministry*. Ed. by R. N. Longenecker. Grand Rapids: Eerdmans, 1997, 213–237.

T. Haraguchi. 'Words of Blessing and Curse: A Rhetorical Study of Galatians'. *AJT* 18/1 (2004): 33–50.

T. Harrison. *Divinity and History: The Religion of Herodotus*. Oxford Classical Monographs. Oxford: Clarendon, 2000.

A. E. Harvey. 'Forty Strokes Save One: Social Aspects of Judaizing and Apostasy'. In *Alternative Approaches to New Testament Study*. Ed. by A. E. Harvey. London: SPCK, 1985, 79–96.

R. B. Hays. 'Christology and Ethics in Galatians: The Law of Christ'. *CBQ* 49 (1987): 268–90.

R. B. Hays. *Echoes of Scripture in the Letters of Paul*. New Haven, Conn.: Yale University Press, 1989.

R. B. Hays. 'The Letter to the Galatians: Introduction, Commentary, and Reflections'. In *The New Interpreter's Bible: A Commentary in Twelve Volumes*. Ed. by L. E. Keck. Vol. 11. Nashville, Tenn.: Abingdon, 2000, 181–348.

R. B. Hays. *The Faith of Jesus Christ: An Investigation of the Narrative Substructure of Galatians 3:1–4:11*. 2nd ed.; Grand Rapids: Eerdmans, 2002.

U. Heckel. *Der Segen im Neuen Testament: Begriff, Formeln, Gesten; Mit einem praktisch-theologischen Ausblick*. WUNT 150. Tübingen: Mohr, 2002.

M. Hengel. *The Pre-Christian Paul*. Translated by J. Bowden. Philadelphia and London: Trinity Press International and SCM, 1991.

I. J. Hesselink. 'John Calvin on the Law and Christian Freedom'. *ExAud* 11 (1995): 77–89.

I.-G. Hong. *The Law in Galatians*. JSNTSup 81. Sheffield: JSOT, 1993.

I.-G. Hong. 'Being "Under the Law" in Galatians'. *EvRevT* 26/4 (2002): 354–72.

M. D. Hooker. 'Interchange in Christ'. *JTS* 22 (1971): 349–61.

W. Horbury. '1 Thessalonians ii.3 as Rebutting the Charge of False Prophecy'. *JTS* 33 (1982): 492–508.

W. Horbury. 'Extirpation and Excommunication'. *VT* 35/1 (1985): 13–38.

G. Howard. *Paul: Crisis in Galatia*. 2nd ed.; SNTSMS. 35. Cambridge: Cambridge University Press, 1990.

H. Hübner. 'Das ganze und das eine Gesetz. Zum Problemkreis Paulus und die Stoa'. *KuD* 21 (1975): 239–56.

H. Hübner. *Law in Paul's Thought*. Translated by J. C. G. Greig. Edinburgh: T & T Clark, 1984.

H. Hübner. *Biblische Theologie des Neuen Testaments. Band 2. Die Theologie des Paulus und ihre neutestamentliche Wirkungsgeschichte.* Göttingen: Vandenhoeck & Ruprecht, 1993.
F. Jacoby. *Atthis: The Local Chronicles of Ancient Athens.* Oxford: Clarendon, 1949.
L. A. Jervis. *Galatians.* NIBCNT 9. Peabody, Mass.: Hendrickson, 1999.
R. Jewett. 'The Agitators and the Galatian Congregations'. *NTS* 17 (1971): 198–212.
R. Jewett. *Paul's Anthropological Terms. A Study of Their Use in Conflict Settings.* Leiden: Brill, 1971.
K. H. Jobes. 'Jerusalem, Our Mother: Metalepsis and Intertextuality in Galatians 4:21-31'. *WTJ* 55 (1993): 299–320.
L. T. Johnson. 'The New Testament's Anti-Jewish Slander and the Conventions of Ancient Polemic'. *JBL* 108 (1989): 419–444.
L. T. Johnson. 'Taciturnity and True Religion: James 1:26-27'. In *Greeks, Romans, and Christians: Essays in Honor of Abraham J. Malherbe.* Ed. by D. L. Balch, E. Ferguson and W. A. Meeks. Minneapolis: Fortress, 1990, 329–39.
E. Kamlah. *Die Form der katalogischen Paränese im Neuen Testament.* Tübingen: Mohr, 1964.
E. Käsemann. *Perspectives on Paul.* Translated by M. Kohl. London: SCM, 1969.
H. C. Kee, ed. *The Cambridge Annotated Study Apocrypha: New Revised Standard Version.* Cambridge: Cambridge University Press, 1994.
S. C. Keesmaat. *Paul and his Story: (Re)Interpreting the Exodus Tradition.* JSNTSup 181. Sheffield: Sheffield Academic, 1999.
G. A. Kennedy. *New Testament Interpretation through Rhetorical Criticism.* Chapel Hill, N.C.: University of North Carolina Press, 1984.
P. H. Kern. *Rhetoric and Galatians: Assessing an Approach to Paul's Epistle.* SNTSMS 101. Cambridge: Cambridge University Press, 1998.
K. Kertelge. 'Freiheitsbotschaft und Liebesgebot im Galaterbrief'. In *Neues Testament und Ethik: Für Rudolf Schnackenburg.* Ed. by H. Merklein. Freiburg/Basel/Wien: Herder, 1989, 326–37.
E. F. Kevan. *The Grace of Law: a Study in Puritan Theology.* London: The Carey Kingsgate Press Limited, 1964.
S. Kim. *Paul and the New Perspective: Second Thoughts on the Origin of Paul's Gospel.* WUNT 140. Tübingen: Mohr, 2002.
H. J. Klauck. 'Die kleinasiatischen Beichtinschriften und das Neue Testament'. In *Geschichte-Tradition-Reflexion, Band 3: Festschrift für Martin Hengel zum 70. Geburtstag.* Ed. by H. Cancik, H. Lichtenberger and P. Schäfer. Tübingen: Mohr, 1996, 63–87.
D.-A. Koch. *Die Schrift als Zeuge des Evangeliums: Untersuchungen zur Verwendung und zum Verständnis der Schrift bei Paulus.* Beiträge zur Historischen Theologie 69. Tübingen: Mohr, 1986.
E. H.-S. Kok. *"The Truth of the Gospel": A Study in Galatians 2:15-21.* Hong Kong: Alliance Bible Seminary, 2000.
D. W. Kuck. '"Each Will Bear His Own Burden": Paul's Creative Use of an Apocalyptic Motif'. *NTS* 40 (1994): 289–297.
K. Kuula. *The Law, the Covenant and God's Plan: Volume 1 – Paul's Polemical Treatment of the Law in Galatians.* Publications of the Finnish Exegetical Society 72. Helsinki and Göttingen: Finish Exegetical Society and Vandenhoeck & Rupercht, 1999.
Y.-G. Kwon. *Eschatology in Galatians: Rethinking Paul's Response to the Crisis in Galatia.* WUNT 2/183. Tübingen: Mohr, 2004.

J. Lambrecht. 'Paul's Coherent Admonition in Gal 6, 1-6: Mutual Help and Individual Attentiveness'. *Bib* 78/1 (1997): 35–56.

B. C. Lategan. 'Is Paul Defending His Apostleship in Galatians? The Function of Galatians 1.11-12 and 2.19-20 in the Development of Paul's Argument'. *NTS* 34 (1988): 411–30.

B. C. Lategan. 'Is Paul Developing a Specifically Christian Ethics in Galatians?'. In *Greeks, Romans, and Christians: Essays in Honor of Abraham J. Malherbe*. Ed. by D. L. Balch, E. Ferguson and W. A. Meeks. Minneapolis: Fortress, 1990, 318–27.

B. C. Lategan. 'Formulas in the Language of Paul: A Study of Prepositional Phrases in Galatians'. *Neot* 25/1 (1991): 75–87.

B. C. Lategan. 'The Argumentative Situation of Galatians'. *Neot* 26 (1992): 257–77.

R. Lattimore. *Themes in Greek and Latin Epitaphs*. Illinois Studies in Language and Literature 28. Urbana, Ill.: University of Illinois Press, 1942.

S. Légasse. *L'Épître de Paul aux Galates*. Lectio Divina Commentaires 9. Paris: Cerf, 2000.

J.-P. Lémonon. 'Dans l'Épître aux Galates Paul considère-t-il la loi mosaïque comme bonne?'. In *La Loi dans l'un et l'autre testament*. Ed. C. Focant. LD 168. Paris: Cerf, 1997, 243–70.

J. Lieu. 'Circumcision, Women and Salvation'. *NTS* 40 (1994): 358–370.

J. B. Lightfoot. *Saint Paul's Epistle to the Galatians: A Revised Text with Introduction, Notes, and Dissertations*. London: Macmillan, 1896.

M. Limbeck. *Das Gesetz im alten und neuen Testament*. Darmstadt: Wissenschaftliche Buchgesellschaft, 1997.

B. W. Longenecker. *The Triumph of Abraham's God: The Transformation of Identity in Galatians*. Edinburgh: T & T Clark, 1998.

B. W. Longenecker. '"Until Christ is Formed in You": Suprahuman Forces and Moral Character in Galatians'. *CBQ* 61 (1999): 92–108.

R. N. Longenecker. *Galatians*. WBC 41. Waco, Tex.: Word, 1990.

J. P. Louw and E. A. Nida. *Greek-English Lexicon of the New Testament Based on Semantic Domains*. 2 Vols. New York: United Bible Society, 1988.

D. Lührmann. *Galatians: A Continental Commentary*. Translated by O. C. Dean, Jr. Minneapolis: Fortress, 1992.

D. J. Lull. '"The Law Was Our Pedagogue": A Study in Galatians 3:19-25'. *JBL* 105 (1986): 481–98.

W. Lütgert. *Gesetz und Geist: Eine Untersuchung zur Vorgeschichte des Galaterbriefs*. Gütersloh: Bertelsmann, 1919.

G. Lyons. *Pauline Autobiography: Toward a New Understanding*. SBLDS 73. Atlanta: Scholars, 1985.

R. MacMullen. 'The Epigraphic Habit in the Roman Empire'. *AJP* 103 (1982): 233–46.

B. J. Malina. *The New Testament World: Insights from Cultural Anthropology*. Rev. ed.; Louisville, Ky.: Westminster/John Knox, 1993.

B. J. Malina and J. H. Neyrey. *Portraits of Paul: An Archaeology of Ancient Personality*. Louisville, Ky.: Westminster/John Knox, 1996.

J. Marcus. 'The Circumcision and the Uncircumcision in Rome'. *NTS* 35 (1989): 67–81.

J. Marcus. '"Under the Law": The Background of a Pauline Expression'. *CBQ* 63 (2001): 72–83.

B. D. Marshall. 'Christ and the Cultures: the Jewish People and Christian Theology'. In *Cambridge Companion to Christian Doctrine*. Ed. by C. E. Gunton. New York: Cambridge University Press, 1997, 81–100.

B. L. Martin. *Christ and the Law in Paul*. NovTSup 62. Leiden: Brill, 1989.

T. W. Martin. 'Apostasy to Paganism: The Rhetorical Stasis of the Galatian Controversy'. *JBL* 114/3 (1995): 437–61.

T. W. Martin. 'Whose Flesh? What Temptation? (Galatians 4.13-14)'. *JSNT* 74 (1999): 65–91.

T. W. Martin. 'The Covenant of Circumcision (Genesis 17:9-14) and the Situational Antithesis in Galatians 3:28'. *JBL* 122/1 (2003): 111–125.

J. L. Martyn. 'Apocalyptic Antinomies in Paul's Letter to the Galatians'. *NTS* 31 (1985): 410–424.

J. L. Martyn. 'A Law-Observant Mission to Gentiles: The Background of Galatians'. *SJT* 38 (1985): 307–24.

J. L. Martyn. 'The Covenants of Hagar and Sarah'. In *Faith and History: Essays in Honor of Paul W. Meyer.* Ed. by J. T. Carroll, C. H. Cosgrove and E. E. Johnson. Atlanta: Scholars, 1990, 160–192.

J. L. Martyn. 'Events in Galatia: Modified Covenantal Nomism versus God's Invasion of the Cosmos in the Singular Gospel: A Response to J. D. G. Dunn and B. R. Gaventa'. In *Pauline Theology. I. Thessalonians, Philippians, Galatians, Philemon.* Ed. by J. M. Bassler. Minneapolis: Fortress, 1991, 160–79.

J. L. Martyn. *Galatians: A New Translation with Introduction and Commentary.* AB 33A. New York: Doubleday, 1997.

Justin Martyr. *Dialogue with Trypho.* Translated by T. B. Falls. Rev. and with a new introduction by Thomas P. Halton. Edited by Michael Slusser. Washington, D.C.: The Catholic University of America Press, 2003.

J. A. Mata. 'El ser Amados nos hace Libres para Amar'. *Estudios teológicos* 17 (1982): 69–118.

F. J. Matera. 'The Culmination of Paul's Argument to the Galatians: 5:1–6:17'. *JSNT* 32 (1988): 79–91.

F. J. Matera. *Galatians.* SP 9. Collegeville, Minn.: Glazier, 1992.

R. B. Matlock. *Unveiling the Apocalyptic Paul: Paul's Interpreters and the Rhetoric of Criticism.* JSNTSup 127. Sheffield: Sheffield Academic, 1996.

B. H. McLean. *The Cursed Christ: Mediterranean Expulsion Rituals and Pauline Soteriology.* JSNTSup 126. Sheffield: Sheffield Academic, 1996.

W. A. Meeks. '"And Rose Up to Play": Midrash and Paraenesis in 1 Corinthians 10:1-22'. *JSNT* 16 (1982): 64–78.

O. Merk. 'Der Beginn der Paränese im Galaterbrief'. *ZNW* 60 (1969): 83–104.

J.-P. Migne, ed. *Jerome's Commentarii in quattuor Epistolas S. Pauli: Ad Galatas, ad Ephesios, ad Titum, ad Philemonem.* PL 26; Paris, 1845.

M. M. Mitchell. 'Rhetorical Shorthand in Pauline Argumentation: The Functions of "The Gospel" in the Corinthian Correspondence'. In *Gospel in Paul: Studies on Corinthians, Galatians and Romans for Richard N. Longenecker.* Ed. by L. A. Jervis and P. Richardson. JSNTSup 108. Sheffield: Sheffield Academic, 1994, 63–88.

M. M. Mitchell. 'Reading Rhetoric with Patristic Exegesis: John Chrysostom on Galatians'. In *Antquity and Humanity: Essays on Ancient Religion and Philosophy Presented to Hans Dieter Betz on his 70th Birthday.* Ed. by A. Y. Collins. Tübingen: Mohr, 2001, 333–355.

S. Mitchell. *Anatolia: Land, Men, and Gods in Asia Minor.* 2 vols. Oxford: Clarendon Press, 1993.

D. Mitternacht. *Forum für Sprachlose: Eine kommunikationspsychologische und epistolärrhetorische Untersuchung des Galaterbriefs.* CBNTS 30. Stockholm: Almquist & Wiksell International, 1999.

D. Mitternacht. 'Foolish Galatians? – A Recipient-Oriented Assessment of Paul's Letter'. In *The Galatians Debate: Contemporary Issues in Rhetorical and Historical Interpretation.* Ed. by M. D. Nanos. Peabody, Mass.: Hendrickson, 2002, 408–33.

K. A. Morland. *The Rhetoric of Curse in Galatians: Paul Confronts Another Gospel*. Emory Studies in Early Christianity. Atlanta: Scholars, 1995.

C. F. D. Moule. *An Idiom Book of the Greek New Testament*. 2nd ed.; Cambridge: Cambridge University Press, 1959.

J. Muddiman. 'An Anatomy of Galatians'. In *Crossing the Boundaries: Essays in Biblical Interpretation in Honour of Michael Goulder*. Ed. by S. E. Porter, P. Joyce and D. E. Orton. BibIntSer 8. Leiden: Brill, 1994, 257–70.

K. Müller. *Tora für die Völker: Die noachidischen Gebote und Ansätze zu ihrer Rezeption im Christentum*. SKI 15. Berlin: Institut Kirche und Judentum, 1998.

J. Murphy-O'Connor. *Paul: A Critical Life*. Oxford: Oxford University Press, 1996.

J. Murphy-O'Connor. *Paul: His Story*. Oxford: Oxford University Press, 2004.

M. Murray. *'Playing a Jewish Game': Gentile Christian Judaizing in the First and Second Centuries CE*. SSEJC 13. Ontario: Wilfrid Laurer University Press, 2004.

F. Mussner. *Der Galaterbrief*. HTKNT 11. Freiburg: Herders, 1974.

M. D. Nanos. *The Irony of Galatians: Paul's Letter in First-Century Context*. Minneapolis: Fortress, 2002.

E. Nestle and K. Aland, eds. *Novum Testamentum Graece*. 27th ed. Stuttgart: Deutsche Bibelgesellschaft, 1994.

J. H. Neyrey. 'Bewitched in Galatia: Paul and Cultural Anthropology'. *CBQ* 50 (1988): 72–100.

J. H. Neyrey. *Paul, in Other Words: A Cultural Reading of His Letters*. Louisville, Ky.: Westminster/John Knox, 1991.

K.-W. Niebuhr. *Heidenapostel aus Israel: Die jüdische Identität des Paulus nach ihrer Darstellung in seinen Briefen*. WUNT 62. Tübingen: Mohr, 1992.

B. Nitzan. *Qumran Prayer and Religious Poetry*. STDJ XII. Leiden: Brill, 1994.

A. Oepke. *Der Brief des Paulus an die Galater*. 5th ed.; THNT 9. Berlin: Evangelische Verlagsanstalt, 1984.

N. Pardee. 'The Curse that Saves (*Didache* 16.5)'. In *The Didache in Context: Essays on its Text, History, and Transmission*. Ed. by C. N. Jefford. NovTSup 77. Leiden: Brill, 1995, 156–76.

R. Parker. *Miasma: Pollution and Purification in Early Greek Religion*. Oxford: Clarendon Press, 1996.

S. Pedersen. 'Agape: Der eschatologische Hauptbegriff bei Paulus'. In *Paulinische Literatur und Theologie: Anlässlich der 50. jährigen Gründungs-Feier der Universität von Aarhus*. Ed. by S. Pedersen. Skandinavische Beiträge. Göttingen: Vandenhoeck & Ruprecht, 1980, 159–86.

C. Perelman and L. Olbrechts-Tyteca. *The New Rhetoric: A Treatise in Argumentation*. Translated by J. Wilkinson and P. Weaver. Notre Dame: University of Notre Dame Press, 1969.

C. Perrot. 'La Loi et son accomplissement selon Ga 5,13-26'. In *La Foi agissant par l'Amour*. Ed. by A. Vanhoye. Série Monographique de Benedictina 13. Rome: Abbaye de S. Paul, 1996, 123–42.

R. Pettazzoni. *Essays on the History of Religions*. Leiden: Brill, 1954.

G. Petzl. 'Die Beichtinschriften Westkleinasiens'. *Epigraphica Anatolica* 22 (1994): v–xxi, 1–178.

C. Pigeon. '"La Loi du Christ" en Galates 6,2'. *SR* 29/4 (2000): 425–438.

H. W. Pleket. 'Religious History as the History of Mentality: The "Believer" as Servant of the Deity in the Greek World'. In *Faith, Hope and Worship: Aspects of Religious Mentality in the Ancient World*. Ed. by H. S. Versnel. Vol. 2. Studies in Greek and Roman Religion. Leiden: Brill, 1981, 152–92.

E. Plumer. *Augustine's Commentary on Galatians: Introduction, Translation (with Facing Latin Text), and Notes.* Oxford Early Christian Studies. Oxford: Oxford University Press, 2003.

J. S. Pobee. *Persecution and Martyrdom in the Theology of Paul.* JSNTSup 6. Sheffield: JSOT Press, 1985.

K. Preisendanz. 'Fluchtafeln (Defixion)'. In *RAC.* Ed. by T. Kluser et al. Vol. 8. Stuttgart: Anton Hiersemann, 1972, cols. 1–29.

E. Qimron and J. Strugnell. *Qumran Cave 4.V: Miqṣat Ma'asé Ha-Torah.* DJD X. Oxford: Clarendon, 1994.

H. Rackham, ed. *Aristotle. Politics.* LCL. Vol. 21. Cambridge, Mass.: Harvard University Press, 1990.

H. Rackham, ed. *Pliny. Natural History.* LCL. 10 Vols. Cambridge, Mass.: Harvard University Press, 1938–62.

A. Rahlfs, ed. *Septuaginta.* Stuttgart: Deutsche Bibelgesellschaft, 1993.

H. Räisänen. *Paul and the Law.* 2nd ed.; WUNT 29. Tübingen: Mohr, 1987.

F. P. Ramos. *La Libertad en la Carta a los Gálatas: Estudio exegético-teológico.* Publicaciones de la Universidad Pontificia Comillas. Madrid: EAPSA, 1977.

W. M. Ramsay. *A Historical Commentary on St. Paul's Epistle to the Galatians.* London: Hodder & Stoughton, 1899.

M. Rastoin. *Tarse et Jérusalem: La double Culture de l'Apôtre Paul en Galates 3,6-4,7.* AnBib 152. Rome: Editrice Pontificio Istituto Biblico, 2003.

W. Reinbold. 'Gal 3,6-14 und das Problem der Erfüllbarkeit des Gesetzes bei Paulus'. *ZNW* 91 (2000): 91–106.

E. Reinmuth. *Geist und Gesetz. Studien zu Voraussetzungen und Inhalt der paulinischen Paränese.* Theologische Arbeiten 44. Berlin: Evangelische Verlagsanstalt, 1985.

M. Ricl. 'CIG 4142–A Forgotten Confession-Inscription from North-West Phrygia'. *Epigraphica Anatolica* 29 (1997): 35–43.

H. N. Ridderbos. *The Epistle of Paul to the Churches of Galatia.* NICNT. Grand Rapids: Eerdmans, 1953.

R. Riesner. *Paul's Early Period: Chronology, Mission Strategy, Theology.* Grand Rapids: Eerdmans, 1998.

J. D. Robb. 'Galatians V. 23: An Explanation'. *ExpTim* 56 (1944–45): 279–280.

L. Robert. 'Malédictions funéraires grecques'. In *Opera Minora Selecta: Épigraphie et Antiquités Grecques.* Vol. 5. Amsterdam: Hakkert, 1989, 697–745.

J. H. Ropes. *The Singular Problem of the Epistle to the Galatians.* HTS 14. Cambridge, Mass.: Harvard University Press, 1929.

W. B. Russell. *The Flesh/Spirit Conflict in Galatians.* Lanham, Md.: University Press of America, 1997.

E. P. Sanders. *Paul and Palestinian Judaism: A Comparison of Patterns of Religion.* Philadelphia: Fortress, 1977.

E. P. Sanders. *Paul, the Law, and the Jewish People.* Philadelphia: Fortress, 1983.

K. O. Sandnes. *Paul – One of the Prophets?: A Contribution to the Apostle's Self-Understanding.* WUNT 2/43. Tübingen: Mohr, 1991.

R. Schäfer. *Paulus bis zum Apostelkonzil: Ein Beitrag zur Einleitung in den Galaterbrief, zur Geschichte der Jesusbewegung und zur Pauluschronologie.* WUNT 2/179. Tübingen: Mohr, 2004.

S. Schewe. *Die Galater zurückgewinnen: Paulinische Strategien in Galater 5 und 6.* FRLANT 208. Göttingen: Vandenhoeck & Ruprecht, 2005.

H. Schlier. *Der Brief an die Galater.* KEK 7. Göttingen: Vandenhoeck & Ruprecht, 1962.

W. Schmithals. *Paul and the Gnostics.* Translated by J. E. Steely. Nashville, Tenn.: Abingdon, 1972.

E. J. Schnabel. *Law and Wisdom from Ben Sira to Paul: A Tradition Historical Inquiry into the Relation of Law, Wisdom, and Ethics.* WUNT 2/16. Tübingen: Mohr, 1985.

E. J. Schnabel. 'Divine Tyranny and Public Humiliation: A Suggestion for the Interpretation of the Lydian and Phrygian Confession Inscriptions'. *NovT* 45/2 (2003): 160–188.

U. Schnelle. *Paulus: Leben und Denken.* Berlin: Gruyter, 2003.

H. J. Schoeps. *Paul: The Theology of the Apostle in the Light of Jewish Religious History.* Translated by H. Knight. London: Lutterworth Press, 1961.

W. Schrage. 'Probleme paulinischer Ethik anhand von Gal 5,25-6,10'. In *La Foi agissant par l'amour.* Ed. A. Vanhoye. Rome: Abbaye de S. Paul, 1996, 155–94.

T. R. Schreiner. 'Is Perfect Obedience to the Law Possible? A Re-examination of Galatians 3:10'. *JETS* 27 (1984): 151–60.

T. R. Schreiner. *The Law and its Fulfillment: A Pauline Theology of Law.* Grand Rapids: Baker, 1993.

E. Schürer. *The History of the Jewish People in the Age of Jesus Christ (175 B.C.–A.D. 135).* Revised and edited by Geza Vermes, Fergus Millar and Martin Goodman. 4 Vols. Edinburgh: T & T Clark, 1986.

E. Schweizer. 'υἱός κτλ.'. In *TDNT.* Ed. by G. Friedrich. Vol. 8. Grand Rapids: Eerdmans, 1972, 334–99.

J. M. Scott. *Adoption as Sons of God: An Exegetical Investigation into the Background of ΥΙΟΘΕΣΙΑ in the Pauline Corpus.* WUNT 2/48. Tübingen: Mohr, 1992.

J. M. Scott. '"For as Many as are of Works of the Law are Under a Curse" (Galatians 3:10)'. In *Paul and the Scritpures of Israel.* Ed. by C. A. Evans and J. A. Sanders. JSNTSup 83. Sheffield: Sheffield Academic, 1993, 187–221.

J. M. Scott. *Paul and the Nations: The Old Testament and Jewish Background of Paul's Mission to the Nations with Special Reference to the Destination of Galatians.* WUNT 84. Tübingen: Mohr, 1995.

J. M. Scott. *2 Corinthians.* NIBCNT 8. Peabody, Mass.: Hendrickson, 1998.

A. F. Segal. *Paul the Convert: The Apostolate and Apostasy of Saul the Pharisee.* New Haven, Conn.: Yale University Press, 1990.

A. F. Segal. 'Universalism in Judaism and Christianity'. In *Paul in His Hellenistic Context.* Ed. by T. Engberg-Pedersen. Edinburgh: T & T Clark, 1994, 1–29.

G. Shaw. *The Cost of Authority: Manipulation and Freedom in the New Testament.* Philadelphia: Fortress, 1983.

M. Silva. *Interpreting Galatians: Explorations in Exegetical Method.* 2nd ed.; Grand Rapids: Baker, 2001.

V. M. Smiles. *The Gospel and the Law in Galatia: Paul's Response to Jewish Christian Separatism and the Threat of Galatian Apostasy.* Collegeville, Minn.: Liturgical, 1998.

J. F. M. Smit. 'The Letter of Paul to the Galatians: A Deliberative Speech'. *NTS* 35 (1989): 1–26.

B. D. Smith. *Paul's Seven Explanations of the Suffering of the Righteous.* Studies in Biblical Literature 47. New York: Peter Lang, 2002.

T. Söding. *Das Liebesgebot bei Paulus: Die Mahnung zur Agape im Rahmen der paulinischen Ethik.* NTA 26. Münster: Aschendorff, 1995.

T. Söding. 'Die Gegner des Apostels Paulus in Galatien'. In *Das Wort vom Kreuz: Studien zur paulinischen Theologie.* WUNT 93. Tübingen: Mohr, 1997, 132–52.

T. Söding. 'Verheißung und Erfüllung im Lichte paulinischer Theologie'. *NTS* 46 (2001): 146–70.

A. Souter, ed. *Pelagius's Expositions of Thirteen Epistles of St. Paul*. Text and Studies 9. Cambridge: Cambridge University Press, 1926
C. D. Stanley. '"Under a Curse": A Fresh Reading of Galatians 3.10-14'. *NTS* 36 (1990): 481–511.
C. D. Stanley. *Paul and the Language of Scripture: Citation Technique in the Pauline Epistles and Contemporary Literature*. SNTMS 69. Cambridge: Cambridge University Press, 1992.
C. D. Stanley. *Arguing with Scripture: The Rhetoric of Quotations in the Letters of Paul*. London: T & T Clark, 2004.
G. N. Stanton. 'The Law of Moses and the Law of Christ – Galatians 3.1-6.2'. In *Paul and the Mosaic Law*. Ed. by J. D. G. Dunn. Tübingen: Mohr, 1996, 99–116.
G. N. Stanton. 'What is the Law of Christ?'. *ExAud* 17 (2001): 47–59.
G. N. Stanton. *Jesus and Gospel*. Cambridge: Cambridge University Press, 2004.
M. Stern. *Greek and Latin Authors on Jews and Judaism, Volume 1: From Herodotus to Plutarch*. Jerusalem: Israel Academy of Sciences and Humanities, 1976.
M. L. Stirewalt. *Paul: The Letter Writer*. Grand Rapids: Eerdmans, 2003.
C. K. Stockhausen. '2 Corinthians 3 and the Principles of Pauline Exegesis'. In *Paul and the Scriptures of Israel*. Ed. by C. A. Evans and J. A. Sanders. JSNTSup 83. Sheffield: JSOT Press, 1993,
D. A. Stoike. '"The Law of Christ": A Study of Paul's Use of the Expression in Galatians 6'. Th.D. diss., Claremont School of Theology, 1971.
J. G. Strelan. 'Burden-Bearing and the Law of Christ: A Re-Examination of Galatians 6:2'. *JBL* 94 (1975): 266–76.
J. H. M. Strubbe. '"Cursed by He that Moves My Bones"'. In *Magika Hiera: Ancient Greek Magic and Religion*. Ed. by C. A. Faraone and D. Obbink. Oxford: Oxford University Press, 1991, 33–59.
J. H. M. Strubbe. 'Curses Against Violation of the Grave in Jewish Epitaphs from Asia Minor'. In *Studies in Early Jewish Epigraphy*. Ed. by J. W. van Henten and P. W. van der Horst. AGJU 21. Leiden: Brill, 1994, 70–127.
D. Stuart. *Hosea-Jonah*. WBC 31. Waco, Tex.: Word, 1987.
P. Stuhlmacher. 'The Law as a Topic of Biblical Theology'. In *Reconciliation, Law, and Rigtheousness: Essays in Biblical Theology*. Philadelphia: Fortress, 1986, 110–33.
P. Stuhlmacher. *Biblische Theologie des Neuen Testaments. Band I. Grundlegung: Von Jesus zu Paulus*. Göttingen: Vandenhoeck & Ruprecht, 1992.
A. Suhl. 'Der Galaterbrief – Situation und Argumentation'. In *ANRW*. Ed. by W. Haase. Part 2. *Principat*, 25.4. New York: de Gruyter, 1987, 3067–3134.
A. Suhl. 'Die Galater und der Geist. Kritische Erwägungen zur Situation in Galatien'. In *Jesu Rede von Gott und ihre Nachgeschichte im frühen Christentum. Beiträge zur Verkündigung Jesu und zum Kerygma der Kirche. FS W. Marxsen*. Ed. by D.-A. Koch, G. Sellin and A. Lindemann. Gütersloh: Gütersloher, 1989, 267–96.
J. L. Sumney. *Identifying Paul's Opponents: The Question of Method in 2 Corinthians*. JSNTSup 40. Sheffield: JSOT Press, 1990.
J. L. Sumney. *"Servants of Satan", "False Brothers" and Other Opponents of Paul*. JSNTSup 188. Sheffield: Sheffield Academic, 1999.
P. N. W. Swarup. 'An Eternal Planting, a House of Holiness: The Self-Understanding of the Dead Sea Scrolls Community'. Ph.D. diss., Cambridge University, 2002.
P. N. W. Swarup. *An Eternal Planting, a House of Holiness: The Self-Understanding of the Dead Sea Scrolls Community*. Library of Second Temple Studies; London: T & T Clark, 2006.

H. B. Swete. *Theodori Episcopi Mopsuesteni in Epistolas B. Pauli Commentrii.* Cambridge: Cambridge University Press, 1880.
S. Talmon. 'The "Desert Motif" in the Bible and in Qumran Literature'. In *Biblical Motifs: Origins and Transformations.* Ed. by A. Altmann. Cambridge, Mass.: Harvard University Press, 1966, 31–63.
H. St. J. Thackeray, R. Marcus, A. Wikgren and L. H. Feldman, eds. *Josephus: Works.* LCL. 10 Vols. Cambridge, Mass.: Harvard University Press, 1926–65.
F. Thielman. *From Plight to Solution: A Jewish Framework for Understanding Paul's View of the Law in Galatians and Romans.* NovTSup 61. Leiden: Brill, 1989.
F. Thielman. 'The Coherence of Paul's View of the Law: The Evidence of First Corinthians'. *NTS* 38 (1992): 235–253.
F. Thielman. *Paul & the Law: A Contextual Approach.* Downers Grove, Ill.: InterVarsity, 1994.
F. Thielman. *The Law and the New Testament: The Question of Continuity.* Companions to the New Testament. New York: Crossroad, 1999.
A. C. Thiselton. *The First Epistle to the Corinthians: A Commentary on the Greek Text.* NIGTC. Grand Rapids: Eerdmans, 2000.
I. H. Thomson. *Chiasmus in the Pauline Letters.* JSNTSup 111. Sheffield: Sheffield Academic, 1995.
D. F. Tolmie. *Persuading the Galatians: A Text-Centered Rhetorical Analysis of a Pauline Letter.* WUNT 2/190. Tübingen: Mohr, 2005.
P. J. Tomson. *Paul and the Jewish Law: Halakha in the Letters of the Apostle to the Gentiles.* CRINT. Vol. 1. Section 3, Jewish Traditions in Early Christian Literature. Assen/Maastricht and Minneapolis: Van Gorcum and Fortress, 1990.
P. J. Tomson. 'Paul's Jewish Background in View of his Law Teaching in 1Cor 7'. In *Paul and the Mosaic Law.* Ed. by J. D. G. Dunn. Tübingen: Mohr, 1996, 251–70.
P. J. Tomson. *"If This be From Heaven . . .": Jesus and the New Testament Authors in Their Relationship to Judaism.* Biblical Seminar 76. Sheffield: Sheffield Academic, 2001.
P. R. Trebilco. *Jewish Communities in Asia Minor.* SNTSMS 69. Cambridge: Cambridge University Press, 1991.
G. W. Trompf. *Early Christian Historiography: Narratives of Retributive Justice.* Studies in Religion. London and New York: Continuum, 2000.
C. M. Tuckett. 'Paul, Scripture and Ethics. Some Reflections'. *NTS* 46 (2000): 403–24.
J. B. Tyson. 'Paul's Opponents in Galatia'. *NovT* 4 (1968): 241–254.
H. van de Sandt and D. Flusser. *The Didache: Its Jewish Sources and its Place in Early Judaism and Christianity.* CRINT. Assen and Minneapolis: Royal van Gorcum and Fortress, 2002.
H. van de Sandt. 'An Explanation of Rom. 8,4a'. *Bijdr* 37 (1976): 361–78.
P. W. van der Horst. *Ancient Jewish Epitaphs: An Introductory Survey of a Millennium of Jewish Funerary Epigraphy.* CBET 2. Kampen: Kok Pharos, 1991.
A. van Dülmen. *Die Theologie des Gesetzes bei Paulus.* SBM 5. Stuttgart: Katholisches Bibelwerk, 1968.
H. S. Versnel. 'Beyond Cursing: The Appeal to Justice in Judicial Prayers'. In *Magika Hiera: Ancient Greek Magic and Religion.* Ed. by C. A. Faraone and D. Obbink. New York and Oxford: Oxford University Press, 1991, 60–106.
S. Vollenweider. *Freiheit als neue Schöpfung: Eine Untersuchung zur Eleutheria bei Paulus und in seiner Umwelt.* FRLANT 147. Göttingen: Vandenhoeck & Ruprecht, 1989.
J. S. Vos. 'Paul's Argumentation in Galatians 1–2'. *HTR* 87/1 (1994): 1–16.
J. S. Vos. *Die Kunst der Argumentation bei Paulus: Studien zur antiken Rhetorik.* WUNT 149. Tübingen: Mohr, 2002.

F. Vouga. 'Zur rhetorischen Gattung des Galaterbriefes'. *ZNW* 79 (1988): 291–292.
F. Vouga. 'Der Galaterbrief: Kein Brief an die Galater? Essay über den literarischen Charakter des letzten großen Paulusbriefes'. In *Schrift und Tradition: Festschrift Josef Ernst*. Ed. by K. Backhaus and G. Untergassmair. Paderborn: Schöningh, 1996, 243–58.
F. Vouga. *An die Galater*. HNT 10. Tübingen: Mohr, 1998.
A. H. Wakefield. *Where to Live: The Hermeneutical Significance of Paul's Citations from Scripture in Galatians 3:1-14*. SBLDS 14. Atlanta: Society of Biblical Literature, 2003.
N. Walter. 'Paulus und die Gegner des Christusevangeliums in Galatien'. In *L'apôtre Paul: Personnalité, style, et conception du ministère*. Ed. by A. Vanhoye. BETL 73. Leuven: Leuven University Press, 1986, 351–56.
D. F. Watson. 'The Contributions and Limitations of Greco-Roman Rhetorical Theory for Constructing the Rhetorical and Historical Situations of a Pauline Epistle'. In *The Rhetorical Interpretation of Scripture: Essays from the 1996 Malibu Conference*. Ed. by S. E. Porter and D. L. Stamps. JSNTSupp 180. Sheffield: Sheffield Academic, 1999, 125–51.
F. Watson. *Paul and the Hermeneutics of Faith*. London: T & T Clark, 2004.
H. Weder. 'Die Normativität der Freiheit: Eine Überlegung zu Gal 5:1, 13-25'. In *Paulus, Apostel Jesu Christi: Festschrift für Günter Klein zum 70. Geburtstag*. Ed. by M. Trowitzsch. Tübingen: Mohr, 1998, 129–45.
J. A. D. Weima. 'Gal. 6.11-18: A Hermeneutical Key to the Galatian Letter'. *CTJ* 28 (1993): 90–107.
D. Wenham. *Paul: Follower of Jesus or Founder of Christianity?* Grand Rapids: Eerdmans, 1995.
R. A. Werline. 'The Curses of the Covenant Renewal Ceremony in 1QS 1.16-2.19 and the Prayers of the Condemned'. In *For a Later Generation: The Transformation of Tradition in Israel, Early Judaism, and Early Christianity*. Ed. by R. A. Argall, B. A. Bow and R. A. Werline. Harrisburg, Pa.: Trinity Press International, 2000, 280–88.
G. F. Wessels. 'The Call to Responsible Freedom in Paul's Persuasive Strategy. Galatians 5:13-6:10'. *Neot* 26/2 (1992): 461–474.
S. Westerholm. 'On Fulfilling the Whole Law (Gal 5.14)'. *SEÅ* 51–52 (1986–87): 229–37.
S. Westerholm. *Israel's Law and the Church's Faith: Paul and his Recent Interpreters*. Grand Rapids: Eerdmans, 1988.
E. E. White. *The Context of Human Discourse: A Configurational Criticism of Rhetoric*. Columbia, S.C.: University of South Carolina Press, 1992.
U. Wilckens. 'Zur Entwicklung des paulinischen Gesetzesverständnisses'. *NTS* 28 (1982): 154–90.
W. N. Wilder. *Echoes of the Exodus Narrative in the Context and Background of Galatians 5:18*. Studies in Biblical Literature 23. New York: Peter Lang, 2001.
T. Wiley. *Paul and Gentile Women: Reframing Galatians*. London: Continuum, 2005.
S. K. Williams. *Galatians*. ANTC. Nashville, Tenn.: Abingdon, 1997.
T. A. Wilson. 'Wilderness Apostasy and Paul's Portrayal of the Crisis in Galatians'. *NTS* 50 (2004): 550–571.
T. A. Wilson. 'The Law of Christ and the Law of Moses: Reflections on a Recent Trend in Interpretation'. *CurBR* 5.1 (2006): 129–50.
T. A. Wilson. '"Under Law" in Galatians: A Pauline Theological Abbreviation'. *JTS* 56/2 (2006): 362–92.
M. Winger. *By What Law? The Meaning of Nomos in the Letters of Paul*. SBLDS 128. Atlanta: Scholars, 1992.
M. Winger. 'The Law of Christ'. *NTS* 46 (2000): 537–546.
M. Winger. 'Act One: Paul Arrives in Galatia'. *NTS* 48 (2002): 548–67.

J. R. Wisdom. *Blessing for the Nations and the Curse of the Law: Paul's Citation of Genesis and Deuteronomy in Gal 3.8-10.* WUNT 2/133. Tübingen: Mohr, 2001.

B. Witherington. *Grace in Galatia: A Commentary on St Paul's Letter to the Galatians.* Grand Rapids: Eerdmans, 1998.

T. Witulski. *Die Adressaten des Galaterbriefes: Untersuchungen zur Gemeinde von Antiochia ad Psidiam.* FRLANT 193. Göttingen: Vandenhoeck & Ruprecht, 2000.

J. Wright. 'Spirit and Wilderness: The Interplay of Two Motifs within the Hebrew Bible as Background to Mark 1:2-13'. In *Perspectives on Language and Text: Essays and Poems in Honor of Francis I. Andersen's Sixtieth Birthday July 28, 1985.* Ed. by E. W. Conrad and E. G. Newing. Winona Lake, Ind.: Eisenbrauns, 1987, 269–98.

N. T. Wright. *The Climax of the Covenant: Christ and the Law in Pauline Theology.* Edinburgh: T & T Clark, 1991.

M. Wyschogrod. 'A Jewish Postscript'. In *Encountering Jesus: A Debate on Christology.* Ed. by S. T. Davis. Atlanta: Westminster/John Knox, 1988,

M. Wyschogrod. 'Christianity and Mosaic Law'. *ProEccl* 2/4 (1993): 451–59.

M. Wyschogrod. *Abraham's Promise: Judaism and Jewish-Christian Relations.* Edited by R. K. Soulen. Grand Rapids: Eerdmans, 2004.

N. H. Young. '*Paidagogos*: The Social Setting of a Pauline Metaphor'. *NovT* 29/2 (1987): 150–176.

N. H. Young. 'Who's Cursed – And Why? (Galatians 3:10-14)'. *JBL* 117 (1998): 79–92.

Index of Sources

Old Testament

Genesis
12	58
12.1-3	58
12.3	59, 60
1.3b	60
12.3	62, 68
15	58
15.6	62
17	58, 61, 62
17.1-14	60
17.4	61
17.8	61
17.9-14	61, 62
17.10-14	58, 68
17.13	62
17.14	61, 62, 92
17.22-27	62
21.10	43
22	58

Exodus
10.2	75
16-17	130
18.27	114
32.1-35	132
32	133
32.1-35	133
32.6	133
32.8	132
32.26-28	132
32.39	132
34.7	75
34.15-16	132

Leviticus
19.18	5
26	93
26.16	93
26.17	93
26.19	93
26.20	93
26.22	93
26.29	93
26.29	93
26.31	93
26.32	93
26.33	93
26.36	93
26.37	93
26.39	93
26.43	93
33.43	93

Numbers
11	130, 132
11.1-35	133
11.4-35	131
12	130, 131
12.1-16	133
13-14	130
13.1-14.45	133
16	132
16-17	130
16.1-35	131, 133
21.4-9	133
25.1	133
25.1-5	132, 133
25.2	132, 133
25.7-8	132
25.11-13	132

Deuteronomy
4.26	93
4.30	93

13	25, 26, 58, 67	32.24	93
13.1-2	25	32.25	93
13.3	26	32.35-39	93
13.7	26	32.36	93
13.13-16	67	32.41	93
13.14	26		
15.26	62	*Nehemiah*	
21.23	28, 36	9	140
27-28	54, 93		
27.26	30, 55, 58, 63, 64,	*Proverbs*	
	68, 92, 109, 113	12.25	54
28.1-22	93	17.6	75
28.18	93		
28.20	93	*Isaiah*	
28.22	93	8.12	54
28.23	93	11.1-2	135
28.24	93	27.2-6	135
28.27	93	27.6	135
28.28	93	30.10	66
28.29	93	32.14	135
28.30	93	32.15	113
28.31	93	32.15-16	135
28.32	93	35	136
28.33	93	35.1-2	136
28.34	93	35.10	136
28.35	93	36.6	136
28.41	93	37.30-32	135
28.43	93	40-66	135
28.45	93	41	139
28.45-46	94	41.17-20	136
28.51	93	44.1-4	136
28.53-56	93	44.3	139
28.53-57	54	44.13	113
28.58	55	49.10	139
28.59	93	51.1-3	136, 137
28.59-61	93	51.2	136, 137
28.62	93	54.1	42, 136
28.65	93	55.10-13	136
28.66	93	28.6-11	136
29.19	76	59.12	113
29.20	63	61.1-3	135
29.22	93	61.11	135
29.23	93	64.9	135
30.15	93	65.23	135
30.19-20	60		
30.19	23, 27	*Jeremiah*	
31.17	93	31.27-28	135
31.21	93	31.33	113
31.29	93	32.41	135
32	140	51.25	113

Index of Sources

31.27-28	135		*Hosea*	
31.33	113		2.2-3	135
32.41	135		2.14-16	138
51.25	113		2.19-20	138
			14.5-8	135
Ezekiel				
11.9	113		*Joel*	
14.22-24	135		2.18-32	113, 135
17.22-24	135		2.21-22	138
36.26	113		2.28-29	138
36.26-27	113			
37.14	113		*Amos*	
39.29	113		9.13-15	135
Daniel				
12.12	88			

New Testament

Matthew			2.39	113
5.11-12	87		5.38-39	66
5.17	113		7.2	58
10.22	87		15	6, 54
25.41	127		15.1	56
27.63-64	67		19.7	108
5.11-12	87		20.18	108
5.17	113		27.37	108
10.22	87			
			Romans	
Mark			1.8-15	24
1.2-13	164		1.9	65
11.31-32	66		3.8	94
			4	59, 64
Luke			4.16	58
1.12	54		6.1	94
6.22	87		6.14-15	31, 44
			6.15	94
John			7.7-25	40
7.12	67		8.1-2	119
7.47	67		8.3	39
8.53	58		8.4	110
13.34-35	104		9.1	65
14.27	54		9.6-12	43
			11.32	38
Acts			12.14	85
2.17-21	138		13.8-10	110, 112
2.33	113		16.15	108

1 Corinthians

1.4-9	24
4.9-13	83
4.12	85
5.1-5	26, 27
7.19	6
9.20-21	31, 44
10.1-13	134, 140
12.19	108
15.9	85

2 Corinthians

1.3-11	24
1.23	65
4.7-12	90
4.8-11	83
4.9	85
5.10	108
6.4-6	83
11.22	58
11.23-30	83
11.31	65
12.19	65

Galatians

1-2	51, 65, 85
1-4	3, 12, 85
1.1	65
1.1-4	127
1.1-9	23
1.2	50, 108
1.4	38, 42, 84, 115, 117, 138, 140
1.5	27
1.6	24, 25, 26, 55
1.6-7	24, 25, 27, 48, 128, 129
1.6-9	24, 41, 81
1.7	24, 26, 41, 53, 56, 62
1.8	25
1.8-9	23-27, 29, 30, 43, 44, 57, 143, 144
1.9	25
1.10	65, 66, 85, 100
1.10-12	25
1.11	31, 66
1.11-12	65
1.11-17	65
1.12	66
1.13	80, 81, 84, 85
1.13-24	66
1.15-17	66
1.16	81, 89
1.17-2.10	65
1.20	65
1.22	31
1.23	80, 81, 84
2-4	12
2.1-10	27
2.1-14	85
2.1-15	85
2.3	53
2.4	27, 31, 100, 116
2.5	55, 85
2.11	65
2.14	53
2.15-16	38
5.15-17	93
2.15-21	38, 111, 144
2.15-4.7	81
2.15-5.12	101
2.16	31, 33, 108
2.17	31, 67, 116
2.19	7, 81
2.19-20	8, 81, 84-86, 89, 114, 116, 117
2.20	31, 55, 84, 112, 115
2.21	84, 117
3-4	23
3.1	25, 26, 54, 55, 81, 84, 86, 88, 89, 115, 117
3.1-2	89
3.1-5	10, 24, 41, 81, 87, 88, 117
3.1-14	55
3.2	31, 33, 55, 89
3.3	53, 55, 68, 101, 141, 143
3.4	81, 87, 88
3.5	31, 33, 55, 87, 89
3.6	58
3.6-9	27
3.6-14	55, 58
3.6-18	47
3.6-29	57, 135
3.6-4.7	41
3.6-4.31	56
3.7	31, 33
3.8	31, 33, 37, 38, 57, 58
3.8-9	36
3.9	29, 33, 58

Index of Sources

3.10	28-31, 33-38, 42, 43, 54, 55, 57, 62, 63, 68, 108-110, 113, 114, 122, 142-144	4.1-9	100
		4.1-11	122
		4.2	29
3.10-12	42	4.3	29
3.10-14	23, 28-30, 33-37, 44, 45, 57, 63, 122, 143	4.3-7	127
		4.4	10, 23, 28, 30, 31, 34-37, 44, 114, 121
3.10-4.7	40		
3.11	33	4.4-5	33-36, 40, 42, 84, 85, 115-117, 143, 144
3.11-12	38, 144		
3.12	33, 55	4.5	10, 23, 28-31, 33-35, 37, 44
3.13	28, 29, 31, 33-36, 40, 55, 57, 84, 108, 114-118, 122, 140-144	4.5-6	118
		4.6	29, 87, 113
		4.6-7	27
3.13-14	29, 42, 55, 58, 89, 144	4.7	40, 55, 133
3.14	29, 36, 55, 58, 112-114, 118	4.8	78
		4.8-9	71, 82, 100, 127, 138
3.15-18	39	4.8-11	24
3.17-18	123	4.8-20	81
3.17-21	38	4.9	26, 40, 41
3.18	33, 133	4.10	41
3.19	39	4.11-20	41
3.19-25	37	4.12	85, 86, 115
3.20	39	4.12-15	88
3.21	33, 37-39, 105, 123, 144	4.12-20	24, 81, 85, 86
3.21-25	39	4.13	116
3.22	37, 39, 42, 138	4.13-14	81, 86, 90, 117
3.22-23	38	4.14	31, 64, 86
3.22-25	42	4.15	86, 90
3.22-29	30, 31	4.16	39, 55
3.23	10, 23, 28, 30, 31, 33, 34, 39, 40, 44	4.16-17	86
		4.17	41, 55, 56, 62, 64, 65, 84
3.23-25	7, 29, 36, 37, 143, 144	4.19	81, 87, 115
3.23-29	40, 122, 143	4.20	27
3.23-4.7	47	4.21	10, 23, 28, 30, 33, 34, 40-42, 44, 56, 123
3.23-5.18	33		
3.24	33, 39	4.21-27	38
3.24-25	40	4.21-31	10, 27, 56-59, 122, 135, 143
3.25	37, 144		
3.25-29	29	4.21-5.1	127
3.26	31	4.21-5.4	143
3.26-29	27	4.21-5.12	81
3.26-4.7	69	4.22-30	42, 43
3.27	29	4.23	42, 101
3.28	31, 62, 100	4.24-25	42, 100
3.29	29, 55, 133	4.25	27
4.1	133	4.26	84
4.1-2	40	4.26-27	42
4.1-3	39	4.28-29	43
4.1-5	29, 42	4.29	42, 80, 81, 83, 101, 135
4.1-7	29, 30, 35, 144	4.30	26, 27, 43, 55, 125, 133

5-6	3, 9, 10, 12-15, 23	5.18	5, 7-12, 19, 23, 28, 30, 31, 33, 34, 43, 44, 119-122, 124, 125, 133, 139-143, 145
5.1	7, 8, 100, 110, 127, 138		
5.1-2	101		
5.1-4	144		
5.1-6	3, 30	5.18-21	140
5.1-12	9, 10, 24, 49, 101	5.18-23	124
5.2-4	27, 43, 56, 103, 110	5.19	131
5.2-5	93	5.19-21	6, 27, 43, 101, 119, 125-127, 129-133, 139, 143-144
5.2-6	53, 69		
5.2-12	81	5.21	14, 16, 25, 43, 55, 123, 126, 127, 131, 133, 138
5.3	6, 102, 108, 109		
5.4	103	5.22	125, 136
5.5	33, 68, 138, 140, 141	5.22-23	119-121, 125, 126, 133-141
5.5-6	16, 27, 112, 125, 126, 144	5.22-24	14
5.6	15, 112, 136, 141	5.23	5, 7-10, 12, 13, 19, 112, 119, 122-125, 138-140, 143
5.7	27, 55, 128, 129		
5.7-8	26	5.24	81, 84, 117, 138, 139
5.7-11	43	5.25	120, 143
5.7-12	26, 27, 43, 81	5.25-26	127
5.8	55	5.26	101, 126, 130, 133, 139
5.9	43	5.31	124
5.10	53, 56	6.1	11, 14, 114
5.10-12	85	6.1-2	105, 125
5.11	80-82, 84-86, 115-117	6.1-5	10
5.12	11, 43	6.1-10	115, 129
5.13	8, 100, 101, 105, 119, 127, 129, 133, 139	6.2	4, 5, 7-10, 12, 14, 19, 91, 99, 100, 102-07, 109, 110, 112, 114-119, 125, 139, 141
5.13-14	104, 106, 112, 115, 116, 120, 129, 139		
5.13-15	43, 102	6.3-5	14, 114
5.13-24	128	6.6-8	114
5.13-26	2, 9, 129	6.7-8	14, 43, 125-127, 133
5.13-6.10	2-19, 23, 45, 95, 99, 101, 102, 107, 118, 119, 127, 141-143, 145	6.7-9	16
		6.8	138, 141
		6.9-10	115
5.14	4, 5, 7-12, 14, 19, 57, 91, 99, 100, 102, 105-10, 114, 117-119, 121, 123, 125, 139, 143	6.11	27
		6.11-18	9-11, 23, 24, 81, 101
		6.12	49, 53, 80, 81, 84, 117
		6.12-13	41, 48, 82, 91, 93, 101, 116
5.15	14, 101, 126, 127, 129, 130, 133, 139	6.12-17	81, 85
		6.13	31, 40, 56
5.16	47, 119-121, 125, 127, 143	6.14	81, 84, 85, 117
5.16-17	11	6.14-17	85, 115
5.16-18	10, 14, 119, 141, 144	6.15	93, 112, 136, 144
5.16-24	69, 118, 127-140	6.15-16	28
5.16-25	143	6.16	23, 26-30, 44, 143, 144
5.17	120, 123	6.17	81, 82, 84-86, 116, 117
		6.11-18	9-11, 23, 24, 81, 101
		6.12	49, 53, 80, 81, 84, 117
		6.12-13	41, 48, 82, 91, 93, 101, 116

Ephesians			*James*	
1.3-14	24		1.12	88
1.13	113			
5.16	35		*1 Peter*	
			2.12-20	84
Philippians			3.1	84
1.3-10	24		3.14	54
1.8	65		3.13-16	84
3.6	85		3.14	87
			4.3-5	84
Colossians			4.12-16	84
1.24	90		4.14	88
4.5	35			
			Revelation	
1 Thessalonians			2.4	124
2.5	65		2.14	124
			2.20	124
1 Timothy				
1.16	108			

Apocrypha and Pseudepigrapha

Apocalypse of Abraham			30.21	57
1-8	58		30.21-22	57
			31.17	60
2 Baruch			31.20	60
13.9-10	92			
			Judith	
1 Enoch			8.27	93
6.4-5	25			
			1 Maccabees	
4 Ezra			1.57	57
4.23	57		2.50	57
7.24	57			
			2 Maccabees	
Joseph and Aseneth			1.2-6	93
2.1	90		6.12-16	93
			6.12-17a	94
Jubilees			7.33	93
1	26			
11.15-17	58		*Psalms of Solomon*	
12.23	60		3.3-4	93
15.14	62		7.1-10	93
15.15	62		10.2	93
15.25	61		13.7	93
25.22	60		13.7-10	93
26.24	60			

Sibylline Oracles	
3.529	88
4.209	88
11.282	88

Sirach	
24.23	57
39.8	57
42.2	57
45.18	130

T. Benjamin	
7.4	88

T. Gad	
5.11	88

T. Judah	
15.2	88

T. Reuben	
3.9	88
4.1	88

T. Simeon	
4.3	88

Tobit	
12.16	54
13.9-18	60
13.12	60

Wisdom	
5.2	54
8.5	54

Dead Sea Scrolls

1QH	
14.13b-17a	135
16.4-8a	136

1QM	
2.2	135
13.4-6	26

1QS	
1.16-2.19	26
4.6-8	136
5.8	57
8.5	137
8.13-14	137
9.19-20	137

4Q286-87	26
4Q280	26

4Q398 (MMT)	
C 28-32	68

11QT	
54.8-11	66

CD	
1.5-8	134
1.20	57
12.3	66

Philo of Alexandria

De Praemiis et Poenis	
1-2	92
126	92, 124

De Specialibus Legibus	
1.54-65	66
1.315	65

De Virtutibus
219   58

Flavius Josephus

Antiquitates Judaicae
1.14   92
1.154-57   58
1.20   92
1.23-24   92
2.292   88
2.293   92
4.14   130
4.270   88
4.279   88
4.310   66
5.166   66
5.31   124
6.267   66
7.39   124
9.43   88
13.318   53
13.268   88

13.257-58   53
15.204   88
17.83   88
20.97-99   65

Bellum Judaicum
1.35   88
8.203   84

Contra Apionem
1.259   88
2.210   31
2.174   31

Vita
112-13   53
404   88

Rabbinic Literature

Genesis Rabbah
46.2   58

m. Sanhedrin
7.6   111
7.10-11   66

Makširin
24[b]   111

m. 'Abot
4.9   111
5.17   129

m. Hullim
7.2   111

m. Menaḥot
10.4   111

m. Sukkah
2.7   111

Mek. Amalek
Exod 18.27 111

Indexes

Early Christian Literature

1 Clement
3.2   129

Clement of Alexandria
Paedagogus
30.3.2   32
33.4.10   32

Stromata
1.3   32
2.3   32
4   32
4.2   32

Didache
16.5   99

Gregory of Nyssa
Psalmorum
5.47.17   32   5.47.18

Canticum
6.403.16   32

Justin Martyr
Dialogue with Trypho
10.3   61
45.3.9   32
95.1.6   32

Origen
De Principiis
4.1.6   32
4.2.6   32

Pseudo-Justin Martyr
Quaestiones
409.c.9   32
413.c.9   32
413.d.1   32
458.c.5   32

Classical and Other Ancient Writings

Aristotle
Politica
3.13   123

Cicero
In Verrem
2.5.66   84

Demosthenes
Against Nausimachus
18-20   124
Against Theocrines
51-52   124

Longinus
De sublimitate
33.5.4   31

Lucian
Alexander
8   69

Pliny the Elder
Naturalis Historia
28.4.19   69

Pseudo-Plato
Definitiones
415.c.3   31

Rhetorica ad Herennium
4.28.38   25

Index of Modern Authors

Alexander, P. H.   xiii
Allison, D. C.   111
Arnold, C. E.   70, 77
Asano, A.   70
Ashley, T. R.   128, 129
Baasland, E.   79–80, 86, 87, 92, 105
Bachmann, M.   8, 83
Bammel, E.   101, 128
Barclay, J. M. G.   1, 2, 3, 7, 11–16, 41, 47, 49, 51, 52, 56, 57, 58, 60, 63, 65, 71, 82, 83, 98, 99, 101, 103, 104, 105, 108, 109, 110, 111–112, 114, 118, 119, 120, 121, 125, 127, 131, 132
Barrett, C. K.   38, 60, 63, 64, 67, 98
Bauckham, R.   6
Bayes, J. F.   4
Beale, G. K.   131
Becker, J.   2, 8
Belleville, L. L.   29, 38, 39
Bengel, J. A.   102
Berger, K.   52
Berger, P. L.   92
Betz, H. D.   1, 3, 7, 11, 24, 26, 27, 31, 37, 39, 41, 43, 56, 70, 81, 87, 98, 99, 101, 106, 108, 109, 118, 119–120, 127, 131
Birnbaum, E.   58
Bligh, J.   122
Bockmuehl, M. N. A.   6, 7, 84
Bodel, J.   72
Bonneau, N.   35
Borgen, P.   9, 53, 99
Borse, U.   120
Botha, P. J. J.   25
Bouwman, G.   57
Boyarin, D.   111
Breytenbach, C.   71
Brinsmead, B. H.   101
Brondos, D.   28, 36
Bruce, F. F.   38, 86, 101, 120, 121
Bryant, R. A.   84, 86, 88, 114
Budd, P. J.   130
de W. Burton, E.   25, 36, 37, 82, 87, 99, 106, 107, 108, 118

Calvert, N. L.   58
Calvert-Koyzis, N.   58
Calvin, J.   5
Campbell, R. A.   122
Ciampa, R. E.   56
Cohen, S. J. D.   76
Cole, R. A.   100, 118
Cornu, H. L.   49
Cosgrove, C. H.   38, 41, 86
Cranfield, C. E. B.   4, 44
Cranford, M.   106, 107
Cross, F. M.   135
Cummins, S. A.   80, 84, 85, 88
Das, A. A.   4, 106, 107
Davies, W. D.   56, 102, 111, 138
Davis, B. S.   18, 28, 79, 80, 85, 87, 88
de Boer, W. P.   85
Deidun, T. J.   121
Dodd, B. J.   85, 113
Dodd, C. H.   102
Donaldson, T. L.   29
Drane, J. W.   8
Draper, J. A.   129
du Toit, A.   50
Dunn, J. D. G.   5–6, 7, 10, 14, 25, 38, 48, 80, 82, 102, 107, 106, 108, 118, 119, 122, 138
Eastman, S.   42, 54
Ebeling, G.   5, 101, 123
Eckert, J.   1, 98, 107, 118
Eckstein, H.-J.   37, 38, 58, 123
Elliot, M. A.   64
Elliott, S. M.   10, 17, 48, 70, 71, 77, 78, 79, 92
Engberg-Pedersen, T.   2, 13
Eriksson, A.   27
Esler, P. F.   9, 13, 14, 70, 80, 97, 100, 101, 102, 104, 121, 137
Evans, R. J.   17
Faraone, C. A.   79
Fee, G. D.   2, 10, 77, 88, 120, 123, 128
Finlan, S.   28
Finsterbusch, K.   6, 32, 39, 120

Flusser, D. 6, 111
Fung, R. Y. K. 8, 80, 107
Gager, J. G. 73, 75, 76, 78, 79
Gaston, L. 32
Gathercole, S. J. 16
Gaventa, B. R. 10, 85, 85
George, T. 4, 5
Goddard, A. J. 80, 85, 87, 90
Gordon, R. 77
Gordon, T. D. 39
Gorman, M. J. 86, 114
Goulder, M. 47
Graf, F. 76, 79
Hafemann, S. J. 31, 37, 39, 80, 85, 88, 128
Hall, R. G. 3, 24, 53
Hamerton-Kelly, R. G. 9, 100
Hansen, G. W. 1, 9, 43, 58, 59, 108
Haraguchi, T. 59
Harvey, A. E. 90
Hays, R. B. 3, 30, 36, 41, 82, 85, 101, 108, 113, 134
Heckel, U. 25, 28, 88
Hengel, M. 63
Hesselink, I. J. 5
Hong, I.-G. 4, 5, 31, 50, 97, 99, 101, 103, 104, 118, 121
Hooker, M. D. 36
Horbury, W. 43, 62, 65, 66, 67
Howard, G. 9, 10, 107
Hübner, H. 100, 106, 107, 108
Jacoby, F. vii
Jervis, L. A. 63
Jewett, R. 12, 14, 49, 99
Jobes, K. H. 43
Johnson, L. T. 33, 50
Kamlah, E. 124
Käsemann, E. 139
Keesmaat, S. C. 86
Kennedy, G. A. 3, 24
Kern, P. H. 3
Kertelge, K. 111
Kevan, E. F. 5
Kim, S. 101
Klauck, H. J. 77
Koch, D.-A. 107
Kok, E. H.-S. 58
Kuck, D. W. 16
Kuula, K. 38, 97

Kwon, Y.-G. 9, 13, 14, 15, 16, 17, 24, 49, 70, 86, 111, 119
Lambrecht, J. 103
Lategan, B. C. 10, 12, 31, 58
Lattimore, R. 72, 73, 76
Légasse, S. 100, 108
Lémonon, J.-P. 97, 108
Lieu, J. 49
Lightfoot, J. B. 10, 25, 37, 70, 82
Limbeck, M. 101
Longenecker, B. W. 2, 10, 55, 65, 85, 103, 104, 109, 111
Longenecker, R. N. 25, 37, 48, 50, 63, 80, 82, 86, 109, 107, 108, 118, 121, 127, 151
Louw, J. P. 53
Luckmann, T. 92
Lührmann, D. 1, 10, 58
Lull, D. J. 39
Lütgert, W. 12
Lyons, G. 51, 65, 81, 85
MacMullen, R. 72
Malina, B. J. 70
Marcus, J. 28, 31, 32
Marshall, B. D. 144
Martin, B. L. 4
Martin, T. W. 24, 62, 86, 107
Martyn, J. L. 1, 8–9, 10, 24, 25, 26, 27, 29, 30, 34, 48, 53, 54, 58, 59, 60, 61, 63, 64, 65, 80, 82, 84, 86, 87, 99, 101, 103, 108, 110, 111, 118, 122, 126, 134, 136, 137, 142
Mata, J. A. 100
Matera, F. J. 2, 9, 38, 57, 58, 80, 82, 99, 108
Matlock, R. B. 126
McLean, B. H. 43
Meeks, W. A. 130
Merk, O. 1
Mitchell, M. M. 3, 34
Mitchell, S. 70, 72, 76, 78, 79
Mitternacht, D. 41, 48, 50, 81, 85
Morland, K. A. 18, 24, 25, 28, 45, 103
Moule, C. F. D. 119
Muddiman, J. 81, 84
Müller, K. 6, 7
Murphy-O'Connor, J. 10, 58
Murray, M. 13, 48, 58
Mussner, F. 1, 2, 10, 25, 82, 85, 104, 105, 106, 119

Nanos, M. D. 40, 48, 81, 87
Neyrey, J. H. 7, 70
Nida, E. A. 53
Niebuhr, K.-W. 84
Nitzan, B. 26
Oepke, A. 90, 118
Olbrechts-Tyteca, L. 69
Pardee, N. 24, 122
Parker, R. 90
Pedersen, S. 111
Perelman, C. 69
Perrot, C. 98, 101, 106, 109
Pettazzoni, R. 78
Petzl, G. 78
Pigeon, C. 101, 112
Pleket, H. W. 77
Plumer, E. 5
Pobee, J. S. 82
Preisendanz, K. 79
Räisänen, H. 108
Ramos, F. P. 101
Ramsay, W. M. 70
Rastoin, M. 121
Reinbold, W. 107
Reinmuth, E. 6
Ricl, M. 78
Ridderbos, H. N. 4, 5, 31, 41, 82, 87, 118, 123
Riesner, R. 71, 80
Robb, J. D. 121
Robert, L. 72, 76
Ropes, J. H. 12
Russell, W. B. 9
Sanders, E. P. 5, 15, 49, 60, 84, 103, 107, 138
Sandnes, K. O. 25, 26, 66, 80
Schäfer, R. 48
Schewe, S. 2-3, 14, 15, 16, 17
Schlier, H. 38, 58, 90, 99, 108, 118
Schmithals, W. 14, 49
Schnabel, E. J. 5, 77, 78, 91, 108
Schnelle, U. 97, 100, 104
Schoeps, H. J. 107
Schrage, W. 113
Schreiner, T. R. 4, 107
Schürer, E. 76
Schweizer, E. 37
Scott, J. M. 31, 37, 42, 71, 129
Segal, A. F. 6, 48
Shaw, G. 100

Shulam, J. 49
Silva, M. 51, 65
Smiles, V. M. 58, 63, 97
Smit, J. F. M. 3
Smith, B. D. 88
Söding, T. 8, 49, 50, 84, 111
Souter, A. 102
Stanley, C. D. 28, 57, 60, 63, 107, 137
Stanton, G. N. 41, 58, 60, 61, 71, 82, 83, 101, 103, 104, 105
Stern, M. 53
Stirewalt, M. L. 25, 27, 49, 106
Stockhausen, C. K. 60
Stoike, D. A. 100
Strelan, J. G. 113
Strubbe, J. H. M. 25, 72, 73, 74, 75, 76, 90
Stuart, D. 92
Stuhlmacher, P. 7, 101, 102
Suhl, A. 2, 8, 10
Sumney, J. L. 48, 49, 52, 58, 60, 63
Swarup, P. N. W. 135-136
Swete, H. B. 102
Talmon, S. 135
Thackeray, H. St. J. 160
Thielman, F. 4, 7, 10, 37, 99, 102, 108, 109, 110
Thiselton, A. C. 27
Thomson, I. H. 14, 124, 125
Tolmie, D. F. 3, 17
Tomson, P. J. 6
Trebilco, P. R. 74, 75, 76
Trompf, G. W. 79, 92
Tuckett, C. M. 137
Tyson, J. B. 51
van de Sandt, H. 6, 108, 111, 112
Versnel, H. S. 77
Vollenweider, S. 108
Vos, J. S. 24, 26, 61
Vouga, F. 3, 27, 71, 97, 98
Wakefield, A. H. 14, 63
Walter, N. 48
Watson, F. 60
Weder, H. 108
Weima, J. A. D. 81
Wenham, D. 102
Werline, R. A. 26
Wessels, G. F. 10
Westerholm, S. 7, 8, 9, 39, 99, 101, 108, 123, 143

Whitaker, G. H.   147
White, E. E.   16
Wilckens, U.   4, 8
Wilder, W. N.   42, 118, 120, 127
Wiley, T.   48, 49
Williams, S. K.   10, 99, 117, 118, 119, 121, 139
Wilson, T. A.   23, 98, 100, 118, 125, 138
Winger, M.   1, 25, 97, 101, 111, 121, 121, 122
Wisdom, J. R.   67
Witherington, B.   10, 50, 82, 98, 99, 106, 108 110, 121, 129
Witulski, T.   71
Wright, J.   132
Wright, N. T.   36
Wyschogrod, M.   6
Young, N. H.   28, 39, 63

Index of Subjects and Key Terms

Abraham 58-62
- blessing of 29, 39, 47, 55, 59, 62, 67
- covenant with 58
- inheritance of 43
- seed of 29
- sons of 27, 43
Agitators
- identity of 48-49, 52
- observance of the Law 49
Allegory of Sarah and Hagar 40-43, 61, 135
Antinomianism 14
Apocalyptic 128, 137
Apostasy 24, 26, 41, 131-33,
Blessing 18, 23, 26, 27, 29, 36, 39, 42, 44, 47, 55, 60, 86, 135, 143-44
Christ
- cross/crucifixion of 81, 84, 85, 116, 137,
- Law of 5, 10, 99, 102-106, 114, 117-118, 143,
Circumcision 9, 10, 11, 13, 18, 27, 28, 41, 44, 47, 49, 53, 56-62, 68, 69, 79, 81, 93, 99, 101, 116, 127, 142, 144
Covenant
- new 113, 137
- Sinai 38, 42, 43
- renewal 26-27
Curse
- threat of 33, 41, 44, 47-48, 52, 56-67, 70, 76, 79, 94, 101, 106, 107-117, 133, 138
- of the Law 16, 18, 19, 23-44, 62, 69, 89-94, 119-140
Ethics 1, 7, 10, 11, 13, 14, 15, 111, 122, 141, 145
Exodus 100, 127, 129, 133, 135, 136, 139
Faith 27, 28, 30, 38, 39, 55, 59, 81, 94, 99, 110, 118, 136, 140, 144
Flesh
- desire of the 9, 47, 69, 120, 125, 126, 144
- works of the 6, 43, 119, 126, 127, 129, 131, 132, 138,

Freedom 43, 83, 100, 101, 119, 129, 133, 139
Gospel 8, 24, 25, 27, 41, 43, 55, 57, 59, 65, 71, 83, 86, 88, 99, 107, 116, 128
Idolatry 58, 131, 132
Imperial cult 82
Israel 5, 6, 28, 38, 39, 40, 60, 68, 104, 127, 130, 133, 135
Justification 69, 81, 118
Law
- fulfilment of the 4, 7, 9, 19, 99-117, 118, 125, 139, 143
- under sin 38
- works of the 55, 63, 81, 89, 110
Libertinism 13, 101
Magic 26, 76
Mirror-reading 50-52, 56, 101
Obedience 101, 108, 120, 137
Persecution 41, 80-94, 116-117, 131, 142
Promise 27, 29, 39, 43, 55, 58, 112, 125, 133-138, 140
Prophecy 25, 65-66, 113, 138
Reception-history 83
Redemption 29, 30, 34, 55, 127, 135, 136, 140, 144
Retribution 72, 79, 80,
Rhetoric 1, 2, 3, 13, 18, 23, 24, 31-33, 40, 71, 81, 86, 89, 99, 107, 116, 127
Righteousness 38, 68, 111, 134, 135, 136
Salvation 5, 53, 134
Scripture 37, 38, 43, 47, 54, 56-64
Shorthand 23, 31-34, 37, 40, 44, 122, 127, 142,
Slavery 41, 42, 100, 101
Spirit
- leading of 12, 19, 119-140
- fruit of 5, 12, 119-122, 133-140
Suffering 79-94, 115-117
Supersessionism 144
Synagogue 43, 56, 83, 84

www.ingramcontent.com/pod-product-compliance
Lightning Source LLC
Chambersburg PA
CBHW051930160426
43198CB00012B/2092